Ansible: Up and Running

Lorin Hochstein

Beijing · Cambridge · Farnham · Köln · Sebastopol · Tokyo

Ansible: Up and Running

by Lorin Hochstein

Printed in the United States of America.

Published by O'Reilly Media, Inc., 1005 Gravenstein Highway North, Sebastopol, CA 95472.

O'Reilly books may be purchased for educational, business, or sales promotional use. Online editions are also available for most titles (*http://safaribooksonline.com*). For more information, contact our corporate/institutional sales department: 800-998-9938 or corporate@oreilly.com.

Editor: Brian Anderson
Production Editor: Melanie Yarbrough
Copyeditor: Carla Thornton
Proofreader: Marta Justak

Indexer: WordCo Indexing Services
Interior Designer: David Futato
Cover Designer: Ellie Volkhausen
Illustrator: Rebecca Demarest

May 2015:   First Edition

Revision History for the First Edition
2015-04-28:   First Release

See *http://oreilly.com/catalog/errata.csp?isbn=9781491915325* for release details.

978-1-491-91532-5

[LSI]

Table of Contents

Foreword

Ansible started as a simple side project in February of 2012, and its rapid growth has been a pleasant surprise. It is now the work product of about a thousand people (and the ideas of many more than that), and it is widely deployed in almost every country. It's not unusual in a computer meet-up to find a handful (at least) of people who use it.

Ansible is perhaps exciting because it really isn't. Ansible doesn't really attempt to break new ground, but rather to distill a lot of existing ideas that other smart folks had already figured out and make them a bit more accessible.

Ansible sought a middle ground between somewhat computer-sciencey IT automation approaches (themselves a reaction to tedious large commercial suites) and hack-and-slash scripting that just got things done. Also, how can we replace a configuration management system, a deployment project, an orchestration project, and our library of arbitrary but important shell scripts with a single system? That was the idea.

Could we remove major architectural components from the IT automation stack? Eliminating management demons and relying instead on OpenSSH meant the system could start managing a computer fleet immediately, without having to set up anything on the managed machines. Further, the system was apt to be more reliable and secure.

I had noticed that in trying to automate systems previously, things that should be simple were often hard, and that writing automation content could often create a time-sucking force that kept me from things I wanted to spend more time doing. And I didn't want the system to take months to become an expert with, either.

In particular, I personally enjoy writing new software, but piloting automation systems, a bit less. In short, I wanted to make automation quicker and leave me more time for the things I cared about. Ansible was not something you were meant to use all day long, but to get in, get out, and get back to doing the things you cared about.

I hope you will like Ansible for many of the same reasons.

Although I spent a large amount of time making sure Ansible's docs were comprehensive, there's always a strong advantage to seeing material presented in a variety of ways, and often in seeing actual practice applied alongside the reference material.

In *Ansible: Up And Running*, Lorin presents Ansible in a very idiomatic way, in exactly the right order in which you might wish to explore it. Lorin has been around Ansible since almost the very beginning, and I'm very grateful for his contributions and input.

I'm also immensely thankful for everyone who has been a part of this project to date, and everyone who will be in the future.

Enjoy the book, and enjoy managing your computer fleet! And remember to install cowsay!

— Michael DeHaan
Creator of Ansible (software), former CTO of Ansible, Inc. (company)
April 2015

Preface

Why I Wrote This Book

When I was writing my first web application, using Django, the popular Python-based framework, I remember the sense of accomplishment when the app was finally working on my desktop. I would run *django manage.py runserver*, point my browser to *http://localhost:8000*, and there was my web application in all its glory.

Then I discovered there were all of these…*things* I had to do, just to get the darned app to run on the Linux server. In addition to installing Django and my app onto the server, I had to install Apache and the mod_python module so that Apache could run Django apps. Then I had to figure out the right Apache configuration file incantation so that it would run my application and serve up the static assets properly.

None of it was hard, it was just a pain to get all of those details right. I didn't want to muck about with configuration files, I just wanted my app to run. Once I got it working, everything was fine…until, several months later, I had to do it again, on a different server, at which point I had to start the process all over again.

Eventually, I discovered that this process was Doing It Wrong. The right way to do this sort of thing has a name, and that name is *configuration management*. The great thing about using configuration management is that it's a way to capture knowledge that always stays up-to-date. No more hunting for the right doc page or searching through your old notes.

Recently, a colleague at work was interested in trying out Ansible for deploying a new project, and he asked me for a reference on how to apply the Ansible concepts in practice, beyond what was available in the official docs. I didn't know what else to recommend, so I decided to write something to fill the gap—and here it is. Alas, this book comes too late for him, but I hope you'll find it useful.

Who Should Read This Book

This book is for anyone who needs to deal with Linux or Unix-like servers. If you've ever used the terms *systems administration, operations, deployment, configuration management*, or (sigh) *DevOps*, then you should find some value here.

Although I have managed my share of Linux servers, my background is in software engineering. This means that the examples in this book tend toward the deployment end of the spectrum, although I'm in agreement with Andrew Clay Shafer ([webops]) that the distinction between deployment and configuration is unresolved.

Navigating This Book

I'm not a big fan of book outlines: Chapter 1 covers so and so, Chapter 2 covers such and such, that sort of thing. I strongly suspect that nobody ever reads them (I never do), and the table of contents is much easier to scan.

This book is written to be read start to finish, with later chapters building on the earlier ones. It's written largely in a tutorial style, so you should be able to follow along on your own machine. Most of the examples are focused on web applications.

Conventions Used in This Book

The following typographical conventions are used in this book:

Italic
> Indicates new terms, URLs, email addresses, filenames, and file extensions.

`Constant width`
> Used for program listings, as well as within paragraphs to refer to program elements such as variable or function names, databases, data types, environment variables, statements, and keywords.

`Constant width bold`
> Shows commands or other text that should be typed literally by the user.

`Constant width italic`
> Shows text that should be replaced with user-supplied values or by values determined by context.

 This icon signifies a tip, suggestion, or general note.

This icon indicates a warning or caution.

Online Resources

Code samples from this book are available at this book's GitHub page (*http://github.com/lorin/ansiblebook*). There is ample official Ansible documentation (*http://docs.ansible.com*) available for reference.

I maintain a few Ansible quick reference pages on GitHub (*https://github.com/lorin/ansible-quickref*) as well.

The Ansible code is on GitHub, split across three repositories:

- Main repo (*https://github.com/ansible/ansible*)
- Core modules (*https://github.com/ansible/ansible-modules-core*)
- Extra modules (*https://github.com/ansible/ansible-modules-extras*)

Bookmark the Ansible module index (*http://bit.ly/1Dt75tg*); you'll be referring to it constantly as you use Ansible. Ansible Galaxy (*https://galaxy.ansible.com*) is a repository of Ansible roles contributed by the community. The Ansible Project Google Group (*http://bit.ly/1Dt79ZT*) is the place to go if you have any questions about Ansible.

If you're interested in contributing to Ansible development, check out the Ansible Development Google Group (*http://bit.ly/1Dt79ZT*).

For real-time help with Ansible, there's an active *#ansible* IRC channel on *irc.freenode.net*.

Supplemental material (code examples, exercises, etc.) is available for download at *https://github.com/lorin/ansiblebook*.

This book is here to help you get your job done. In general, if example code is offered with this book, you may use it in your programs and documentation. You do not need to contact us for permission unless you're reproducing a significant portion of the code. For example, writing a program that uses several chunks of code from this book does not require permission. Selling or distributing a CD-ROM of examples from O'Reilly books does require permission. Answering a question by citing this book and quoting example code does not require permission. Incorporating a significant amount of example code from this book into your product's documentation does require permission.

We appreciate, but do not require, attribution. An attribution usually includes the title, author, publisher, and ISBN. For example: "*Ansible: Up and Running* by Lorin Hochstein (O'Reilly). Copyright 2015 Lorin Hochstein, 978-1-491-91532-5."

If you feel your use of code examples falls outside fair use or the permission given above, feel free to contact us at *permissions@oreilly.com*.

Safari® Books Online

 *Safari Books Online* is an on-demand digital library that delivers expert content in both book and video form from the world's leading authors in technology and business.

Technology professionals, software developers, web designers, and business and creative professionals use Safari Books Online as their primary resource for research, problem solving, learning, and certification training.

Safari Books Online offers a range of plans and pricing for enterprise, government, education, and individuals.

Members have access to thousands of books, training videos, and prepublication manuscripts in one fully searchable database from publishers like O'Reilly Media, Prentice Hall Professional, Addison-Wesley Professional, Microsoft Press, Sams, Que, Peachpit Press, Focal Press, Cisco Press, John Wiley & Sons, Syngress, Morgan Kaufmann, IBM Redbooks, Packt, Adobe Press, FT Press, Apress, Manning, New Riders, McGraw-Hill, Jones & Bartlett, Course Technology, and hundreds more. For more information about Safari Books Online, please visit us online.

How to Contact Us

Please address comments and questions concerning this book to the publisher:

> O'Reilly Media, Inc.
> 1005 Gravenstein Highway North
> Sebastopol, CA 95472
> 800-998-9938 (in the United States or Canada)
> 707-829-0515 (international or local)
> 707-829-0104 (fax)

We have a web page for this book, where we list errata, examples, and any additional information. You can access this page at *http://bit.ly/ansible-up-and-running*.

To comment or ask technical questions about this book, send email to *bookquestions@oreilly.com*.

For more information about our books, courses, conferences, and news, see our website at *http://www.oreilly.com*.

Find us on Facebook: *http://facebook.com/oreilly*

Follow us on Twitter: *http://twitter.com/oreillymedia*

Watch us on YouTube: *http://www.youtube.com/oreillymedia*

Acknowledgments

Thanks to Jan-Piet Mens, Matt Jaynes, and John Jarvis for reviewing drafts of the book and providing feedback. Thanks to Isaac Saldana and Mike Rowan at SendGrid for being so supportive of this endeavor. Thanks to Michael DeHaan for creating Ansible and shepherding the community that sprang up around it, as well as for providing feedback on the book, including an explanation of why he chose to use the name "Ansible." Thanks to my editor, Brian Anderson, for his endless patience in working with me.

Thanks to Mom and Dad for their unfailing support; my brother Eric, the actual writer in the family; and my two sons, Benjamin and Julian. Finally, thanks to my wife, Stacy, for everything.

## CHAPTER 1

Introduction

It's an interesting time to be working in the IT industry. We don't deliver software to our customers by installing a program on a single machine and calling it a day.[1] Instead, we are all slowly turning into system engineers.

We now deploy software applications by stringing together services that run on a distributed set of computing resources and communicate over different networking protocols. A typical application can include web servers, application servers, memory-based caching systems, task queues, message queues, SQL databases, NoSQL datastores, and load balancers.

We also need to make sure we have the appropriate redundancies in place, so that when failures happen (and they will), our software systems will handle these failures gracefully. Then there are the secondary services that we also need to deploy and maintain, such as logging, monitoring, and analytics, as well as third-party services we need to interact with, such as infrastructure-as-a-service endpoints for managing virtual machine instances.[2]

You can wire up these services by hand: spinning up the servers you need, SSHing to each one, installing packages, editing config files, and so forth, but it's a pain. It's time-consuming, error-prone, and just plain dull to do this kind of work manually, especially around the third or fourth time. And for more complex tasks, like standing up an OpenStack cloud inside your application, doing it by hand is madness. There's a better way.

---

1 OK, nobody ever really delivered software like that.

2 Check out *The Practice of Cloud System Administration* and *Designing Data-Intensive Applications* for excellent books on building and maintaining these types of distributed systems.

If you're reading this, you're probably already sold on the idea of configuration management and considering adopting Ansible as your configuration management tool. Whether you're a developer deploying your code to production, or you're a systems administrator looking for a better way to automate, I think you'll find Ansible to be an excellent solution to your problem.

A Note About Versions

All of the example code in this book was tested against version 1.8.4 of Ansible, which was the most recent release as of this writing. As backward compatibility is a major goal of the Ansible project, these examples should work unmodified in future versions of Ansible.

What's with the Name "Ansible"?

It's a science fiction reference. An *ansible* is a fictional communication device that can transfer information faster than the speed of light. The author Ursula K. Le Guin invented the concept in her book *Rocannon's World*, and other sci-fi authors have since borrowed the idea from Le Guin.

More specifically, Michael DeHaan took the name Ansible from the book *Ender's Game* by Orson Scott Card. In that book, the ansible was used to control a large number of remote ships at once, over vast distances. Think of it as a metaphor for controlling remote servers.

Ansible: What Is It Good For?

Ansible is often described as a *configuration management* tool, and is typically mentioned in the same breath as *Chef, Puppet,* and *Salt.* When we talk about configuration management, we are typically talking about writing some kind of state description for our servers, and then using a tool to enforce that the servers are, indeed, in that state: the right packages are installed, configuration files contain the expected values and have the expected permissions, the right services are running, and so on. Like other configuration management tools, Ansible exposes a domain-specific language (DSL) that you use to describe the state of your servers.

These tools also can be used for doing *deployment* as well. When people talk about deployment, they are usually referring to the process of taking software that was written in-house, generating binaries or static assets (if necessary), copying the required files to the server(s), and then starting up the services. *Capistrano* and *Fabric* are two examples of open-source deployment tools. Ansible is a great tool for doing deployment as well as configuration management. Using a single tool for both configuration management and deployment makes life simpler for the folks responsible for operations.

Some people talk about the need for *orchestration* of deployment. This is where multiple remote servers are involved, and things have to happen in a specific order. For example, you need to bring up the database before bringing up the web servers, or you need to take web servers out of the load balancer one at a time in order to upgrade them without downtime. Ansible's good at this as well, and is designed from the ground up for performing actions on multiple servers. Ansible has a refreshingly simple model for controlling the order that actions happen in.

Finally, you'll hear people talk about *provisioning* new servers. In the context of public clouds such as Amazon EC2, this refers to spinning up a new virtual machine instance. Ansible's got you covered here, with a number of modules for talking to clouds, including EC2, Azure, Digital Ocean, Google Compute Engine, Linode, and Rackspace, as well as any clouds that support the OpenStack APIs.

 Confusingly, the *Vagrant* tool, which we'll discuss later in this chapter, uses the term "provisioner" to refer to a tool that does the configuration management. So, Vagrant refers to Ansible as a kind of provisioner, where I think of Vagrant as a provisioner, since Vagrant is responsible for starting up virtual machines.

How Ansible Works

Figure 1-1 shows a sample use case of Ansible in action. A user we'll call Stacy is using Ansible to configure three Ubuntu-based web servers to run nginx. She has written an Ansible script called *webservers.yml*. In Ansible, a script is called a *playbook*. A playbook describes which *hosts* (what Ansible calls *remote servers*) to configure, and an ordered list of *tasks* to perform on those hosts. In this example, the hosts are web1, web2, and web3, and the tasks are things such as:

- Install nginx
- Generate an nginx configuration file
- Copy over the security certificate
- Start the nginx service

In the next chapter, we'll discuss what's actually in this playbook. Stacy executes the playbook using the *ansible-playbook* command. In the example, the playbook is named *webservers.yml*, and is executed by typing:

```
$ ansible-playbook webservers.yml
```

Ansible will make SSH connections in parallel to web1, web2, and web3. It will execute the first task on the list on all three hosts simultaneously. In this example, the first task is installing the nginx apt package (since Ubuntu uses the apt package manager), so the task in the playbook would look something like this:

```
- name: install nginx
  apt: name=nginx
```

Ansible will:

1. Generate a Python script that installs the nginx package.

2. Copy the script to web1, web2, and web3.

3. Execute the script on web1, web2, web3.

4. Wait for the script to complete execution on all hosts.

Ansible will then move to the next task in the list, and go through these same four steps. It's important to note that:

- Ansible runs each task in parallel across all hosts.

- Ansible waits until all hosts have completed a task before moving to the next task.

- Ansible runs the tasks in the order that you specify them.

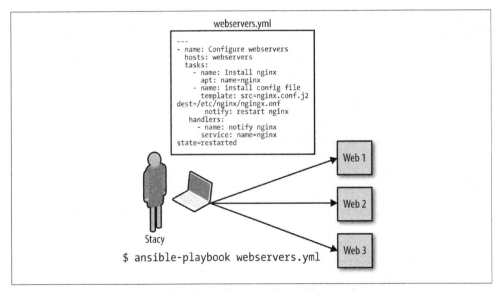

Figure 1-1. Running an Ansible playbook to configure three web servers

What's So Great About Ansible?

There are several open source configuration management tools out there to choose from. Here are some of the things that drew me to Ansible in particular.

Easy-to-Read Syntax

Recall that Ansible configuration management scripts are called *playbooks*. Ansible's playbook syntax is built on top of YAML, which is a data format language that was designed to be easy for humans to read and write. In a way, YAML is to JSON what Markdown is to HTML.

I like to think of Ansible playbooks as *executable documentation*. It's like the README file that describes the commands you had to type out to deploy your software, except that the instructions will never go out-of-date because they are also the code that gets executed directly.

Nothing to Install on the Remote Hosts

To manage a server with Ansible, the server needs to have SSH and Python 2.5 or later installed, or Python 2.4 with the Python *simplejson* library installed. There's no need to preinstall an agent or any other software on the host.

The control machine (the one that you use to control remote machines) needs to have Python 2.6 or later installed.

 Some modules might require Python 2.5 or later, and some might have additional prerequisites. Check the documentation for each module to see whether it has specific requirements.

Push-Based

Some configuration management systems that use agents, such as Chef and Puppet, are "pull-based" by default. Agents installed on the servers periodically check in with a central service and pull down configuration information from the service. Making configuration management changes to servers goes something like this:

1. You: make a change to a configuration management script.

2. You: push the change up to a configuration management central service.

3. Agent on server: wakes up after periodic timer fires.

4. Agent on server: connects to configuration management central service.

5. Agent on server: downloads new configuration management scripts.

6. Agent on server: executes configuration management scripts locally which change server state.

In contrast, Ansible is "push-based" by default. Making a change looks like this:

1. You: make a change to a playbook.
2. You: run the new playbook.
3. Ansible: connects to servers and executes modules, which changes server state.

As soon as you run the `ansible-playbook` command, Ansible connects to the remote server and does its thing.

The push-based approach has a significant advantage: you control when the changes happen to the servers. You don't need to wait around for a timer to expire. Advocates of the pull-based approach claim that pull is superior for scaling to large numbers of servers and for dealing with new servers that can come online anytime. However, as we'll discuss later in the book, Ansible has been used successfully in production with thousands of nodes, and has excellent support for environments where servers are dynamically added and removed.

If you really prefer using a pull-based model, Ansible has official support for pull mode, using a tool it ships with called *ansible-pull*. I don't cover pull mode in this book, but you can read more about it in the official documentation (*http://docs.ansible.com/playbooks_intro.html#ansible-pull*).

Ansible Scales Down

Yes, Ansible can be used to manage hundreds or even thousands of nodes. But what got me hooked is how it scales down. Using Ansible to configure a single node is easy; you simply write a single playbook. Ansible obeys Alan Kay's maxim: "Simple things should be simple, complex things should be possible."

Built-in Modules

You can use Ansible to execute arbitrary shell commands on your remote servers, but Ansible's real power comes from the collection of modules it ships with. You use modules to perform tasks such as installing a package, restarting a service, or copying a configuration file.

As we'll see later, Ansible modules are *declarative*; you use them to describe the state you want the server to be in. For example, you would invoke the user module like this to ensure there was an account named "deploy" in the "web" group:

```
user: name=deploy group=web
```

Modules are also *idempotent*. If the "deploy" user doesn't exist, then Ansible will create it. If it does exist, then Ansible won't do anything. Idempotence is a nice property because it means that it's safe to run an Ansible playbook multiple times against a server. This is a big improvement over the homegrown shell script approach, where running the shell script a second time might have a different (and likely unintended) effect.

What About Convergence?

Books on configuration management often mention the concept of *convergence*. Convergence in configuration management is most closely associated with Mark Burgess and the *CFEngine* configuration management system he authored.

If a configuration management system is convergent, then the system may run multiple times to put a server into its desired state, with each run bringing the server closer to that state.

This idea of convergence doesn't really apply to Ansible, as Ansible doesn't have a notion of running multiple times to configure servers. Instead, Ansible modules are implemented in such a way that running an Ansible playbook a single time should put each server into the desired state.

If you're interested in what Ansible's author thinks of the idea of convergence, see Michael DeHaan's post (*http://bit.ly/1InGh1A*) in the Ansible Project newsgroup, entitled, "Idempotence, convergence, and other silly fancy words we use too often."

Very Thin Layer of Abstraction

Some configuration management tools provide a layer of abstraction so that you can use the same configuration management scripts to manage servers running different operating systems. For example, instead of having to deal with a specific package manager like yum or apt, the configuration management tool exposes a "package" abstraction that you use instead.

Ansible isn't like that. You have to use the apt module to install packages on apt-based systems and the yum module to install packages on yum-based systems.

Although this might sound like a disadvantage, in practice, I've found that it makes Ansible easier to work with. Ansible doesn't require that I learn a new set of abstractions that hide the differences between operating systems. This makes Ansible's surface area smaller; there's less you need to know before you can start writing playbooks.

If you really want to, you can write your Ansible playbooks to take different actions, depending on the operating system of the remote server. But I try to avoid that when

I can, and instead I focus on writing playbooks that are designed to run on a specific operating system, such as Ubuntu.

The primary unit of reuse in the Ansible community is the module. Because the scope of a module is small and can be operating-system specific, it's straightforward to implement well-defined, shareable modules. The Ansible project is very open to accepting modules contributed by the community. I know because I've contributed a few.

Ansible playbooks aren't really intended to be reused across different contexts. In Chapter 8, we'll discuss *roles*, which is a way of collecting playbooks together so they are more reusable, as well as Ansible Galaxy, which is an online repository of these roles.

In practice, though, every organization sets up its servers a little bit differently, and you're best off writing playbooks for your organization rather than trying to reuse generic playbooks. I believe the primary value of looking at other people's playbooks is for examples to see how things are done.

What Is Ansible, Inc.'s Relationship to Ansible?

The name *Ansible* refers to both the software and the company that runs the open source project. Michael DeHaan, the creator of Ansible the software, is the former CTO of Ansible the company. To avoid confusion, I'll refer to the software as *Ansible* and to the company as *Ansible, Inc.*

Ansible, Inc. sells training and consulting services for Ansible, as well as a proprietary web-based management tool called *Ansible Tower*.

Is Ansible Too Simple?

When I was working on this book, my editor mentioned to me that "some folks who use the XYZ configuration management tool call Ansible a for-loop over SSH scripts." If you're considering switching over from another config management tool, you might be concerned at this point about whether Ansible is powerful enough to meet your needs.

As you'll soon learn, Ansible provides a lot more functionality than shell scripts. As I mentioned, Ansible's modules provide idempotence, and Ansible has excellent support for templating, as well as defining variables at different scopes. Anybody who thinks Ansible is equivalent to working with shell scripts has never had to maintain a non-trivial program written in shell. I'll always choose Ansible over shell scripts for config management tasks if given a choice.

And if you're worried about the scalability of SSH? As we'll discuss in Chapter 9, Ansible uses SSH multiplexing to optimize performance, and there are folks out there who are managing thousands of nodes with Ansible.[3]

 I'm not familiar enough with the other tools to describe their differences in detail. If you're looking for a head-to-head comparison of config management tools, check out *Taste Test: Puppet, Chef, Salt, Ansible* by Matt Jaynes. As it happens, Matt prefers Ansible.

What Do I Need to Know?

To be productive with Ansible, you need to be familiar with basic Linux system administration tasks. Ansible makes it easy to automate your tasks, but it's not the kind of tool that "automagically" does things that you otherwise wouldn't know how to do.

For this book, I assumed my readers would be familiar with at least one Linux distribution (e.g., Ubuntu, RHEL/CentOS, SUSE), and that they would know how to:

- Connect to a remote machine using SSH
- Interact with the bash command-line shell (pipes and redirection)
- Install packages
- Use the sudo command
- Check and set file permissions
- Start and stop services
- Set environment variables
- Write scripts (any language)

If these concepts are all familiar to you, then you're good to go with Ansible.

I won't assume you have knowledge of any particular programming language. For instance, you don't need to know Python to use Ansible unless you want to write your own module.

Ansible uses the YAML file format and uses the Jinja2 templating languages, so you'll need to learn some YAML and Jinja2 to use Ansible, but both technologies are easy to pick up.

---

3 For example, see "Using Ansible at Scale to Manage a Public Cloud" (*http://www.slideshare.net/JesseKeating/ ansiblefest-rax*) by Jesse Keating, formerly of Rackspace.

What Isn't Covered

This book isn't an exhaustive treatment of Ansible. It's designed to get you productive in Ansible as quickly as possible and describe how to perform certain tasks that aren't obvious from glancing over the official documentation.

I don't cover the official Ansible modules in detail. There are over 200 of these, and the official Ansible reference documentation on the modules is quite good.

I only cover the basic features of the templating engine that Ansible uses, Jinja2, primarily because I find that I generally only need to use the basic features of Jinja2 when I use Ansible. If you need to use more advanced Jinja2 features in your templates, I recommend you check out the official Jinja2 documentation (*http:// jinja.pocoo.org/docs/dev/*).

I don't go into detail about some features of Ansible that are mainly useful when you are running Ansible on an older version of Linux. This includes features such as the *paramiko* SSH client and *accelerated mode*. For these issues, I mention them in passing and put links to the official documentation.

In version 1.7, Ansible added support for managing Windows servers. I don't cover the Windows support in this book because I don't have experience managing Windows servers with Ansible, and because I think this is still a niche use. A proper treatment of using Ansible with Windows hosts probably deserves its own book.

I don't discuss Ansible Tower, which is a commercial web-based tool for managing Ansible, developed by Ansible, Inc. This book focuses on Ansible itself, which is fully open source, including all of the modules.

Finally, there are several features of Ansible I don't cover simply to keep the book a manageable length. These features include pull mode, logging, connecting to hosts using protocols other than SSH, and prompting the user for passwords or input. I encourage you to check out the official docs to find out more about these features.

Installing Ansible

If you're running on a Linux machine, all of the major Linux distributions package Ansible these days, so you should be able to install it using your native package manager, although this might be an older version of Ansible. If you're running on Mac OS X, I recommend you use the excellent Homebrew package manager to install Ansible.

If all else fails, you can install it using *pip*, Python's package manager. You can install it as root by running:

```
$ sudo pip install ansible
```

If you don't want to install Ansible as root, you can safely install it into a Python *virtualenv*. If you're not familiar with virtualenvs, you can use a newer tool called *pipsi* that will automatically install Ansible into a virtualenv for you:

```
$ wget https://raw.githubusercontent.com/mitsuhiko/pipsi/master/get-pipsi.py
$ python get-pipsi.py
$ pipsi install ansible
```

If you go the pipsi route, you'll need to update your PATH environment variable to include *~/.local/bin*. Some Ansible plug-ins and modules might require additional Python libraries. If you've installed with pipsi, and you wanted to install *docker-py* (needed by the Ansible Docker modules) and *boto* (needed by the Ansible EC2 modules), you'd do it like this:

```
$ cd ~/.local/venvs/ansible
$ source bin/activate
$ pip install docker-py boto
```

If you're feeling adventurous and want to use the bleeding-edge version of Ansible, you can grab the development branch from GitHub:

```
$ git clone https://github.com/ansible/ansible.git --recursive
```

If you're running Ansible from the development branch, you'll need to run these commands each time to set up your environment variables, including your PATH variable so that your shell knows where the *ansible* and *ansible-playbooks* programs are.

```
$ cd ./ansible
$ source ./hacking/env-setup
```

For more details on installation see:

- Official Ansible install docs (*http://docs.ansible.com/intro_installation.html*)
- Pip (*http://pip.readthedocs.org/*)
- Virtualenv (*http://docs.python-guide.org/en/latest/dev/virtualenvs/*)
- Pipsi (*https://github.com/mitsuhiko/pipsi*)

Setting Up a Server for Testing

You'll need to have SSH access and root privileges on a Linux server to follow along with the examples in this book. Fortunately, these days it's easy to get low-cost access to a Linux virtual machine through a public cloud service such as Amazon EC2, Google Compute Engine, Microsoft Azure,[4] Digital Ocean, Rackspace, SoftLayer, HP Public Cloud, Linode…you get the idea.

Using Vagrant to Set Up a Test Server

If you'd prefer not to spend the money on a public cloud, I recommend you install Vagrant on your machine. Vagrant is an excellent open source tool for managing virtual machines. You can use Vagrant to boot a Linux virtual machine inside of your laptop, and we can use that as a test server.

Vagrant has built-in support for provisioning virtual machines with Ansible, but we'll talk about that in detail in Chapter 11. For now, we'll just manage a Vagrant virtual machine as if it were a regular Linux server.

Vagrant needs the VirtualBox virtualizer to be installed on your machine. Download VirtualBox (*http://www.virtualbox.org*) and then download Vagrant (*http://www.vagrantup.com*).

I recommend you create a directory for your Ansible playbooks and related files. In the following example, I've named mine *playbooks*.

Run the following commands to create a Vagrant configuration file (Vagrantfile) for an Ubuntu 14.04 (Trusty Tahr) 64-bit virtual machine image,[5] and boot it.

```
$ mkdir playbooks
$ cd playbooks
$ vagrant init ubuntu/trusty64
$ vagrant up
```

 The first time you do vagrant up, it will download the virtual machine image file, which might take a while depending on your Internet connection.

If all goes well, the output should look like this:

```
A `Vagrantfile` has been placed in this directory. You are now
ready to `vagrant up` your first virtual environment! Please read
the comments in the Vagrantfile as well as documentation on
`vagrantup.com` for more information on using Vagrant.

Bringing machine 'default' up with 'virtualbox' provider...
==> default: Box 'ubuntu/trusty64' could not be found. Attempting to
find and install...
```

---

4 Yes, Azure supports Linux servers.

5 Vagrant uses the terms *machine* to refer to a virtual machine and *box* to refer to a virtual machine image.

```
    default: Box Provider: virtualbox
    default: Box Version: >= 0
==> default: Loading metadata for box 'ubuntu/trusty64'
    default: URL: https://vagrantcloud.com/ubuntu/trusty64
==> default: Adding box 'ubuntu/trusty64' (v14.04) for provider: virtualbox
    default: Downloading: https://vagrantcloud.com/ubuntu/trusty64/version/1/
             provider/virtualbox.box
==> default: Successfully added box 'ubuntu/trusty64' (v14.04) for 'virtualbox'!
==> default: Importing base box 'ubuntu/trusty64'...
==> default: Matching MAC address for NAT networking...
==> default: Checking if box 'ubuntu/trusty64' is up to date...
==> default: Setting the name of the VM: playbooks_default_1423013257297_44645
==> default: Clearing any previously set forwarded ports...
==> default: Clearing any previously set network interfaces...
==> default: Preparing network interfaces based on configuration...
    default: Adapter 1: nat
==> default: Forwarding ports...
    default: 22 => 2222 (adapter 1)
==> default: Booting VM...
==> default: Waiting for machine to boot. This may take a few minutes...
    default: SSH address: 127.0.0.1:2222
    default: SSH username: vagrant
    default: SSH auth method: private key
    default: Warning: Connection timeout. Retrying...
==> default: Machine booted and ready!
==> default: Checking for guest additions in VM...
==> default: Mounting shared folders...
    default: /vagrant => /Users/lorinhochstein/dev/ansiblebook/ch01/playbooks
```

You should be able to SSH into your new Ubuntu 14.04 virtual machine by running:

```
$ vagrant ssh
```

If this works, you should see a login screen like this:

```
Welcome to Ubuntu 14.04.1 LTS (GNU/Linux 3.13.0-35-generic x86_64)

 * Documentation:  https://help.ubuntu.com/

  System information as of Sun Aug 31 04:07:21 UTC 2014

  System load:  0.0              Processes:           73
  Usage of /:   2.7% of 39.34GB  Users logged in:     0
  Memory usage: 25%              IP address for eth0: 10.0.2.15
  Swap usage:   0%

  Graph this data and manage this system at:
    https://landscape.canonical.com/

  Get cloud support with Ubuntu Advantage Cloud Guest:
    http://www.ubuntu.com/business/services/cloud

0 packages can be updated.
0 updates are security updates.
```

```
Last login: Sun Aug 31 04:07:21 2014 from 10.0.2.2
```

Type **exit** to quit the SSH session.

This approach lets us interact with the shell, but Ansible needs to connect to the virtual machine using the regular SSH client, not the `vagrant ssh` command.

Tell Vagrant to output the SSH connection details by typing:

```
$ vagrant ssh-config
```

On my machine, the output looks like this:

```
Host default
   HostName 127.0.0.1
   User vagrant
   Port 2222
   UserKnownHostsFile /dev/null
   StrictHostKeyChecking no
   PasswordAuthentication no
   IdentityFile /Users/lorinhochstein/dev/ansiblebook/ch01/playbooks/.vagrant/
   machines/default/virtualbox/private_key
   IdentitiesOnly yes
   LogLevel FATAL
```

The important lines are:

```
   HostName 127.0.0.1
   User vagrant
   Port 2222
   IdentityFile /Users/lorinhochstein/dev/ansiblebook/ch01/playbooks/.vagrant/
   machines/default/virtualbox/private_key
```

 Vagrant 1.7 changed how it handled private SSH keys. Starting with 1.7, Vagrant generates a new private key for each machine. Earlier versions used the same key, which was in the default location of *~/.vagrant.d/insecure_private_key*. The examples in this book use Vagrant 1.7.

In your case, every field should likely be the same except for the path of the IdentityFile.

Confirm that you can start an SSH session from the command line using this information. In my case, the SSH command is:

```
$ ssh vagrant@127.0.0.1 -p 2222 -i /Users/lorinhochstein/dev/ansiblebook/ch01/
playbooks/.vagrant/machines/default/virtualbox/private_key
```

You should see the Ubuntu login screen. Type **exit** to quit the SSH session.

Telling Ansible About Your Test Server

Ansible can manage only the servers it explicitly knows about. You provide Ansible with information about servers by specifying them in an inventory file.

Each server needs a name that Ansible will use to identify it. You can use the hostname of the server, or you can give it an alias and pass some additional arguments to tell Ansible how to connect to it. We'll give our Vagrant server the alias of test server.

Create a file called *hosts* in the *playbooks* directory. This file will serve as the inventory file. If you're using a Vagrant machine as your test server, your *hosts* file should look like Example 1-1. I've broken the file contents up across multiple lines so that it fits on the page, but it should be all on one line in your file, without any backslashes.

Example 1-1. playbooks/hosts

```
testserver ansible_ssh_host=127.0.0.1 ansible_ssh_port=2222 \
  ansible_ssh_user=vagrant \
  ansible_ssh_private_key_file=.vagrant/machines/default/virtualbox/private_key
```

Here we see one of the drawbacks of using Vagrant. We have to explicitly pass in extra arguments to tell Ansible how to connect. In most cases, we won't need this extra data.

Later on in this chapter, we'll see how we can use the *ansible.cfg* file to avoid having to be so verbose in the inventory file. In later chapters, we'll see how to use Ansible variables to similar effect.

If you have an Ubuntu machine on Amazon EC2 with a hostname like ec2-203-0-113-120.compute-1.amazonaws.com, then your inventory file will look something like (all on one line):

```
testserver ansible_ssh_host=ec2-203-0-113-120.compute-1.amazonaws.com \
  ansible_ssh_user=ubuntu ansible_ssh_private_key_file=/path/to/keyfile.pem
```

 Ansible supports the ssh-agent program, so you don't need to explicitly specify SSH key files in your inventory files. See "SSH Agent" on page 273 for more details if you haven't used ssh-agent before.

We'll use the ansible command-line tool to verify that we can use Ansible to connect to the server. You won't use the ansible command very often; it's mostly used for ad hoc, one-off things.

Let's tell Ansible to connect to the server named `testserver` described in the inventory file named *hosts* and invoke the `ping` module:

```
$ ansible testserver -i hosts -m ping
```

If your local SSH client has host key verification enabled, you might see something that looks like this the first time Ansible tries to connect to the server:

```
The authenticity of host '[127.0.0.1]:2222 ([127.0.0.1]:2222)' \
can't be established.
RSA key fingerprint is e8:0d:7d:ef:57:07:81:98:40:31:19:53:a8:d0:76:21.
Are you sure you want to continue connecting (yes/no)?
```

You can just type **yes**.

If it succeeded, output will look like this:

```
testserver | success >> {
    "changed": false,
    "ping": "pong"
}
```

 If Ansible did not succeed, add the `-vvvv` flag to see more details about the error:

```
$ ansible testserver -i hosts -m ping -vvvv
```

We can see that the module succeeded. The `"changed": false` part of the output tells us that executing the module did not change the state of the server. The `"ping": "pong"` text is output that is specific to the *ping* module.

The ping module doesn't actually do anything other than check that Ansible can start an SSH session with the servers. It's a useful tool for testing that Ansible can connect to the server.

Simplifying with the ansible.cfg File

We had to type a lot of text in the inventory file to tell Ansible about our test server. Fortunately, Ansible has a number of ways you can specify these sorts of variables so we don't have to put them all in one place.

Right now, we'll use one such mechanism, the *ansible.cfg* file, to set some defaults so we don't need to type as much.

Example 1-2 shows an *ansible.cfg* file that specifies the location of the inventory file (*hostfile*), the user to SSH (*remote_user*), and the SSH private key (*private_key_file*). This assumes you're using Vagrant. If you're using your own server, you'll need to set the *remote_user* and *private_key_file* values accordingly.

Our example configuration also disables SSH host key checking. This is convenient when dealing with Vagrant machines; otherwise, we need to edit our *~/.ssh/ known_hosts* file every time we destroy and recreate a Vagrant machine. However, disabling host key checking can be a security risk when connecting to other servers over the network. If you're not familiar with host keys, they are covered in detail in Appendix A.

Example 1-2. ansible.cfg

```
[defaults]
hostfile = hosts
remote_user = vagrant
private_key_file = .vagrant/machines/default/virtualbox/private_key
host_key_checking = False
```

systems administrator and aren't using version control yet, this is a perfect opportunity to get started.

With our default values set, we no longer need to specify the SSH user or key file in our *hosts* file. Instead, it simplifies to:

```
testserver ansible_ssh_host=127.0.0.1 ansible_ssh_port=2222
```

We can also invoke ansible without passing the `-i hostname` arguments, like so:

```
$ ansible testserver -m ping
```

I like to use the *ansible* command-line tool to run arbitrary commands on remote machines, like parallel SSH. You can execute arbitrary commands with the *command* module. When invoking this module, you also need to pass an argument to the module with the `-a` flag, which is the command to run.

For example, to check the uptime of our server, we can use:

```
$ ansible testserver -m command -a uptime
```

Output should look like this:

```
testserver | success | rc=0 >>
 17:14:07 up  1:16,  1 user,  load average: 0.16, 0.05, 0.04
```

The *command* module is so commonly used that it's the default module, so we can omit it:

```
$ ansible testserver -a uptime
```

If our command contains spaces, we need to quote it so that the shell passes the entire string as a single argument to Ansible. For example, to view the last several lines of the */var/log/dmesg* logfile:

```
$ ansible testserver -a "tail /var/log/dmesg"
```

The output from my Vagrant machine looks like this:

```
testserver | success | rc=0 >>
[    5.170544] type=1400 audit(1409500641.335:9): apparmor="STATUS" operation=
"profile_replace" profile="unconfined" name="/usr/lib/NetworkManager/nm-dhcp-c
lient.act on" pid=888 comm="apparmor_parser"
[    5.170547] type=1400 audit(1409500641.335:10): apparmor="STATUS" operation=
"profile_replace" profile="unconfined" name="/usr/lib/connman/scripts/dhclient-
script" pid=888 comm="apparmor_parser"
[    5.222366] vboxvideo: Unknown symbol drm_open (err 0)
[    5.222370] vboxvideo: Unknown symbol drm_poll (err 0)
[    5.222372] vboxvideo: Unknown symbol drm_pci_init (err 0)
[    5.222375] vboxvideo: Unknown symbol drm_ioctl (err 0)
[    5.222376] vboxvideo: Unknown symbol drm_vblank_init (err 0)
[    5.222378] vboxvideo: Unknown symbol drm_mmap (err 0)
```

```
[    5.222380] vboxvideo: Unknown symbol drm_pci_exit (err 0)
[    5.222381] vboxvideo: Unknown symbol drm_release (err 0)
```

If we need root access, we pass in the -s flag to tell Ansible to *sudo* as root. For example, to access */var/log/syslog* requires root access:

```
$ ansible testserver -s -a "tail /var/log/syslog"
```

The output looks something like this:

```
testserver | success | rc=0 >>
Aug 31 15:57:49 vagrant-ubuntu-trusty-64 ntpdate[1465]: /
adjust time server 91.189
94.4 offset -0.003191 sec
Aug 31 16:17:01 vagrant-ubuntu-trusty-64 CRON[1480]: (root) CMD (   cd /
&& run-p
rts --report /etc/cron.hourly)
Aug 31 17:04:18 vagrant-ubuntu-trusty-64 ansible-ping: Invoked with data=None
Aug 31 17:12:33 vagrant-ubuntu-trusty-64 ansible-ping: Invoked with data=None
Aug 31 17:14:07 vagrant-ubuntu-trusty-64 ansible-command: Invoked with executable
None shell=False args=uptime removes=None creates=None chdir=None
Aug 31 17:16:01 vagrant-ubuntu-trusty-64 ansible-command: Invoked with executable
None shell=False args=tail /var/log/messages removes=None creates=None chdir=None
Aug 31 17:17:01 vagrant-ubuntu-trusty-64 CRON[2091]: (root) CMD (   cd /
&& run-pa
rts --report /etc/cron.hourly)
Aug 31 17:17:09 vagrant-ubuntu-trusty-64 ansible-command: Invoked with /
executable=
N one shell=False args=tail /var/log/dmesg removes=None creates=None chdir=None
Aug 31 17:19:01 vagrant-ubuntu-trusty-64 ansible-command: Invoked with /
executable=
None shell=False args=tail /var/log/messages removes=None creates=None chdir=None
Aug 31 17:22:32 vagrant-ubuntu-trusty-64 ansible-command: Invoked with /
executable=
one shell=False args=tail /var/log/syslog removes=None creates=None chdir=None
```

We can see from this output that Ansible writes to the syslog as it runs.

You aren't just restricted to the *ping* and *command* modules when using the *ansible* command-line tool: you can use any module that you like. For example, you can install nginx on Ubuntu using the follow command:

```
$ ansible testserver -s -m apt -a name=nginx
```

 If installing nginx fails for you, you might need to update the package lists. To tell Ansible to do the equivalent of apt-get update before installing the package, change the argument from name=nginx to "name=nginx update_cache=yes"

You can restart nginx by doing:

```
$ ansible testserver -s -m service -a "name=nginx \
    state=restarted"
```

We need the -s argument to use sudo because only root can install the nginx package and restart services.

Moving Forward

To recap, in this introductory chapter, we've covered the basic concepts of Ansible at a high level, including how it communicates with remote servers and how it differs from other configuration management tools. We've also seen how to use the *ansible* command-line tool to perform simple tasks on a single host.

However, using *ansible* to run commands against single hosts isn't terribly interesting. In the next chapter, we'll cover playbooks, where the real action is.

## CHAPTER 2

Playbooks: A Beginning

Most of your time in Ansible will be spent writing *playbooks*. A playbook is the term that Ansible uses for a configuration management script. Let's look at an example: installing the nginx web server and configuring it for secure communication.

If you're following along in this chapter, you should end up with the files listed here:

- *playbooks/ansible.cfg*
- *playbooks/hosts*
- *playbooks/Vagrantfile*
- *playbooks/web-notls.yml*
- *playbooks/web-tls.yml*
- *playbooks/files/nginx.key*
- *playbooks/files/nginx.crt*
- *playbooks/files/nginx.conf*
- *playbooks/templates/index.html.j2*
- *playbooks/templates/nginx.conf.j2*

Some Preliminaries

Before we can run this playbook against our Vagrant machine, we need to expose ports 80 and 443, so we can access them. As shown in Figure 2-1, we are going to configure Vagrant so that requests to ports 8080 and 8443 on our local machine are forwarded to ports 80 and 443 on the Vagrant machine. This will allow us to access the web server running inside Vagrant at *http://localhost:8080* and *https://localhost:8443*.

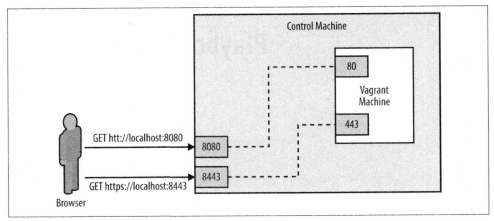

Figure 2-1. Exposing ports on Vagrant machine

Modify your *Vagrantfile* so it looks like this:

```
VAGRANTFILE_API_VERSION = "2"

Vagrant.configure(VAGRANTFILE_API_VERSION) do |config|
  config.vm.box = "ubuntu/trusty64"
  config.vm.network "forwarded_port", guest: 80, host: 8080
  config.vm.network "forwarded_port", guest: 443, host: 8443
end
```

This maps port 8080 on your local machine to port 80 of the Vagrant machine, and port 8443 on your local machine to port 443 on the Vagrant machine. Once you make the changes, tell Vagrant to have them go into effect by running:

```
$ vagrant reload
```

You should see output that includes:

```
==> default: Forwarding ports...
    default: 80 => 8080 (adapter 1)
    default: 443 => 8443 (adapter 1)
    default: 22 => 2222 (adapter 1)
```

A Very Simple Playbook

For our first example playbook, we'll configure a host to run an nginx web server. For this example, we won't configure the web server to support TLS encryption. This will make setting up the web server simpler, but a proper website should have TLS encryption enabled, and we'll cover how to do that later on in this chapter.

First, we'll see what happens when we run the playbook in Example 2-1, and then we'll go over the contents of the playbook in detail.

Example 2-1. web-notls.yml

```
- name: Configure webserver with nginx
  hosts: webservers
  sudo: True
  tasks:
    - name: install nginx
      apt: name=nginx update_cache=yes

    - name: copy nginx config file
      copy: src=files/nginx.conf dest=/etc/nginx/sites-available/default

    - name: enable configuration
      file: >
        dest=/etc/nginx/sites-enabled/default
        src=/etc/nginx/sites-available/default
        state=link

    - name: copy index.html
      template: src=templates/index.html.j2 dest=/usr/share/nginx/html/index.html
        mode=0644

    - name: restart nginx
      service: name=nginx state=restarted
```

Why Do You Use "True" in One Place and "Yes" in Another?

Sharp-eyed readers might have noticed that Example 2-1 uses True in one spot in the playbook (to enable sudo) and yes in another spot in the playbook (to update the apt cache).

Ansible is pretty flexible on how you represent truthy and falsey values in playbooks. Strictly speaking, module arguments (like update_cache=yes) are treated differently from values elsewhere in playbooks (like sudo: True). Values elsewhere are handled by the YAML parser and so use the YAML conventions of truthiness, which are:

YAML truthy
    true, True, TRUE, yes, Yes, YES, on, On, ON, y, Y

YAML falsey
    false, False, FALSE, no, No, NO, off, Off, OFF, n, N

Module arguments are passed as strings and use Ansible's internal conventions, which are:

---

module arg truthy
    yes, on, 1, true

module arg falsey
    no, off, 0, false

I tend to follow the examples in the official Ansible documentation. These typically use yes and no when passing arguments to modules (since that's consistent with the module documentation), and True and False elsewhere in playbooks.

Specifying an nginx Config File

This playbook requires two additional files before we can run it. First, we need to define an nginx configuration file.

Nginx ships with a configuration file that works out of the box if you just want to serve static files. But you'll almost always need to customize this, so we'll overwrite the default configuration file with our own as part of this playbook. As we'll see later, we'll need to modify this configuration file to support TLS. Example 2-2 shows a basic nginx config file. Put it in *playbooks/files/nginx.conf*.[1]

Example 2-2. files/nginx.conf

```
server {
        listen 80 default_server;
        listen [::]:80 default_server ipv6only=on;

        root /usr/share/nginx/html;
        index index.html index.htm;

        server_name localhost;

        location / {
                try_files $uri $uri/ =404;
        }
}
```

An Ansible convention is to keep files in a subdirectory named *files* and Jinja2 templates in a subdirectory named *templates*. I'll follow this convention throughout the book.

---

1 Note that while we call this file *nginx.conf*, it replaces the *sites-enabled/default* nginx server block config file, not the main */etc/nginx.conf* config file.

Creating a Custom Homepage

Let's add a custom homepage. We're going to use Ansible's template functionality so that Ansible will generate the file from a template. Put the file shown in Example 2-3 in *playbooks/templates/index.html.j2*.

Example 2-3. playbooks/templates/index.html.j2

```
<html>
  <head>
    <title>Welcome to ansible</title>
  </head>
  <body>
  <h1>nginx, configured by Ansible</h1>
  <p>If you can see this, Ansible successfully installed nginx.</p>

  <p>{{ ansible_managed }}</p>
  </body>
</html>
```

This template references a special Ansible variable named *ansible_managed*. When Ansible renders this template, it will replace this variable with information about when the template file was generated. Figure 2-2 shows a screenshot of a web browser viewing the generated HTML.

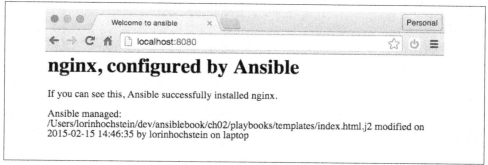

Figure 2-2. Rendered HTML

Creating a Webservers Group

Let's create a "webservers" group in our inventory file so that we can refer to this group in our playbook. For now, this group will contain our testserver.

Inventory files are in the *.ini* file format. We'll go into this format in detail later in the book. Edit your *playbooks/hosts* file to put a [webservers] line above the testserver line, as shown in Example 2-4. This indicates that testserver is in the webservers group.

Example 2-4. playbooks/hosts

```
[webservers]
testserver ansible_ssh_host=127.0.0.1 ansible_ssh_port=2222
```

You should now be able to ping the webservers group using the `ansible` command-line tool:

```
$ ansible webservers -m ping
```

The output should look like this:

```
testserver | success >> {
    "changed": false,
    "ping": "pong"
}
```

Running the Playbook

The `ansible-playbook` command executes playbooks. To run the playbook, do:

```
$ ansible-playbook web-notls.yml
```

Example 2-5 shows what the output should look.

Example 2-5. Output of ansible-playbook

```
PLAY [Configure webserver with nginx] ********************************

GATHERING FACTS *****************************************************************
ok: [testserver]

TASK: [install nginx] **********************************************************
changed: [testserver]

TASK: [copy nginx config file] *************************************************
changed: [testserver]

TASK: [enable configuration] ***************************************************
ok: [testserver]

TASK: [copy index.html] ********************************************************
changed: [testserver]

TASK: [restart nginx] **********************************************************
changed: [testserver]

PLAY RECAP *********************************************************************
testserver                 : ok=6    changed=4    unreachable=0    failed=0
```

Cowsay

If you have the *cowsay* program installed on your local machine, then Ansible output will look like this instead:

```
 _____
< PLAY [Configure webserver with nginx] >
 -----------------------------------------
        \   ^__^
         \  (oo)_____
            (__)\       )\/\
                ||----w |
                ||     ||
```

If you don't want to see the cows, you can disable cowsay by setting the ANSIBLE_NOCOWS environment variable like this:

```
$ export ANSIBLE_NOCOWS=1
```

You can also disable cowsay by adding the following to your *ansible.cfg* file.

```
[defaults]
nocows = 1
```

If you didn't get any errors,[2] you should be able to point your browser to *http://local host:8080* and see the custom HTML page, as shown in Figure 2-2.

 If your playbook file is marked as executable and starts with a line that looks like this:[3]

```
#!/usr/bin/env ansible-playbook
```

then you can execute it by invoking it directly, like this:

```
$ ./web-notls.yml
```

---

2 If you encountered an error, you might want to skip to Chapter 14 for assistance on debugging.

3 Colloquially referred to as a "shebang."

Playbooks Are YAML

Ansible playbooks are written in YAML syntax. YAML is a file format similar in intent to JSON, but generally easier for humans to read and write. Before we go over the playbook, let's cover the concepts of YAML that are most important for writing playbooks.

Start of File

YAML files are supposed to start with three dashes to indicate the beginning of the document:

```
---
```

However, if you forget to put those three dashes at the top of your playbook files, Ansible won't complain.

Comments

Comments start with a number sign and apply to the end of the line, the same as in shell scripts, Python, and Ruby:

```
# This is a YAML comment
```

Strings

In general, YAML strings don't have to be quoted, although you can quote them if you prefer. Even if there are spaces, you don't need to quote them. For example, this is a string in YAML:

```
this is a lovely sentence
```

The JSON equivalent is:

```
"this is a lovely sentence"
```

There are some scenarios in Ansible where you will need to quote strings. These typically involve the use of {{ braces }} for variable substitution. We'll get to those later.

Booleans

YAML has a native Boolean type, and provides you with a wide variety of strings that can be interpreted as true or false, which we covered in "Why Do You Use "True" in One Place and "Yes" in Another?" on page 23.

Personally, I always use True and False in my Ansible playbooks.

For example, this is a Boolean in YAML:

```
True
```

The JSON equivalent is:

```
true
```

Lists

YAML lists are like arrays in JSON and Ruby or lists in Python. Technically, these are called *sequences* in YAML, but I call them *lists* here to be consistent with the official Ansible documentation.

They are delimited with hyphens, like this:

```
- My Fair Lady
- Oklahoma
- The Pirates of Penzance
```

The JSON equivalent is:

```
[
  "My Fair Lady",
  "Oklahoma",
  "The Pirates of Penzance"
]
```

(Note again how we didn't have to quote the strings in YAML, even though they have spaces in them.)

YAML also supports an inline format for lists, which looks like this:

```
[My Fair Lady, Oklahoma, The Pirates of Penzance]
```

Dictionaries

YAML *dictionaries* are like objects in JSON, dictionaries in Python, or hashes in Ruby. Technically, these are called *mappings* in YAML, but I call them *dictionaries* here to be consistent with the official Ansible documentation.

They look like this:

```
address: 742 Evergreen Terrace
city: Springfield
state: North Takoma
```

The JSON equivalent is:

```
{
    "address": "742 Evergreen Terrace",
    "city": "Springfield",
    "state": "North Takoma"
}
```

YAML also supports an inline format for dictionaries, which looks like this:

```
{address: 742 Evergreen Terrace, city: Springfield, state: North Takoma}
```

Line Folding

When writing playbooks, you'll often encounter situations where you're passing many arguments to a module. For aesthetics, you might want to break this up across multiple lines in your file, but you want Ansible to treat the string as if it were a single line.

You can do this with YAML using line folding with the greater than (>) character. The YAML parser will replace line breaks with spaces. For example:

```
address: >
    Department of Computer Science,
    A.V. Williams Building,
    University of Maryland
city: College Park
state: Maryland
```

The JSON equivalent is:

```
{
    "address": "Department of Computer Science, A.V. Williams Building,
                University of Maryland",
    "city": "College Park",
    "state": "Maryland"
}
```

Anatomy of a Playbook

Let's take a look at our playbook from the perspective of a YAML file. Here it is again, in Example 2-6.

Example 2-6. web-notls.yml

```
- name: Configure webserver with nginx
  hosts: webservers
  sudo: True
  tasks:
    - name: install nginx
      apt: name=nginx update_cache=yes

    - name: copy nginx config file
      copy: src=files/nginx.conf dest=/etc/nginx/sites-available/default

    - name: enable configuration
      file: >
        dest=/etc/nginx/sites-enabled/default
        src=/etc/nginx/sites-available/default
        state=link

    - name: copy index.html
      template: src=templates/index.html.j2 dest=/usr/share/nginx/html/index.html
        mode=0644

    - name: restart nginx
      service: name=nginx state=restarted
```

In Example 2-7, we see the JSON equivalent of this file.

Example 2-7. JSON equivalent of web-notls.yml

```
[
  {
    "name": "Configure webserver with nginx",
    "hosts": "webservers",
    "sudo": true,
    "tasks": [
      {
        "name": "Install nginx",
        "apt": "name=nginx update_cache=yes"
      },
      {
        "name": "copy nginx config file",
        "template": "src=files/nginx.conf dest=/etc/nginx/
        sites-available/default"
      },
      {
```

```
      "name": "enable configuration",
      "file": "dest=/etc/nginx/sites-enabled/default src=/etc/nginx/sites-available
/default state=link"
    },
    {
      "name": "copy index.html",
      "template" : "src=templates/index.html.j2 dest=/usr/share/nginx/html/
      index.html mode=0644"
    },
    {
      "name": "restart nginx",
      "service": "name=nginx state=restarted"
    }
  ]
 }
]
```

 A valid JSON file is also a valid YAML file. This is because YAML allows strings to be quoted, considers `true` and `false` to be valid Booleans, and has inline lists and dictionary syntaxes that are the same as JSON arrays and objects. But don't write your playbooks as JSON—the whole point of YAML is that it's easier for people to read.

Plays

Looking at either the YAML or JSON representation, it should be clear that a playbook is a list of dictionaries. Specifically, a playbook is a list of *plays*.

Here's the play[4] from our example:

```
- name: Configure webserver with nginx
  hosts: webservers
  sudo: True
  tasks:
    - name: install nginx
      apt: name=nginx update_cache=yes

    - name: copy nginx config file
      copy: src=files/nginx.conf dest=/etc/nginx/sites-available/default

    - name: enable configuration
      file: >
        dest=/etc/nginx/sites-enabled/default
        src=/etc/nginx/sites-available/default
        state=link
```

---

4 Actually, it's a list that contains a single play.

```
- name: copy index.html
  template: src=templates/index.html.j2
           dest=/usr/share/nginx/html/index.html mode=0644


- name: restart nginx
  service: name=nginx state=restarted
```

Every play must contain:

- A set of *hosts* to configure
- A list of *tasks* to be executed on those hosts

Think of a play as the thing that connects hosts to tasks.

In addition to specifying hosts and tasks, plays also support a number of optional settings. We'll get into those later, but three common ones are:

name
: A comment that describes what the play is about. Ansible will print this out when the play starts to run.

sudo
: If true, Ansible will run every task by sudo'ing as (by default) the root user. This is useful when managing Ubuntu servers, since by default you cannot SSH as the root user.

vars
: A list of variables and values. We'll see this in action later in this chapter.

Tasks

Our example playbook contains one play that has five tasks. Here's the first task of that play:

```
- name: install nginx
  apt: name=nginx update_cache=yes
```

The name is optional, so it's perfectly valid to write a task like this:

```
- apt: name=nginx update_cache=yes
```

Even though names are optional, I recommend you use them because they serve as good reminders for the intent of the task. (Names will be very useful when somebody else is trying to understand your playbook, including yourself in six months.) As we've seen, Ansible will print out the name of a task when it runs. Finally, as we'll see in Chapter 14, you can use the --start-at-task <task name> flag to tell ansible-playbook to start a playbook in the middle of a task, but you need to reference the task by name.

Every task must contain a key with the name of a module and a value with the arguments to that module. In the preceding example, the module name is *apt* and the arguments are `name=nginx update_cache=yes`.

These arguments tell the apt module to install the package named *nginx* and to update the package cache (the equivalent of doing an `apt-get update`) before installing the package.

It's important to understand that, from the point of view of the YAML parser used by the Ansible frontend, the arguments are treated as a string, not as a dictionary. This means that if you want to break up arguments into multiple lines, you need to use the YAML folding syntax, like this:

```
- name: install nginx
  apt: >
      name=nginx
      update_cache=yes
```

Ansible also supports a task syntax that will let you specify module arguments as a YAML dictionary, which is helpful when using modules that support complex arguments. We'll cover that in "Complex Arguments in Tasks: A Brief Digression" on page 99.

Ansible also supports an older syntax that uses `action` as the key and puts the name of the module in the value. The preceding example also can be written as:

```
- name: install nginx
  action: apt name=nginx update_cache=yes
```

Modules

Modules are scripts[5] that come packaged with Ansible and perform some kind of action on a host. Admittedly, that's a pretty generic description, but there's enormous variety across Ansible modules. The modules we use in this chapter are:

apt
  Installs or removes packages using the apt package manager.

copy
  Copies a file from local machine to the hosts.

file
  Sets the attribute of a file, symlink, or directory.

service
  Starts, stops, or restarts a service.

---

5 The modules that ship with Ansible all are written in Python, but modules can be written in any language.

template
> Generates a file from a template and copies it to the hosts.

Viewing Ansible Module Documentation

Ansible ships with the `ansible-doc` command-line tool, which shows documentation about modules. Think of it as man pages for Ansible modules. For example, to show the documentation for the *service* module, run:

```
$ ansible-doc service
```

If you use Mac OS X, there's a wonderful documentation viewer called Dash (*http://kapeli.com/dash*) that has support for Ansible. Dash indexes all of the Ansible module documentation. It's a commercial tool ($19.99 as of this writing), but I find it invaluable.

Recall from the first chapter that Ansible executes a task on a host by generating a custom script based on the module name and arguments, and then copies this script to the host and runs it.

There are over 200 modules that ship with Ansible, and this number grows with every release. You can also find third-party Ansible modules out there, or write your own.

Putting It All Together

To sum up, a playbook contains one or more plays. A play associates an unordered set of hosts with an ordered list of task_. Each task is associated with exactly one module.

Figure 2-3 is an entity-relationship diagram that depicts this relationship between playbooks, plays, hosts, tasks, and modules.

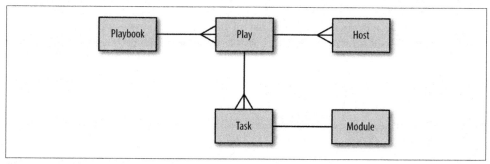

Figure 2-3. Entity-relationship diagram

Did Anything Change? Tracking Host State

When you run ansible-playbook, Ansible outputs status information for each task it executes in the play.

Looking back at Example 2-5, notice that the status for some of the tasks is *changed*, and the status for some others is *ok*. For example, the install nginx task has status *changed*, which appears as yellow on my terminal.

```
TASK: [install nginx] ********************************************************
changed: [testserver]
```

The enable configuration, on the other hand, has status *ok*, which appears as green on my terminal:

```
TASK: [enable configuration] *************************************************
ok: [testserver]
```

Any Ansible task that runs has the potential to change the state of the host in some way. Ansible modules will first check to see if the state of the host needs to be changed before taking any action. If the state of the host matches the arguments of the module, then Ansible takes no action on the host and responds with a state of *ok*.

On the other hand, if there is a difference between the state of the host and the arguments to the module, then Ansible will change the state of the host and return *changed*.

In the example output just shown, the *install nginx* task was changed, which meant that before I ran the playbook, the *nginx* package had not previously been installed on the host. The *enable configuration* task was unchanged, which meant that there was already a configuration file on the server that was identical to the file I was copying over. The reason for this is that the *nginx.conf* file I used in my playbook is the same as the *nginx.conf* file that gets installed by the *nginx* package on Ubuntu.

As we'll see later in this chapter, Ansible's detection of state change can be used to trigger additional actions through the use of *handlers*. But, even without using handlers, it is still a useful form of feedback to see whether your hosts are changing state as the playbook runs.

Getting Fancier: TLS Support

Let's move on to a more complex example: We're going to modify the previous playbook so that our webservers support TLS. The new features here are:

- Variables
- Handlers

TLS versus SSL

You might be familiar with the term *SSL* rather than *TLS* in the context of secure web servers. SSL is an older protocol that was used to secure communications between browsers and web servers, and it has been superseded by a newer protocol named TLS.

Although many continue to use the term *SSL* to refer to the current secure protocol, in this book, I use the more accurate *TLS*.

Example 2-8 shows what our playbook looks like with TLS support.

Example 2-8. web-tls.yml

```
- name: Configure webserver with nginx and tls
  hosts: webservers
  sudo: True
  vars:
    key_file: /etc/nginx/ssl/nginx.key
    cert_file: /etc/nginx/ssl/nginx.crt
    conf_file: /etc/nginx/sites-available/default
    server_name: localhost
  tasks:
    - name: Install nginx
      apt: name=nginx update_cache=yes cache_valid_time=3600

    - name: create directories for ssl certificates
      file: path=/etc/nginx/ssl state=directory

    - name: copy TLS key
      copy: src=files/nginx.key dest={{ key_file }} owner=root mode=0600
      notify: restart nginx

    - name: copy TLS certificate
      copy: src=files/nginx.crt dest={{ cert_file }}
      notify: restart nginx

    - name: copy nginx config file
      template: src=templates/nginx.conf.j2 dest={{ conf_file }}
      notify: restart nginx

    - name: enable configuration
      file: dest=/etc/nginx/sites-enabled/default src={{ conf_file }} state=link
      notify: restart nginx

    - name: copy index.html
      template: src=templates/index.html.j2 dest=/usr/share/nginx/html/index.html
            mode=0644
```

```
handlers:
  - name: restart nginx
    service: name=nginx state=restarted
```

Generating TLS certificate

We need to manually generate a TLS certificate. In a production environment, you'd purchase your TLS certificate from a certificate authority. We'll use a self-signed certificate, since we can generate those for free.

Create a *files* subdirectory of your *playbooks* directory, and then generate the TLS certificate and key:

```
$ mkdir files
$ openssl req -x509 -nodes -days 3650 -newkey rsa:2048 \
    -subj /CN=localhost \
    -keyout files/nginx.key -out files/nginx.crt
```

It should generate the files *nginx.key* and *nginx.crt* in the *files* directory. The certificate has an expiration date of 10 years (3,650 days) from the day you created it.

Variables

The play in our playbook now has a section called *vars*:

```
vars:
  key_file: /etc/nginx/ssl/nginx.key
  cert_file: /etc/nginx/ssl/nginx.crt
  conf_file: /etc/nginx/sites-available/default
  server_name: localhost
```

This section defines four variables and assigns a value to each variable.

In our example, each value is a string (e.g., `/etc/nginx/ssl/nginx.key`), but any valid YAML can be used as the value of a variable. You can use lists and dictionaries in addition to strings and Booleans.

Variables can be used in tasks, as well as in template files. You reference variables using the `{{ braces }}` notation. Ansible will replace these braces with the value of the variable.

Consider this task in the playbook:

```
  - name: copy TLS key
    copy: src=files/nginx.key dest={{ key_file }} owner=root mode=0600
```

Ansible will substitute `{{ key_file }}` with `/etc/nginx/ssl/nginx.key` when it executes this task.

When Quoting Is Necessary

If you reference a variable right after specifying the module, the YAML parser will misinterpret the variable reference as the beginning of an in-line dictionary. Consider the following example:

```
- name: perform some task
  command: {{ myapp }} -a foo
```

Ansible will try to parse the first part of {{ myapp }} -a foo as a dictionary instead of a string, and will return an error. In this case, you must quote the arguments:

```
- name: perform some task
  command: "{{ myapp }} -a foo"
```

A similar problem arises if your argument contains a colon. For example:

```
- name: show a debug message
  debug: msg="The debug module will print a message: neat, eh?"
```

The colon in the msg argument trips up the YAML parser. To get around this, you need to quote the entire argument string.

Unfortunately, just quoting the argument string won't resolve the problem, either.

```
- name: show a debug message
  debug: "msg=The debug module will print a message: neat, eh?"
```

This will make the YAML parser happy, but the output isn't what you expect:

```
TASK: [show a debug message] **********************************************
ok: [localhost] => {
    "msg": "The"
}
```

The debug module's *msg* argument requires a quoted string to capture the spaces. In this particular case, we need to quote both the whole argument string and the *msg* argument. Ansible supports alternating single and double quotes, so you can do this:

```
- name: show a debug message
  debug: "msg='The debug module will print a message: neat, eh?'"
```

This yields the expected output:

```
TASK: [show a debug message] **********************************************
ok: [localhost] => {
    "msg": "The debug module will print a message: neat, eh?"
}
```

Ansible is pretty good at generating meaningful error messages if you forget to put quotes in the right places and end up with invalid YAML.

Generating the Nginx Configuration Template

If you've done web programming, you've likely used a template system to generate HTML. In case you haven't, a template is just a text file that has some special syntax for specifying variables that should be replaced by values. If you've ever received an automated email from a company, they're probably using an email template as shown in Example 2-9.

Example 2-9. An email template

```
Dear {{ name }},

You have {{ num_comments }} new comments on your blog: {{ blog_name }}.
```

Ansible's use case isn't HTML pages or emails—it's configuration files. You don't want to hand-edit configuration files if you can avoid it. This is especially true if you have to reuse the same bits of configuration data (say, the IP address of your queue server or your database credentials) across multiple configuration files. It's much better to take the info that's specific to your deployment, record it in one location, and then generate all of the files that need this information from templates.

Ansible uses the Jinja2 template engine to implement templating. If you've ever used a templating library such as Mustache, ERB, or the Django template system, Jinja2 will feel very familiar.

Nginx's configuration file needs information about where to find the TLS key and certificate. We're going to use Ansible's templating functionality to define this configuration file so that we can avoid hard-coding values that might change.

In your *playbooks* directory, create a *templates* subdirectory and create the file *templates/nginx.conf.j2*, as shown in Example 2-10.

Example 2-10. templates/nginx.conf.j2

```
server {
        listen 80 default_server;
        listen [::]:80 default_server ipv6only=on;

        listen 443 ssl;

        root /usr/share/nginx/html;
        index index.html index.htm;

        server_name {{ server_name }};
        ssl_certificate {{ cert_file }};
        ssl_certificate_key {{ key_file }};

        location / {
```

```
            try_files $uri $uri/ =404;
        }
}
```

We use the .j2 extension to indicate that the file is a Jinja2 template. However, you can use a different extension if you like; Ansible doesn't care.

In our template, we reference three variables:

server_name
> The hostname of the web server (e.g., www.example.com)

cert_file
> The path to the TLS certificate

key_file
> The path to the TLS private key

We define these variables in the playbook.

Ansible also uses the Jinja2 template engine to evaluate variables in playbooks. Recall that we saw the {{ conf_file }} syntax in the playbook itself.

 Early versions of Ansible used a dollar sign ($) to do variable interpolation in playbooks instead of the braces. You used to dereference variable *foo* by writing $foo, where now you write {{ foo }}. The dollar sign syntax has been deprecated; if you encounter it in an example playbook you find on the Internet, then you're looking at older Ansible code.

You can use all of the Jinja2 features in your templates, but we won't cover them in detail here. Check out the Jinja2 Template Designer Documentation (*http://jinja.pocoo.org/docs/dev/templates/*) for more details. You probably won't need to use those advanced templating features, though. One Jinja2 feature you probably will use with Ansible is filters; we'll cover those in a later chapter.

Handlers

Looking back at our *web-tls.yml* playbook, note that there are two new playbook elements we haven't discussed yet. There's a handlers section that looks like this:

```
handlers:
- name: restart nginx
  service: name=nginx state=restarted
```

In addition, several of the tasks contain a notify key. For example:

```
- name: copy TLS key
  copy: src=files/nginx.key dest={{ key_file }} owner=root mode=0600
  notify: restart nginx
```

Handlers are one of the conditional forms that Ansible supports. A handler is similar to a task, but it runs only if it has been notified by a task. A task will fire the notification if Ansible recognizes that the task has changed the state of the system.

A task notifies a handler by passing the handler's name as the argument. In the preceding example, the handler's name is restart nginx. For an nginx server, we'd need to restart it[6] if any of the following happens:

- The TLS key changes
- The TLS certificate changes
- The configuration file changes
- The contents of the *sites-enabled* directory change

We put a notify statement on each of the tasks to ensure that Ansible restarts nginx if any of these conditions are met.

A few things to keep in mind about handlers

Handlers only run after all of the tasks are run, and they only run once, even if they are notified multiple times. They always run in the order that they appear in the play, not the notification order.

The official Ansible docs mention that the only common uses for handlers are for restarting services and for reboots. Personally, I've only ever used them for restarting services. Even then, it's a pretty small optimization, since we can always just unconditionally restart the service at the end of the playbook instead of notifying it on change, and restarting a service doesn't usually take very long.

Another pitfall with handlers that I've encountered is that they can be troublesome when debugging a playbook. It goes something like this:

1. I run a playbook.
2. One of my tasks with a *notify* on it changes state.
3. An error occurs on a subsequent task, stopping Ansible.
4. I fix the error in my playbook.
5. I run Ansible again.

---

6 Alternatively, we could reload the configuration file using state=reloaded instead of restarting the service.

6. None of the tasks report a state change the second time around, so Ansible doesn't run the handler.

Running the Playbook

As before, we use the `ansible-playbook` command to run the playbook.

```
$ ansible-playbook web-tls.yml
```

The output should look something like this:

```
PLAY [Configure webserver with nginx and tls] ********************************

GATHERING FACTS **************************************************************
ok: [testserver]

TASK: [Install nginx] ********************************************************
changed: [testserver]

TASK: [create directories for tls certificates] *****************************
changed: [testserver]

TASK: [copy TLS key] ********************************************************
changed: [testserver]

TASK: [copy TLS certificate] ************************************************
changed: [testserver]

TASK: [copy nginx config file] **********************************************
changed: [testserver]

TASK: [enable configuration] ************************************************
ok: [testserver]

NOTIFIED: [restart nginx] ***************************************************
changed: [testserver]

PLAY RECAP ******************************************************************
testserver                 : ok=8    changed=6    unreachable=0    failed=0
```

Point your browser to *https://localhost:8443* (don't forget the "s" on https). If you're using Chrome, like I am, you'll get a ghastly message that says something like, "Your connection is not private" (see Figure 2-4).

Figure 2-4. Browsers like Chrome don't trust self-signed TLS certificates

Don't worry, though; that error is expected, as we generated a self-signed TLS certificate, and web browsers like Chrome only trust certificates that have been issued from a proper authority.

We covered a lot of the "what" of Ansible in this chapter, describing what Ansible will do to your hosts. The handlers we discussed here are just one form of control flow that Ansible supports. In a later chapter, we'll see iteration and conditionally running tasks based on the values of variables.

In the next chapter, we'll talk about the "who"; in other words, how to describe the hosts that your playbooks will run against.

## CHAPTER 3

Inventory: Describing Your Servers

So far, we've been working with only one server (or *host*, as Ansible calls it). In reality, you're going to be managing multiple hosts. The collection of hosts that Ansible knows about is called the *inventory*.

The Inventory File

The default way to describe your hosts in Ansible is to list them in text files, called *inventory files*. A very simple inventory file might just contain a list of hostnames, as shown in Example 3-1.

Example 3-1. A very simple inventory file

```
ontario.example.com
newhampshire.example.com
maryland.example.com
virginia.example.com
newyork.example.com
quebec.example.com
rhodeisland.example.com
```

 Ansible uses your local SSH client by default, which means that it will understand any aliases that you set up in your SSH config file. This does not hold true if you configure Ansible to use the Paramiko connection plug-in instead of the default SSH plug-in.

There is one host that Ansible automatically adds to the inventory by default: *localhost*. Ansible understands that localhost refers to your local machine, so it will interact with it directly rather than connecting by SSH.

Although Ansible adds the localhost to your inventory automatically, you have to have at least one other host in your inventory file; otherwise, ansible-playbook will terminate with the error:

```
ERROR: provided hosts list is empty
```

In the case where you have no other hosts in your inventory file, you can explicitly add an entry for localhost like this:

```
localhost ansible_connection=local
```

Preliminaries: Multiple Vagrant Machines

To talk about inventory, we need to interact with multiple hosts. Let's configure Vagrant to bring up three hosts. We'll unimaginatively call them vagrant1, vagrant2, and vagrant3.

Before you modify your existing Vagrantfile, make sure you destroy your existing virtual machine by running:

```
$ vagrant destroy --force
```

If you don't include the --force option, Vagrant will prompt you to confirm that you want to destroy the virtual machine.

Next, edit your Vagrantfile so it looks like Example 3-2.

Example 3-2. Vagrantfile with three servers

```
VAGRANTFILE_API_VERSION = "2"

Vagrant.configure(VAGRANTFILE_API_VERSION) do |config|
  # Use the same key for each machine
  config.ssh.insert_key = false

  config.vm.define "vagrant1" do |vagrant1|
    vagrant1.vm.box = "ubuntu/trusty64"
    vagrant1.vm.network "forwarded_port", guest: 80, host: 8080
    vagrant1.vm.network "forwarded_port", guest: 443, host: 8443
  end
  config.vm.define "vagrant2" do |vagrant2|
    vagrant2.vm.box = "ubuntu/trusty64"
    vagrant2.vm.network "forwarded_port", guest: 80, host: 8081
    vagrant2.vm.network "forwarded_port", guest: 443, host: 8444
  end
  config.vm.define "vagrant3" do |vagrant3|
    vagrant3.vm.box = "ubuntu/trusty64"
    vagrant3.vm.network "forwarded_port", guest: 80, host: 8082
    vagrant3.vm.network "forwarded_port", guest: 443, host: 8445
  end
end
```

Vagrant 1.7+ defaults to using a different SSH key for each host. Example 3-2 contains the line to revert to the earlier behavior of using the same SSH key for each host:

```
config.ssh.insert_key = false
```

Using the same key on each host simplifies our Ansible setup because we can specify a single SSH key in the *ansible.cfg* file. You'll need to edit the *host_key_checking* value in your *ansible.cfg*. Your file should look like Example 3-3.

Example 3-3. ansible.cfg

```
[defaults]
hostfile = inventory
remote_user = vagrant
private_key_file = ~/.vagrant.d/insecure_private_key
host_key_checking = False
```

For now, we'll assume each of these servers can potentially be a web server, so Example 3-2 maps ports 80 and 443 inside each Vagrant machine to a port on the local machine.

You should be able to bring up the virtual machines by running:

```
$ vagrant up
```

If all went well, the output should look something like this:

```
Bringing machine 'vagrant1' up with 'virtualbox' provider...
Bringing machine 'vagrant2' up with 'virtualbox' provider...
Bringing machine 'vagrant3' up with 'virtualbox' provider...
...
    vagrant3: 80 => 8082 (adapter 1)
    vagrant3: 443 => 8445 (adapter 1)
    vagrant3: 22 => 2201 (adapter 1)
==> vagrant3: Booting VM...
==> vagrant3: Waiting for machine to boot. This may take a few minutes...
    vagrant3: SSH address: 127.0.0.1:2201
    vagrant3: SSH username: vagrant
    vagrant3: SSH auth method: private key
    vagrant3: Warning: Connection timeout. Retrying...
==> vagrant3: Machine booted and ready!
==> vagrant3: Checking for guest additions in VM...
==> vagrant3: Mounting shared folders...
    vagrant3: /vagrant => /Users/lorinhochstein/dev/oreilly-ansible/playbooks
```

Let's create an inventory file that contains these three machines.

First, we need to know what ports on the local machine map to the SSH port (22) inside of each VM. Recall we can get that information by running:

```
$ vagrant ssh-config
```

The output should look something like this:

```
Host vagrant1
  HostName 127.0.0.1
  User vagrant
  Port 2222
  UserKnownHostsFile /dev/null
  StrictHostKeyChecking no
  PasswordAuthentication no
  IdentityFile /Users/lorinhochstein/.vagrant.d/insecure_private_key
  IdentitiesOnly yes
  LogLevel FATAL

Host vagrant2
  HostName 127.0.0.1
  User vagrant
  Port 2200
  UserKnownHostsFile /dev/null
  StrictHostKeyChecking no
  PasswordAuthentication no
  IdentityFile /Users/lorinhochstein/.vagrant.d/insecure_private_key
  IdentitiesOnly yes
  LogLevel FATAL

Host vagrant3
  HostName 127.0.0.1
  User vagrant
  Port 2201
  UserKnownHostsFile /dev/null
  StrictHostKeyChecking no
  PasswordAuthentication no
  IdentityFile /Users/lorinhochstein/.vagrant.d/insecure_private_key
  IdentitiesOnly yes
  LogLevel FATAL
```

We can see that vagrant1 uses port 2222, vagrant2 uses port 2200, and vagrant3 uses port 2201.

Modify your *hosts* file so it looks like this:

```
vagrant1 ansible_ssh_host=127.0.0.1 ansible_ssh_port=2222
vagrant2 ansible_ssh_host=127.0.0.1 ansible_ssh_port=2200
vagrant3 ansible_ssh_host=127.0.0.1 ansible_ssh_port=2201
```

Now, make sure that you can access these machines. For example, to get information about the network interface for vagrant2, run:

```
$ ansible vagrant2 -a "ip addr show dev eth0"
```

On my machine, the output looks like this:

```
vagrant2 | success | rc=0 >>
2: eth0: <BROADCAST,MULTICAST,UP,LOWER_UP> mtu 1500 qdisc pfifo_fast state UP
group default qlen 1000
    link/ether 08:00:27:fe:1e:4d brd ff:ff:ff:ff:ff:ff
    inet 10.0.2.15/24 brd 10.0.2.255 scope global eth0
```

```
    valid_lft forever preferred_lft forever
    inet6 fe80::a00:27ff:fefe:1e4d/64 scope link
    valid_lft forever preferred_lft forever
```

Behavioral Inventory Parameters

To describe our Vagrant machines in the Ansible inventory file, we had to explicitly specify the hostname (127.0.0.1) and port (2222, 2200, or 2201) that Ansible's SSH client should connect to.

Ansible calls these variables *behavioral inventory parameters*, and there are several of them you can use when you need to override the Ansible defaults for a host (see Table 3-1).

Table 3-1. Behavioral inventory parameters

Name	Default	Description
ansible_ssh_host	name of host	Hostname or IP address to SSH to
ansible_ssh_port	22	Port to SSH to
ansible_ssh_user	root	User to SSH as
ansible_ssh_pass	*none*	Password to use for SSH authentication
ansible_connection	smart	How Ansible will connect to host (see below)
ansible_ssh_private_key_file	*none*	SSH private key to use for SSH authentication
ansible_shell_type	sh	Shell to use for commands (see below)
ansible_python_interpreter	*/usr/bin/python*	Python interpreter on host (see below)
ansible_*_interpreter	*none*	Like ansible_python_interpreter for other languages (see below)

For some of these options, the meaning is obvious from the name, but others require additional explanation.

ansible_connection

Ansible supports multiple *transports*, which are mechanisms that Ansible uses to connect to the host. The default transport, *smart*, will check to see if the locally installed SSH client supports a feature called *ControlPersist*. If the SSH client supports ControlPersist, Ansible will use the local SSH client. If the SSH client doesn't support

ControlPersist, then the smart transport will fall back to using a Python-based SSH client library called *paramiko*.

ansible_shell_type

Ansible works by making SSH connections to remote machines and then invoking scripts. By default, Ansible assumes that the remote shell is the Bourne shell located at */bin/sh*, and will generate the appropriate command-line parameters that work with Bourne shell.

Ansible also accepts `csh`, `fish`, and (on Windows) `powershell` as valid values for this parameter. I've never encountered a need for changing the shell type.

ansible_python_interpreter

Because the modules that ship with Ansible are implemented in Python 2, Ansible needs to know the location of the Python interpreter on the remote machine. You might need to change this if your remote host does not have a Python 2 interpreter at */usr/bin/python*. For example, if you are managing hosts that run Arch Linux, you will need to change this to */usr/bin/python2*, because Arch Linux installs Python 3 at */usr/bin/python*, and Ansible modules are not (yet) compatible with Python 3.

ansible_*_interpreter

If you are using a custom module that is not written in Python, you can use this parameter to specify the location of the interpreter (e.g., */usr/bin/ruby*). We'll cover this in Chapter 10.

Changing Behavioral Parameter Defaults

You can override some of the behavioral parameter default values in the [`defaults`] section of the *ansible.cfg* file (Table 3-2). Recall that we used this previously to change the default SSH user.

Table 3-2. Defaults that can be overridden in ansible.cfg

Behavioral inventory parameter	ansible.cfg option
ansible_ssh_port	remote_port
ansible_ssh_user	remote_user
ansible_ssh_private_key_file	private_key_file
ansible_shell_type	executable (see the following paragraph)

The ansible.cfg `executable` config option is not exactly the same as the `ansible_shell_type` behavioral inventory parameter. Instead, the executable specifies the full path of the shell to use on the remote machine (e.g., */usr/local/bin/fish*). Ansible will look at the name of the base name of this path (in the case of */usr/local/bin/fish*, the basename is *fish*) and use that as the default value for `ansible_shell_type`.

Groups and Groups and Groups

When performing configuration tasks, we typically want to perform actions on groups of hosts, rather than on an individual host.

Ansible automatically defines a group called *all* (or ***), which includes all of the hosts in the inventory. For example, we can check if the clocks on the machines are roughly synchronized by running:

```
$ ansible all -a "date"
```

or

```
$ ansible '*' -a "date"
```

The output on my system looks like this:

```
vagrant3 | success | rc=0 >>
Sun Sep  7 02:56:46 UTC 2014

vagrant2 | success | rc=0 >>
Sun Sep  7 03:03:46 UTC 2014

vagrant1 | success | rc=0 >>
Sun Sep  7 02:56:47 UTC 2014
```

We can define our own groups in the inventory file. Ansible uses the *.ini* file format for inventory files. In the *.ini* format, configuration values are grouped together into sections.

Here's how we would specify that our vagrant hosts are in a group called *vagrant*, along with the other example hosts we mentioned at the beginning of the chapter:

```
ontario.example.com
newhampshire.example.com
maryland.example.com
virginia.example.com
newyork.example.com
quebec.example.com
rhodeisland.example.com

[vagrant]
vagrant1 ansible_ssh_host=127.0.0.1 ansible_ssh_port=2222
vagrant2 ansible_ssh_host=127.0.0.1 ansible_ssh_port=2200
vagrant3 ansible_ssh_host=127.0.0.1 ansible_ssh_port=2201
```

We could have also listed the vagrant hosts at the top, and then also in a group, like this:

```
maryland.example.com
newhampshire.example.com
newyork.example.com
ontario.example.com
quebec.example.com
rhodeisland.example.com
vagrant1 ansible_ssh_host=127.0.0.1 ansible_ssh_port=2222
vagrant2 ansible_ssh_host=127.0.0.1 ansible_ssh_port=2200
vagrant3 ansible_ssh_host=127.0.0.1 ansible_ssh_port=2201
virginia.example.com

[vagrant]
vagrant1
vagrant2
vagrant3
```

Example: Deploying a Django App

Imagine you're responsible for deploying a Django-based web application that processes long-running jobs. The app needs to support the following services:

- The actual Django web app itself, run by a Gunicorn HTTP server.
- An nginx web server, which will sit in front of Gunicorn and serve static assets.
- A Celery task queue that will execute long-running jobs on behalf of the web app.
- A RabbitMQ message queue that serves as the backend for Celery.
- A Postgres database that serves as the persistent store.

 In later chapters, we will work through a detailed example of deploying this kind of Django-based application, although our example won't use Celery or RabbitMQ.

We need to deploy this application into different types of environments: production (the real thing), staging (for testing on hosts that our team has shared access to), and vagrant (for local testing).

When we deploy to production, we want the entire system to respond quickly and be reliable, so we:

- Run the web application on multiple hosts for better performance and put a load balancer in front of them.

- Run task queue servers on multiple hosts for better performance.

- Put Gunicorn, Celery, RabbitMQ, and Postgres all on separate servers.

- Use two Postgres hosts, a primary and a replica.

Assuming we have one load balancer, three web servers, three task queues, one RabbitMQ server, and two database servers, that's 10 hosts we need to deal with.

For our staging environment, imagine that we want to use fewer hosts than we do in production in order to save costs, especially since the staging environment is going to see a lot less activity than production. Let's say we decide to use only two hosts for staging; we'll put the web server and task queue on one staging host, and RabbitMQ and Postgres on the other.

For our local vagrant environment, we decide to use three servers: one for the web app, one for a task queue, and one that will contain RabbitMQ and Postgres.

Example 3-4 shows a possible inventory file that groups our servers by environment (production, staging, vagrant) and by function (web server, task queue, etc.).

Example 3-4. Inventory file for deploying a Django app

```
[production]
delaware.example.com
georgia.example.com
maryland.example.com
newhampshire.example.com
newjersey.example.com
newyork.example.com
northcarolina.example.com
pennsylvania.example.com
rhodeisland.example.com
virginia.example.com

[staging]
ontario.example.com
quebec.example.com

[vagrant]
vagrant1 ansible_ssh_host=127.0.0.1 ansible_ssh_port=2222
vagrant2 ansible_ssh_host=127.0.0.1 ansible_ssh_port=2200
vagrant3 ansible_ssh_host=127.0.0.1 ansible_ssh_port=2201

[lb]
delaware.example.com

[web]
georgia.example.com
newhampshire.example.com
newjersey.example.com
```

```
ontario.example.com
vagrant1

[task]
newyork.example.com
northcarolina.example.com
maryland.example.com
ontario.example.com
vagrant2

[rabbitmq]
pennsylvania.example.com
quebec.example.com
vagrant3

[db]
rhodeisland.example.com
virginia.example.com
quebec.example.com
vagrant3
```

We could have first listed all of the servers at the top of the inventory file, without specifying a group, but that isn't necessary, and that would've made this file even longer.

Note that we only needed to specify the behavioral inventory parameters for the Vagrant instances once.

Aliases and Ports

We described our Vagrant hosts like this:

```
[vagrant]
vagrant1 ansible_ssh_host=127.0.0.1 ansible_ssh_port=2222
vagrant2 ansible_ssh_host=127.0.0.1 ansible_ssh_port=2200
vagrant3 ansible_ssh_host=127.0.0.1 ansible_ssh_port=2201
```

The names vagrant1, vagrant2, and vagrant3 here are *aliases*. They are not the real hostnames, but instead are useful names for referring to these hosts.

Ansible supports doing <hostname>:<port> syntax when specifying hosts, so we could replace the line that contains vagrant1 with 127.0.0.1:2222.

However, we can't actually run what you see in Example 3-5.

Example 3-5. This doesn't work

```
[vagrant]
127.0.0.1:2222
127.0.0.1:2200
127.0.0.1:2201
```

The reason is that Ansible's inventory can associate only a single host with *127.0.0.1*, so the vagrant group would contain only one host instead of three.

Groups of Groups

Ansible also allows you to define groups that are made up of other groups. For example, both the web servers and the task queue servers will need to have Django and its dependencies. We might find it useful to define a "django" group that contains both of these two groups. You would add this to the inventory file:

```
[django:children]
web
task
```

Note that the syntax changes when you are specifying a group of groups, as opposed to a group of hosts. That's so Ansible knows to interpret *web* and *task* as groups and not as hosts.

Numbered Hosts (Pets versus Cattle)

The inventory file shown in Example 3-4 looks complex. In reality, it describes only 15 different hosts, which doesn't sound like a large number in this cloudy scale-out world. However, even dealing with 15 hosts in the inventory file can be cumbersome because each host has a completely different hostname.

Bill Baker of Microsoft came up with the distinction between treating servers as *pets* versus treating them like *cattle*.[1] We give pets distinctive names, and we treat and care for them as individuals. On the other hand, when we discuss cattle, we refer to them by identification number.

The cattle approach is much more scalable, and Ansible supports it well by supporting numeric patterns. For example, if your 20 servers were named *web1.example.com*, *web2.example.com*, and so on, then you could specify them in the inventory file like this:

```
[web]
web[1:20].example.com
```

If you prefer to have a leading zero (e.g., *web01.example.com*), then specify a leading zero in the range, like this:

```
[web]
web[01:20].example.com
```

---

1 This term has been popularized by Randy Bias of Cloudscaling (*http://bit.ly/1P3nHB2*).

Ansible also supports using alphabetic characters to specify ranges. If you wanted to use the convention *web-a.example.com*, *web-b.example.com*, and so on, for your 20 servers, then you could do this:

```
[web]
web-[a-t].example.com
```

Hosts and Group Variables: Inside the Inventory

Recall how we specified behavioral inventory parameters for Vagrant hosts:

```
vagrant1 ansible_ssh_host=127.0.0.1 ansible_ssh_port=2222
vagrant2 ansible_ssh_host=127.0.0.1 ansible_ssh_port=2200
vagrant3 ansible_ssh_host=127.0.0.1 ansible_ssh_port=2201
```

Those parameters are variables that have special meaning to Ansible. We can also define arbitrary variable names and associated values on hosts. For example, we could define a variable named *color* and set it to a value for each server:

```
newhampshire.example.com color=red
maryland.example.com color=green
ontario.example.com color=blue
quebec.example.com color=purple
```

This variable can then be used in a playbook, just like any other variable.

Personally, I don't often attach variables to specific hosts. On the other hand, I often associate variables with groups.

Circling back to our Django example, the web application and task queue service need to communicate with RabbitMQ and Postgres. We'll assume that access to the Postgres database is secured both at the network layer (so only the web application and the task queue can reach the database) as well as by username and password, where RabbitMQ is secured only by the network layer.

To set everything up, we need to do the following:

- Configure the web servers with the hostname, port, username, password of the primary postgres server, and name of the database.
- Configure the task queues with the hostname, port, username, password of the primary postgres server, and the name of the database.
- Configure the web servers with the hostname and port of the RabbitMQ server.
- Configure the task queues with the hostname and port of the RabbitMQ server.
- Configure the primary postgres server with the hostname, port, and username and password of the replica postgres server (production only).

This configuration info varies by environment, so it makes sense to define these as group variables on the production, staging, and vagrant groups.

Example 3-6 shows one way we can specify this information as group variables in the inventory file.

Example 3-6. Specifying group variables in inventory

```
[all:vars]
ntp_server=ntp.ubuntu.com

[production:vars]
db_primary_host=rhodeisland.example.com
db_primary_port=5432
db_replica_host=virginia.example.com
db_name=widget_production
db_user=widgetuser
db_password=pFmMxcyD;Fc6)6
rabbitmq_host=pennsylvania.example.com
rabbitmq_port=5672


[staging:vars]
db_primary_host=quebec.example.com
db_name=widget_staging
db_user=widgetuser
db_password=L@4Ryz8cRUXedj
rabbitmq_host=quebec.example.com
rabbitmq_port=5672

[vagrant:vars]
db_primary_host=vagrant3
db_primary_port=5432
db_primary_port=5432
db_name=widget_vagrant
db_user=widgetuser
db_password=password
rabbitmq_host=vagrant3
rabbitmq_port=5672
```

Note how group variables are organized into sections named [<group name>:vars].

Also note how we took advantage of the all group that Ansible creates automatically to specify variables that don't change across hosts.

Host and Group Variables: In Their Own Files

The inventory file is a reasonable place to put host and group variables if you don't have too many hosts. But as your inventory gets larger, it gets more difficult to manage variables this way.

Additionally, though Ansible variables can hold Booleans, strings, lists, and dictionaries, in an inventory file, you can specify only Booleans and strings.

Ansible offers a more scalable approach to keep track of host and group variables: You can create a separate variable file for each host and each group. Ansible expects these variable files to be in YAML format.

Ansible looks for host variable files in a directory called *host_vars* and group variable files in a directory called *group_vars*. Ansible expects these directories to be either in the directory that contains your playbooks or in the directory adjacent to your inventory file. In our case, those two directories are the same.

For example, if I had a directory containing my playbooks at */home/lorin/playbooks/* with an inventory file at */home/lorin/playbooks/hosts*, then I would put variables for the *quebec.example.com* host in the file */home/lorin/playbooks/host_vars/quebec.example.com*, and I would put variables for the production group in the file */home/lorin/playbooks/group_vars/production*.

Example 3-7 shows what the */home/lorin/playbooks/group_vars/production* file would look like.

Example 3-7. group_vars/production

```
db_primary_host: rhodeisland.example.com
db_replica_host: virginia.example.com
db_name: widget_production
db_user: widgetuser
db_password: pFmMxcyD;Fc6)6
rabbitmq_host:pennsylvania.example.com
```

Note that we could also use YAML dictionaries to represent these values, as shown in Example 3-8.

Example 3-8. group_vars/production, with dictionaries

```
db:
    user: widgetuser
    password: pFmMxcyD;Fc6)6
    name: widget_production
    primary:
        host: rhodeisland.example.com
        port: 5432
    replica:
        host: virginia.example.com
        port: 5432

rabbitmq:
    host: pennsylvania.example.com
    port: 5672
```

If we choose YAML dictionaries, that changes the way we access the variables:

```
{{ db_primary_host }}
```

versus:

```
{{ db.primary.host }}
```

If you want to break things out even further, Ansible will allow you to define *group_vars/production* as a directory instead of a file, and let you place multiple YAML files that contain variable definitions.

For example, we could put the database-related variables in one file and the RabbitMQ-related variables in another file, as shown in Examples 3-9 and 3-10.

Example 3-9. group_vars/production/db

```
db:
    user: widgetuser
    password: pFmMxcyD;Fc6)6
    name: widget_production
    primary:
        host: rhodeisland.example.com
        port: 5432
    replica:
        host: virginia.example.com
        port: 5432
```

Example 3-10. group_vars/production/rabbitmq

```
rabbitmq:
    host: pennsylvania.example.com
    port: 6379
```

In general, I find it's better to keep things simple rather than split variables out across too many files.

Dynamic Inventory

Up until this point, we've been explicitly specifying all of our hosts in our hosts inventory file. However, you might have a system external to Ansible that keeps track of your hosts. For example, if your hosts run on Amazon EC2, then EC2 tracks information about your hosts for you, and you can retrieve this information through EC2's web interface, its Query API, or through command-line tools such as *awscli*. Other cloud providers have similar interfaces. Or, if you're managing your own servers and are using an automated provisioning system such as Cobbler or Ubuntu MAAS, then your provisioning system is already keeping track of your servers. Or, maybe you have one of those fancy configuration management databases (CMDBs) where all of this information lives.

You don't want to manually duplicate this information in your hosts file, because eventually that file will not jibe with your external system, which is the true source of information about your hosts. Ansible supports a feature called *dynamic inventory* that allows you to avoid this duplication.

If the inventory file is marked executable, Ansible will assume it is a dynamic inventory script and will execute the file instead of reading it.

 To mark a file as executable, use the `chmod +x` command. For example:

```
$ chmod +x dynamic.py
```

The Interface for a Dynamic Inventory Script

An Ansible dynamic inventory script must support two command-line flags:

- `--host=<hostname>` for showing host details
- `--list` for listing groups

Showing host details

To get the details of the individual host, Ansible will call the inventory script like this:

```
$ ./dynamic.py --host=vagrant2
```

The output should contain any host-specific variables, including behavioral parameters, like this:

```
{ "ansible_ssh_host": "127.0.0.1", "ansible_ssh_port": 2200,
  "ansible_ssh_user": "vagrant"}
```

The output is a single JSON object where the names are variable names, and the values are the variable values.

Listing groups

Dynamic inventory scripts need to be able to list all of the groups, and details about the individual hosts. For example, if our script is called *dynamic.py*, Ansible will call it like this to get a list of all of the groups:

```
$ ./dynamic.py --list
```

The output should look something like this:

```
{"production": ["delaware.example.com", "georgia.example.com",
                "maryland.example.com", "newhampshire.example.com",
                "newjersey.example.com", "newyork.example.com",
                "northcarolina.example.com", "pennsylvania.example.com",
                "rhodeisland.example.com", "virginia.example.com"],
 "staging": ["ontario.example.com", "quebec.example.com"],
 "vagrant": ["vagrant1", "vagrant2", "vagrant3"],
 "lb": ["delaware.example.com"],
 "web": ["georgia.example.com", "newhampshire.example.com",
         "newjersey.example.com", "ontario.example.com", "vagrant1"]
 "task": ["newyork.example.com", "northcarolina.example.com",
          "ontario.example.com", "vagrant2"],
 "rabbitmq": ["pennsylvania.example.com", "quebec.example.com", "vagrant3"],
 "db": ["rhodeisland.example.com", "virginia.example.com", "vagrant3"]
}
```

The output is a single JSON object where the names are Ansible group names, and the values are arrays of host names.

As an optimization, the `--list` command can contain the values of the host variables for all of the hosts, which saves Ansible the trouble of making a separate `--host` invocation to retrieve the variables for the individual hosts.

To take advantage of this optimization, the `--list` command should return a key named `_meta` that contains the variables for each host, in this form:

```
"_meta" :
  { "hostvars" :
    "vagrant1" : { "ansible_ssh_host": "127.0.0.1", "ansible_ssh_port": 2222,
                   "ansible_ssh_user": "vagrant"},
    "vagrant2": { "ansible_ssh_host": "127.0.0.1", "ansible_ssh_port": 2200,
                  "ansible_ssh_user": "vagrant"},
    ...
}
```

Writing a Dynamic Inventory Script

One of the handy features of Vagrant is that you can see which machines are currently running using the `vagrant status` command. Assuming we had a Vagrant file that looked like Example 3-2, if we ran `vagrant status`, the output would look like Example 3-11.

Example 3-11. Output of vagrant status

```
$ vagrant status
Current machine states:

vagrant1                  running (virtualbox)
vagrant2                  running (virtualbox)
vagrant3                  running (virtualbox)
```

```
This environment represents multiple VMs. The VMs are all listed
above with their current state. For more information about a specific
VM, run `vagrant status NAME`.
```

Because Vagrant already keeps track of machines for us, there's no need for us to write a list of the Vagrant machines in an Ansible inventory file. Instead, we can write a dynamic inventory script that queries Vagrant about which machines are currently running.

Once we've set up a dynamic inventory script for Vagrant, even if we alter our Vagrantfile to run different numbers of Vagrant machines, we won't need to edit an Ansible inventory file.

Let's work through an example of creating a dynamic inventory script that retrieves the details about hosts from Vagrant.[2]

Our dynamic inventory script is going to need to invoke the `vagrant status` command. The output shown in Example 3-11 is designed for humans to read, rather than for machines to parse. We can get a list of running hosts in a format that is easier to parse with the `--machine-readable` flag, like so:

```
$ vagrant status --machine-readable
```

The output looks like this:

```
1410577818,vagrant1,provider-name,virtualbox
1410577818,vagrant1,state,running
1410577818,vagrant1,state-human-short,running
1410577818,vagrant1,state-human-long,The VM is running. To stop this VM%!(VAGRANT
_COMMA) you can run `vagrant halt` to\nshut it down forcefully%!(VAGRANT_COMMA)
or you can run `vagrant suspend` to simply\nsuspend the virtual machine. In
either case%!(VAGRANT_COMMA to restart it again%!(VAGRANT_COMMA)\nsimply run
`vagrant up`.
1410577818,vagrant2,provider-name,virtualbox
1410577818,vagrant2,state,running
1410577818,vagrant2,state-human-short,running
1410577818,vagrant2,state-human-long,The VM is running. To stop this VM%!(VAGRANT
_COMMA) you can run `vagrant halt` to\nshut it down forcefully%!(VAGRANT_COMMA)
or you can run `vagrant suspend` to simply\nsuspend the virtual machine. In
either case%!(VAGRANT_COMMA) to restart it again%!(VAGRANT_COMMA)\nsimply run
`vagrant up`.
1410577818,vagrant3,provider-name,virtualbox
1410577818,vagrant3,state,running
1410577818,vagrant3,state-human-short,running
1410577818,vagrant3,state-human-long,The VM is running. To stop this VM%!(VAGRANT
_COMMA) you can run `vagrant halt` to\nshut it down forcefully%!(VAGRANT_COMMA)
```

---

2 Yes, there's a Vagrant dynamic inventory script included with Ansible already, but it's helpful to go through the exercise.

or you can run `vagrant suspend` to simply\nsuspend the virtual machine. In either case%!(VAGRANT_COMMA) to restart it again%!(VAGRANT_COMMA)\nsimply run `vagrant up`.

To get details about a particular Vagrant machine, say, vagrant2, we would run:

```
$ vagrant ssh-config vagrant2
```

The output looks like:

```
Host vagrant2
  HostName 127.0.0.1
  User vagrant
  Port 2200
  UserKnownHostsFile /dev/null
  StrictHostKeyChecking no
  PasswordAuthentication no
  IdentityFile /Users/lorinhochstein/.vagrant.d/insecure_private_key
  IdentitiesOnly yes
  LogLevel FATAL
```

Our dynamic inventory script will need to call these commands, parse the outputs, and output the appropriate json. We can use the Paramiko library to parse the output of vagrant ssh-config. Here's an interactive Python session that shows how to use the Paramiko library to do this:

```
>>> import subprocess
>>> import paramiko
>>> cmd = "vagrant ssh-config vagrant2"
>>> p = subprocess.Popen(cmd.split(), stdout=subprocess.PIPE)
>>> config = paramiko.SSHConfig()
>>> config.parse(p.stdout)
>>> config.lookup("vagrant2")
{'identityfile': ['/Users/lorinhochstein/.vagrant.d/insecure_private_key'],
 'loglevel': 'FATAL', 'hostname': '127.0.0.1', 'passwordauthentication': 'no',
 'identitiesonly': 'yes', 'userknownhostsfile': '/dev/null', 'user': 'vagrant',
 'stricthostkeychecking': 'no', 'port': '2200'}
```

 You will need to install the Python Paramiko library in order to use this script. You can do this with pip by running:

```
$ sudo pip install paramiko
```

Example 3-12 shows our complete *vagrant.py* script.

Example 3-12. vagrant.py

```
#!/usr/bin/env python
# Adapted from Mark Mandel's implementation
# https://github.com/ansible/ansible/blob/devel/plugins/inventory/vagrant.py
# License: GNU General Public License, Version 3 <http://www.gnu.org/licenses/>
```

```
import argparse
import json
import paramiko
import subprocess
import sys


def parse_args():
    parser = argparse.ArgumentParser(description="Vagrant inventory script")
    group = parser.add_mutually_exclusive_group(required=True)
    group.add_argument('--list', action='store_true')
    group.add_argument('--host')
    return parser.parse_args()


def list_running_hosts():
    cmd = "vagrant status --machine-readable"
    status = subprocess.check_output(cmd.split()).rstrip()
    hosts = []
    for line in status.split('\n'):
        (_, host, key, value) = line.split(',')
        if key == 'state' and value == 'running':
            hosts.append(host)
    return hosts


def get_host_details(host):
    cmd = "vagrant ssh-config {}".format(host)
    p = subprocess.Popen(cmd.split(), stdout=subprocess.PIPE)
    config = paramiko.SSHConfig()
    config.parse(p.stdout)
    c = config.lookup(host)
    return {'ansible_ssh_host': c['hostname'],
            'ansible_ssh_port': c['port'],
            'ansible_ssh_user': c['user'],
            'ansible_ssh_private_key_file': c['identityfile'][0]}


def main():
    args = parse_args()
    if args.list:
        hosts = list_running_hosts()
        json.dump({'vagrant': hosts}, sys.stdout)
    else:
        details = get_host_details(args.host)
        json.dump(details, sys.stdout)

if __name__ == '__main__':
    main()
```

Pre-Existing Inventory Scripts

Ansible ships with several dynamic inventory scripts that you can use. I can never figure out where my package manager installs these files, so I just grab the ones I need directly off GitHub. You can grab these by going to the Ansible GitHub repo (*https://github.com/ansible/ansible*) and browsing to the *plugins/inventory* directory.

Many of these inventory scripts have an accompanying configuration file. In Chapter 12, we'll discuss the Amazon EC2 inventory script in more detail.

Breaking Out the Inventory into Multiple Files

If you want to have both a regular inventory file and a dynamic inventory script (or, really, any combination of static and dynamic inventory files), just put them all in the same directory and configure Ansible to use that directory as the inventory. You can do this either via the `hostfile` parameter in *ansible.cfg* or by using the `-i` flag on the command line. Ansible will process all of the files and merge the results into a single inventory.

For example, our directory structure could look like this: *inventory/hosts* and *inventory/vagrant.py*.

Our *ansible.cfg* file would contain these lines:

```
[defaults]
hostfile = inventory
```

Adding Entries at Runtime with add_host and group_by

Ansible will let you add hosts and groups to the inventory during the execution of a playbook.

add_host

The *add_host* module adds a host to the inventory. This module is useful if you're using Ansible to provision new virtual machine instances inside of an infrastructure-as-a-service cloud.

Why Do I Need add_host if I'm Using Dynamic Inventory?

Even if you're using dynamic inventory scripts, the *add_host* module is useful for scenarios where you start up new virtual machine instances and configure those instances in the same playbook.

If a new host comes online while a playbook is executing, the dynamic inventory script will not pick up this new host. This is because the dynamic inventory script is executed at the beginning of the playbook, so if any new hosts are added while the playbook is executing, Ansible won't see them.

We'll cover a cloud computing example that uses the *add_host* module in Chapter 12.

Invoking the module looks like this:

```
add_host name=hostname groups=web,staging myvar=myval
```

Specifying the list of groups and additional variables is optional.

Here's the `add_host` command in action, bringing up a new vagrant machine and then configuring the machine:

```
- name: Provision a vagrant machine
  hosts: localhost
  vars:
    box: trusty64
  tasks:
    - name: create a Vagrantfile
      command: vagrant init {{ box }} creates=Vagrantfile

    - name: Bring up a vagrant server
      command: vagrant up

    - name: add the Vagrant hosts to the inventory
      add_host: >
            name=vagrant
            ansible_ssh_host=127.0.0.1
            ansible_ssh_port=2222
            ansible_ssh_user=vagrant
            ansible_ssh_private_key_file=/Users/lorinhochstein/.vagrant.d/
            insecure_private_key

- name: Do something to the vagrant machine
  hosts: vagrant
  sudo: yes
  tasks:
    # The list of tasks would go here
    - ...
```

The *add_host* module adds the host only for the duration of the execution of the playbook. It does not modify your inventory file.

When I do provisioning inside of my playbooks, I like to split it up into two plays. The first play runs against localhost and provisions the hosts, and the second play configures the hosts.

Note that we made use of the `creates=Vagrantfile` parameter in this task:

```
- name: create a Vagrantfile
  command: vagrant init {{ box }} creates=Vagrantfile
```

This tells Ansible that if the *Vagrantfile* file is present, the host is already in the correct state, and there is no need to run the command again. It's a way of achieving idempotence in a playbook that invokes the command module, by ensuring that the (potentially non-idempotent) command is run only once.

group_by

Ansible also allows you to create new groups during execution of a playbook, using the *group_by* module. This lets you create a group based on the value of a variable that has been set on each host, which Ansible refers to as a *fact*.[3]

If Ansible fact gathering is enabled, then Ansible will associate a set of variables with a host. For example, the *ansible_machine* variable will be *i386* for 32-bit x86 machines and *x86_64* for 64-bit x86 machines. If Ansible is interacting with a mix of such hosts, we can create *i386* and *x86_64* groups with the task.

Or, if we want to group our hosts by Linux distribution (e.g., Ubuntu, CentOS), we can use the *ansible_distribution* fact.

```
- name: create groups based on Linux distribution
  group_by: key={{ ansible_distribution }}
```

In Example 3-13, we use `group_by` to create separate groups for our Ubuntu hosts and our CentOS hosts, and then we use the *apt* module to install packages onto Ubuntu and the *yum* module to install packages into CentOS.

Example 3-13. Creating ad-hoc groups based on Linux distribution

```
- name: group hosts by distribution
  hosts: myhosts
  gather_facts: True
```

---

3 We cover facts in more detail in Chapter 4.

```
    tasks:
      - name: create groups based on distro
        group_by: key={{ ansible_distribution }}

- name: do something to Ubuntu hosts
  hosts: Ubuntu
  tasks:
    - name: install htop
      apt: name=htop
    # ...

- name: do something else to CentOS hosts
  hosts: CentOS
  tasks:
    - name: install htop
      yum: name=htop
    # ...
```

Although using group_by is one way to achieve conditional behavior in Ansible, I've never found much use for it. In Chapter 6, we'll see an example of how to use the when task parameter to take different actions based on variables.

That about does it for Ansible's inventory. In the next chapter, we'll cover how to use variables. See Chapter 9 for more details about *ControlPersist*, also known as SSH multiplexing.

## CHAPTER 4

Variables and Facts

Ansible is not a full-fledged programming language, but it does have several programming language features, and one of the most important of these is variable substitution. In this chapter, we'll cover Ansible's support for variables in more detail, including a certain type of variable that Ansible calls a *fact*.

Defining Variables in Playbooks

The simplest way to define variables is to put a `vars` section in your playbook with the names and values of variables. Recall from Example 2-8 that we used this approach to define several configuration-related variables, like this:

```
vars:
    key_file: /etc/nginx/ssl/nginx.key
    cert_file: /etc/nginx/ssl/nginx.crt
    conf_file: /etc/nginx/sites-available/default
    server_name: localhost
```

Ansible also allows you to put variables into one or more files, using a section called `vars_files`. Let's say we wanted to take the preceding example and put the variables in a file named *nginx.yml* instead of putting them right in the playbook. We would replace the `vars` section with a `vars_files` that looks like this:

```
vars_files:
    - nginx.yml
```

The *nginx.yml* file would look like Example 4-1.

Example 4-1. nginx.yml

```
key_file: /etc/nginx/ssl/nginx.key
cert_file: /etc/nginx/ssl/nginx.crt
```

```
conf_file: /etc/nginx/sites-available/default
server_name: localhost
```

We'll see an example of `vars_files` in action in Chapter 6 when we use it to separate out the variables that contain sensitive information.

As we discussed in Chapter 3, Ansible also let you define variables associated with hosts or groups in the inventory file or in separate files that live alongside the inventory file.

Viewing the Values of Variables

For debugging, it's often handy to be able to view the output of a variable. We saw in Chapter 2 how we could use the `debug` module to print out an arbitrary message. We can also use it to output the value of the variable. It works like this:

```
- debug: var=myvarname
```

We'll be using this form of the `debug` module several times in this chapter.

Registering Variables

Often, you'll find that you need to set the value of a variable based on the result of a task. To do so, we create a *registered variable* using the `register` clause when invoking a module. Example 4-2 shows how we would capture the output of the *whoami* command to a variable named *login*.

Example 4-2. Capturing the output of a command to a variable

```
- name: capture output of whoami command
  command: whoami
  register: login
```

In order to use the *login* variable later, we need to know what type of value to expect. The value of a variable set using the register clause is always a dictionary, but the specific keys of the dictionary are different, depending on the module that was invoked.

Unfortunately, the official Ansible module documentation doesn't contain information about what the return values look like for each module. The module docs do often contain examples that use the register clause, which can be helpful. I've found the simplest way to find out what a module returns is to register a variable and then output that variable with the `debug` module:

Let's say we run the playbook shown in Example 4-3.

Example 4-3. whoami.yml

```
- name: show return value of command module
  hosts: server1
  tasks:
    - name: capture output of id command
      command: id -un
      register: login
    - debug: var=login
```

The output of the debug module would look like this:

```
TASK: [debug var=login] ********************************************************
ok: [server1] => {
    "login": {
        "changed": true, ❶
        "cmd": [ ❷
            "id",
            "-un"
        ],
        "delta": "0:00:00.002180",
        "end": "2015-01-11 15:57:19.193699",
        "invocation": {
            "module_args": "id -un",
            "module_name": "command"
        },
        "rc": 0, ❸
        "start": "2015-01-11 15:57:19.191519",
        "stderr": "", ❹
        "stdout": "vagrant", ❺
        "stdout_lines": [ ❻
            "vagrant"
        ],
        "warnings": []
    }
}
```

❶ The changed key is present in the return value of all Ansible modules, and Ansible uses it to determine whether a state change has occurred. For the command and shell module, this will always be set to true unless overridden with the changed_when clause, which we cover in Chapter 7.

❷ The cmd key contains the invoked command as a list of strings.

❸ The rc key contains the return code. If it is non-zero, Ansible will assume the task failed to execute.

❹ The stderr key contains any text written to standard error, as a single string.

❺ The stdout key contains any text written to standard out, as a single string.

❻ The stdout_lines key contains any text written to split by newline. It is a list, where each element of the list is a line of output.

If you're using the register clause with the command module, you'll likely want access to the stdout key, as shown in Example 4-4.

Example 4-4. Using the output of a command in a task

```
- name: capture output of id command
  command: id -un
  register: login
- debug: msg="Logged in as user {{ login.stdout }}"
```

Sometimes it's useful to do something with the output of a failed task. However, if the task fails, then Ansible will stop executing tasks for the failed host. We can use the ignore_errors clause, as shown in Example 4-5, so Ansible does not stop on the error.

Example 4-5. Ignoring when a module returns an error

```
- name: Run myprog
  command: /opt/myprog
  register: result
  ignore_errors: True
- debug: var=result
```

The shell module has the same output structure as the command module, but other modules contain different keys. Example 4-6 shows the output of the apt module when installing a package that wasn't present before.

Example 4-6. Output of apt module when installing a new package

```
ok: [server1] => {
    "result": {
        "changed": true,
        "invocation": {
            "module_args": "name=nginx",
            "module_name": "apt"
        },
        "stderr": "",
        "stdout": "Reading package lists...\nBuilding dependency tree...",
        "stdout_lines": [
            "Reading package lists...",
            "Building dependency tree...",
            "Reading state information...",
            "Preparing to unpack .../nginx-common_1.4.6-1ubuntu3.1_all.deb ...",
```

```
    ...
    "Setting up nginx-core (1.4.6-1ubuntu3.1) ...",
    "Setting up nginx (1.4.6-1ubuntu3.1) ...",
    "Processing triggers for libc-bin (2.19-0ubuntu6.3) ..."
    ]
  }
}
```

Accessing Dictionary Keys in a Variable

If a variable contains a dictionary, then you can access the keys of the dictionary using either a dot (.) or a subscript ([]). Example 4-4 had a variable reference that used the dot notation:

    {{ login.stdout }}

We could have used subscript notation instead:

    {{ login['stdout'] }}

This rule applies to multiple dereferences, so all of the following are equivalent:

    ansible_eth1['ipv4']['address']
    ansible_eth1['ipv4'].address
    ansible_eth1.ipv4['address']
    ansible_eth1.ipv4.address

I generally prefer the dot notation, unless the key is a string that contains a character that's not allowed as a variable name, such as a dot, space, or hyphen.

Ansible uses Jinja2 to implement variable dereferencing, so for more details on this topic, see the Jinja2 documentation on variables (*http://jinja.pocoo.org/docs/dev/templates/#variables*).

Example 4-7 shows the output of the `apt` module when the package was already present on the host.

Example 4-7. Output of apt module when package already present

```
ok: [server1] => {
    "result": {
        "changed": false,
        "invocation": {
            "module_args": "name=nginx",
            "module_name": "apt"
        }
    }
}
```

Note that the `stdout`, `stderr`, and `stdout_lines` keys were present only in the output when the package was not previously installed.

 If your playbooks use registered variables, make sure you know the content of that variable, both for cases where the module changes the host's state and for when the module doesn't change the host's state. Otherwise, your playbook might fail when it tries to access a key in a registered variable that doesn't exist.

Facts

As we've already seen, when Ansible runs a playbook, before the first task runs, this happens:

```
GATHERING FACTS ************************************************
ok: [servername]
```

When Ansible gathers facts, it connects to the host and queries the host for all kinds of details about the host: CPU architecture, operating system, IP addresses, memory info, disk info, and more. This information is stored in variables that are called *facts*, and they behave just like any other variable does.

Here's a simple playbook that will print out the operating system of each server:

```
- name: print out operating system
  hosts: all
  gather_facts: True
  tasks:
  - debug: var=ansible_distribution
```

Here's what the output looks like for servers running Ubuntu and CentOS.

```
PLAY [print out operating system] ********************************************

GATHERING FACTS *************************************************************
ok: [server1]
ok: [server2]

TASK: [debug var=ansible_distribution] ***************************************
ok: [server1] => {
    "ansible_distribution": "Ubuntu"
}
ok: [server2] => {
    "ansible_distribution": "CentOS"
}

PLAY RECAP ******************************************************************
server1                    : ok=2    changed=0    unreachable=0    failed=0
server2                    : ok=2    changed=0    unreachable=0    failed=0
```

You can consult the official Ansible documentation (*http://bit.ly/1G9pVfx*) for a list of some of the available facts. I maintain a more comprehensive list of facts on GitHub (*http://bit.ly/1G9pX7a*).

Viewing All Facts Associated with a Server

Ansible implements fact collecting through the use of a special module called the setup module. You don't need to call this module in your playbooks because Ansible does that automatically when it gathers facts. However, if you invoke it manually with the ansible command-line tool, like this:

```
$ ansible server1 -m setup
```

Then Ansible will output all of the facts, as shown in Example 4-8.

Example 4-8. Output of setup module

```
server1 | success >> {
    "ansible_facts": {
        "ansible_all_ipv4_addresses": [
            "10.0.2.15",
            "192.168.4.10"
        ],
        "ansible_all_ipv6_addresses": [
            "fe80::a00:27ff:fefe:1e4d",
            "fe80::a00:27ff:fe67:bbf3"
        ],
(many more facts)
```

Note how the returned value is a dictionary whose key is ansible_facts and whose value is a dictionary that contains the name and value of the actual facts.

Viewing a Subset of Facts

Because Ansible collects many facts, the setup module supports a filter parameter that lets you filter by fact name by specifying a glob.[1] For example:

```
$ ansible web -m setup -a 'filter=ansible_eth*'
```

The output would look like this:

```
web | success >> {
    "ansible_facts": {
        "ansible_eth0": {
            "active": true,
            "device": "eth0",
```

---

1 A glob is what shells use to match file patterns (e.g., *.txt).

```
        "ipv4": {
            "address": "10.0.2.15",
            "netmask": "255.255.255.0",
            "network": "10.0.2.0"
        },
        "ipv6": [
            {
                "address": "fe80::a00:27ff:fefe:1e4d",
                "prefix": "64",
                "scope": "link"
            }
        ],
        "macaddress": "08:00:27:fe:1e:4d",
        "module": "e1000",
        "mtu": 1500,
        "promisc": false,
        "type": "ether"
    },
    "ansible_eth1": {
        "active": true,
        "device": "eth1",
        "ipv4": {
            "address": "192.168.33.10",
            "netmask": "255.255.255.0",
            "network": "192.168.33.0"
        },
        "ipv6": [
            {
                "address": "fe80::a00:27ff:fe23:ae8e",
                "prefix": "64",
                "scope": "link"
            }
        ],
        "macaddress": "08:00:27:23:ae:8e",
        "module": "e1000",
        "mtu": 1500,
        "promisc": false,
        "type": "ether"
    }
},
"changed": false
}
```

Any Module Can Return Facts

If you look closely at Example 4-8, you'll see that the output is a dictionary whose key
is ansible_facts. The use of ansible_facts in the return value is an Ansible idiom.
If a module returns a dictionary that contains ansible_facts as a key, then Ansible
will create variable names in the environment with those values and associate them
with the active host.

For modules that return facts, there's no need to register variables, since Ansible creates these variables for you automatically. For example, the following tasks would use the ec2_facts module to retrieve Amazon EC2[2] facts about a server and then print out the instance id.

```
- name: get ec2 facts
  ec2_facts:

- debug: var=ansible_ec2_instance_id
```

The output would look like this.

```
TASK: [debug var=ansible_ec2_instance_id] *************************************
ok: [myserver] => {
    "ansible_ec2_instance_id": "i-a3a2f866"
}
```

Note how we did not need to use the register keyword when invoking ec2_facts, since the returned values are facts. There are several modules that ship with Ansible that return facts. We'll see another one of them, the docker module, in Chapter 13.

Local Facts

Ansible also provides an additional mechanism for associating facts with a host. You can place one or more files on the host machine in the */etc/ansible/facts.d* directory. Ansible will recognize the file if it's:

- In *.ini* format
- In JSON format
- An executable that takes no arguments and outputs JSON on standard out

These facts are available as keys of a special variable named ansible_local.

For instance, Example 4-9 shows a fact file in *.ini* format.

Example 4-9. /etc/ansible/facts.d/example.fact

```
[book]
title=Ansible: Up and Running
author=Lorin Hochstein
publisher=O'Reilly Media
```

If we copy this file to */etc/ansible/facts.d/example.fact* on the remote host, we can access the contents of the ansible_local variable in a playbook:

---

2 We'll cover Amazon EC2 in more detail in Chapter 12.

```
  - name: print ansible_local
    debug: var=ansible_local
  - name: print book title
    debug: msg="The title of the book is {{ ansible_local.example.book.title }}"
```

The output of these tasks looks like this:

```
TASK: [print ansible_local] ************************************************
ok: [server1] => {
    "ansible_local": {
        "example": {
            "book": {
                "author": "Lorin Hochstein",
                "publisher": "O'Reilly Media",
                "title": "Ansible: Up and Running"
            }
        }
    }
}

TASK: [print book title] ***************************************************
ok: [server1] => {
    "msg": "The title of the book is Ansible: Up and Running"
}
```

Note the structure of value in the ansible_local variable. Because the fact file is named *example.fact*, the ansible_local variable is a dictionary that contains a key named "example."

Using set_fact to Define a New Variable

Ansible also allows you to set a fact (effectively the same as defining a new variable) in a task using the set_fact module. I often like to use set_fact immediately after register to make it simpler to refer to a variable. Example 4-10 demonstrates how to use set_fact so that a variable can be referred to as snap instead of snap_result.stdout.

Example 4-10. Using set_fact to simplify variable reference

```
- name: get snapshot id
  shell: >
    aws ec2 describe-snapshots --filters
    Name=tag:Name,Values=my-snapshot
    | jq --raw-output ".Snapshots[].SnapshotId"
  register: snap_result

- set_fact: snap={{ snap_result.stdout }}

- name: delete old snapshot
  command: aws ec2 delete-snapshot --snapshot-id "{{ snap }}"
```

Built-in Variables

Ansible defines several variables that are always available in a playbook, shown in Table 4-1.

Table 4-1. Built-in variables

Parameter	Description
hostvars	A dict whose keys are Ansible host names and values are dicts that map variable names to values
inventory_hostname	Name of the current host as known by Ansible
group_names	A list of all groups that the current host is a member of
groups	A dict whose keys are Ansible group names and values are a list of hostnames that are members of the group. Includes `all` and ungrouped groups: `{"all": [...], "web": [...], "ungrouped": [...]}`
play_hosts	A list of inventory hostnames that are active in the current play
ansible_version	A dict with Ansible version info: `{"full": 1.8.2", "major": 1, "minor": 8, "revision": 2, "string": "1.8.2"}`

The `hostvars`, `inventory_hostname`, and `groups` variables merit some additional discussion.

hostvars

In Ansible, variables are scoped by host. It only makes sense to talk about the value of a variable relative to a given host.

The idea that variables are relative to a given host might sound confusing, since Ansible allows you to define variables on a group of hosts. For example, if you define a variable in the *vars* section of a play, you are defining the variable for the set of hosts in the play. But what Ansible is really doing is creating a copy of that variable for each host in the group.

Sometimes, a task that's running on one host needs the value of a variable defined on another host. Consider the scenario where you need to create a configuration file on web servers that contains the IP address of the *eth1* interface of the database server, and you don't know in advance what this IP address is. This IP address is available as the *ansible_eth1.ipv4.address* fact for the database server.

The solution is to use the `hostvars` variable. This is a dictionary that contains all of the variables defined on all of the hosts, keyed by the hostname as known to Ansible.

If Ansible has not yet gathered facts on a host, then you will not be able to access its facts using the hostvars variable, unless fact caching is enabled.[3]

Continuing our example, if our database server is *db.example.com*, then we could put the following in a configuration template:

```
{{ hostvars['db.example.com'].ansible_eth1.ipv4.address }}
```

This would evaluate to the *ansible_eth1.ipv4.address* fact associated with the host named *db.example.com*.

inventory_hostname

The *inventory_hostname* is the hostname of the current host, as known by Ansible. If you have defined an alias for a host, then this is the alias name. For example, if your inventory contains a line like this:

```
server1 ansible_ssh_host=192.168.4.10
```

then the *inventory_hostname* would be server1.

You can output all of the variables associated with the current host with the help of the hostvars and inventory_hostname variables:

```
- debug: var=hostvars[inventory_hostname]
```

Groups

The groups variable can be useful when you need to access variables for a group of hosts. Let's say we are configuring a load balancing host, and our configuration file needs the IP addresses of all of the servers in our web group. Our configuration file would contain a fragment that looks like this:

```
backend web-backend
{% for host in groups.web %}
  server {{ host.inventory_hostname }} {{ host.ansible_default_ipv4.address }}:80
{% endfor %}
```

The generated file would look like this:

```
backend web-backend
  server georgia.example.com 203.0.113.15:80
  server newhampshire.example.com 203.0.113.25:80
  server newjersey.example.com 203.0.113.38:80
```

---

3 See Chapter 9 for information about fact caching.

Setting Variables on the Command Line

Variables set by passing `-e var=value` to `ansible-playbook` have the highest precedence, which means you can use this to override variables that are already defined. Example 4-11 shows how to set the variable named `token` to the value *12345*.

Example 4-11. Setting a variable from the command-line

```
$ ansible-playbook example.yml -e token=12345
```

Use the `ansible-playbook -e var=value` method when you want to want to use a playbook like you would a shell script that takes a command-line argument. The `-e` flag effectively allows you to pass variables as arguments.

Example 4-12 shows a very simple playbook that outputs a message specified by a variable.

Example 4-12. greet.yml

```
- name: pass a message on the command line
  hosts: localhost
  vars:
    greeting: "you didn't specify a message"
  tasks:
    - name: output a message
      debug: msg="{{ greeting }}"
```

If we invoke it like this:

```
$ ansible-playbook greet.yml -e greeting=hiya
```

Then the output looks like this:

```
PLAY [pass a message on the command line] ************************************

TASK: [output a message] ****************************************************
ok: [localhost] => {
    "msg": "hiya"
}

PLAY RECAP ******************************************************************
localhost                  : ok=1    changed=0    unreachable=0    failed=0
```

If you want to put a space in the variable, you'll need two use quotes like this:

```
$ ansible-playbook greet.yml -e 'greeting="hi there"'
```

You've got to put single quotes around the entire `'greeting="hi there"'` so that the shell interprets that as a single argument to pass to Ansible, and you've got to put double quotes around "hi there" so that Ansible treats that message as a single string.

Ansible also allows you to pass a file containing the variables instead of passing them directly on the command line by passing `@filename.yml` as the argument to `-e`, for example, if we had a file that looked like Example 4-13.

Example 4-13. greetvars.yml

```
greeting: hiya
```

Then we can pass this file to the command line like this:

```
$ ansible-playbook greet.yml -e @greetvars.yml
```

Precedence

We've covered several different ways of defining variables, and it can happen that you define the same variable multiple times for a host, using different values. Avoid this when you can, but if you can't, then keep in mind Ansible's precedence rules. When the same variable is defined in multiple ways, the precedence rules determine which value wins.

The basic rules of precedence are:

1. (Highest) `ansible-playbook -e var=value`
2. Everything else not mentioned in this list
3. On a host or group, either defined in inventory file or YAML file
4. Facts
5. In *defaults/main.yml* of a role.[4]

In this chapter, we covered the different ways you can define and access variables and facts. In the next chapter, we'll focus on a realistic example of deploying an application.

---

4 We'll discuss roles in Chapter 8.

## CHAPTER 5

Introducing Mezzanine:
Our Test Application

In Chapter 2, we covered the basics of writing playbooks. But real life is always messier than introductory chapters of programming books, so we're going to work through a complete example of deploying a non-trivial application.

Our example application is an open source content management system (CMS) called Mezzanine (*http://mezzanine.jupo.org*), which is similar in spirit to WordPress. Mezzanine is built on top of Django, the free Python-based framework for writing web applications.

Why Deploying to Production Is Complicated

Let's take a little detour and talk about the differences between running software in development mode on your laptop versus running the software in production.

Mezzanine is a great example of an application that is much easier to run in development mode than it is to deploy. Example 5-1 shows all you need to do to get Mezzanine running on your laptop.[1]

Example 5-1. Running Mezzanine in development mode

```
$ virtualenv venv
$ source venv/bin/activate
$ pip install mezzanine
$ mezzanine-project myproject
```

---

[1] This will install the Python packages into a virtualenv. We'll cover virtualenvs in "Installing Mezzanine and Other Packages into a virtualenv" on page 97.

```
$ cd myproject
$ python manage.py createdb
$ python manage.py runserver
```

You'll be prompted to answer several questions. I answered "yes" to each yes/no question, and accepted the default answer whenever one was available. This was what my interaction looked like:

```
You just installed Django's auth system, which means you don't have any
superusers defined.
Would you like to create one now? (yes/no): yes
Username (leave blank to use 'lorinhochstein'):
Email address: lorin@ansiblebook.com
Password:
Password (again):
Superuser created successfully.

A site record is required.
Please enter the domain and optional port in the format 'domain:port'.
For example 'localhost:8000' or 'www.example.com'.
Hit enter to use the default (127.0.0.1:8000):

Creating default site record: 127.0.0.1:8000 ...

Installed 2 object(s) from 1 fixture(s)

Would you like to install some initial demo pages?
Eg: About us, Contact form, Gallery. (yes/no): yes
```

You should eventually see output on the terminal that looks like this:

```
                .....
           _d^^^^^^^^^b_
        .d''           ``b.
      .p'                 `q.
     .d'                   `b.
    .d'                     `b.    * Mezzanine 3.1.10
    ::                       ::    * Django 1.6.8
    ::      M E Z Z A N I N E ::   * Python 2.7.6
    ::                       ::    * SQLite 3.8.5
    `p.                     .q'    * Darwin 14.0.0
     `p.                   .q'
      `b.                 .d'
        `q..           ..p'
          ^q........p^
             ''''

Validating models...

0 errors found
December 01, 2014 - 02:54:40
Django version 1.6.8, using settings 'mezzanine-example.settings'
```

```
Starting development server at http://127.0.0.1:8000/
Quit the server with CONTROL-C.
```

If you point your browser to *http://127.0.0.1:8000/*, you should see a web page that looks like Figure 5-1.

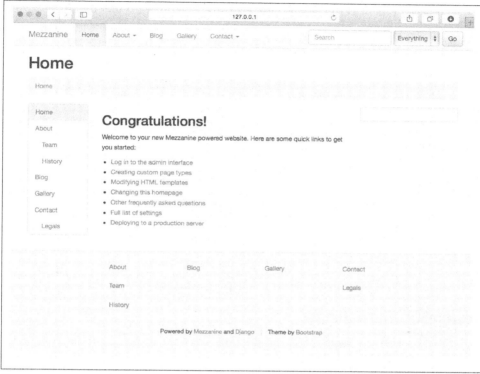

Figure 5-1. Mezzanine after a fresh install

Deploying this application to production is another matter. When you run the `mezzanine-project` command, Mezzanine will generate a Fabric (*http://www.fabfile.org*) deployment script at *myproject/fabfile.py* that you can use to deploy your project to a production server. (Fabric is a Python-based tool that helps automate running tasks via ssh.) The script is over 500 lines long, and that's not counting the included configuration files that are also involved in deployment. Why is deploying to production so much more complex? I'm glad you asked.

When run in development, Mezzanine provides the following simplifications (see Figure 5-2):

- The system uses SQLite as the back-end database, and will create the database file if it doesn't exist.

- The development HTTP server serves up both the static content (images, *.css* files, JavaScript) as well as the dynamically generated HTML.

- The development HTTP server uses the (insecure) http protocol, not (secure) HTTPS.

- The development HTTP server process runs in the foreground, taking over your terminal window.

- The hostname for the HTTP server is always 127.0.0.1 (localhost).

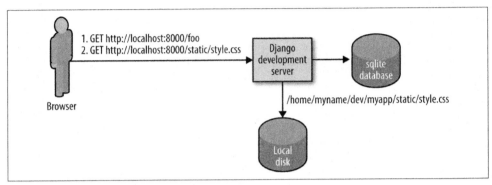

Figure 5-2. Django app in development mode

Now, let's look at what happens when you deploy to production.

PostgreSQL: The Database

SQLite is a serverless database. In production, we want to run a server-based database, because those have better support for multiple, concurrent requests, and server-based databases allow us to run multiple HTTP servers for load balancing. This means we need to deploy a database management system such as MySQL or PostgreSQL (aka simply "Postgres"). Setting up one of these database servers requires more work. We need to:

1. Install the database software.

2. Ensure the database service is running.

3. Create the database inside the database management system.

4. Create a database user who has the appropriate permissions for the database system.

5. Configure our Mezzanine application with the database user credentials and connection information.

Gunicorn: The Application Server

Because Mezzanine is a Django-based application, you can run Mezzanine using Django's HTTP server, referred as the *development server* in the Django documentation. Here's what the Django 1.7 docs have to say about the development server (*http://bit.ly/1G9AbV0*).

> [D]on't use this server in anything resembling a production environment. It's intended only for use while developing. (We're in the business of making Web frameworks, not Web servers.)

Django implements the standard Web Server Gateway Interface (WSGI),[2] so any Python HTTP server that supports WSGI is suitable for running a Django application such as Mezzanine. We'll use Gunicorn, one of the most popular HTTP WSGI servers, which is what the Mezzanine deploy script uses.

Nginx: The Web Server

Gunicorn will execute our Django application, just like the development server does. However, Gunicorn won't serve any of the *static assets* associated with the application. Static assets are files such as images, *.css* files, and JavaScript files. They are called static because they never change, in contrast with the dynamically generated web pages that Gunicorn serves up.

Although Gunicorn can handle TLS encryption, it's common to configure nginx to handle the encryption.[3]

We're going to use nginx as our web server for serving static assets and for handling the TLS encryption, as shown in Figure 5-3. We need to configure nginx as a *reverse proxy* for Gunicorn. If the request is for a static asset, such as a css file, then nginx will serve that file directly from the local file system. Otherwise, nginx will proxy the request to Gunicorn, by making an http request against the Gunicorn service that is running on the local machine. Nginx uses the URL to determine whether to serve a local file or proxy the request to Gunicorn. Note that requests to nginx will be (encrypted) HTTPS, and all requests that nginx proxies to Gunicorn will be (unencrypted) HTTP.

---

2 The WSGI protocol is documented in Python Enhancement Proposal (PEP) 3333 (*https://www.python.org/dev/peps/pep-3333*).

3 Gunicorn 0.17 added support for TLS encryption. Before that you had to use a separate application such as nginx to handle the encryption.

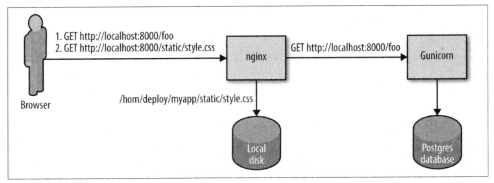

Figure 5-3. Nginx as a reverse proxy

Supervisor: The Process Manager

When we run in development mode, we run the application server in the foreground of our terminal. If we were to close our terminal, the program would terminate. For a server application, we need it to run as a background process so it doesn't terminate, even if we close the terminal session we used to start the process.

The colloquial terms for such a process are *daemon* or *service*. We need to run Gunicorn as a daemon, and we'd like to be able to easily stop it and restart it. There are a number of service managers that can do this job. We're going to use Supervisor, because that's what the Mezzanine deployment scripts use.

At this point, you should have a sense of the steps involved in deploying a web application to production. We'll go over how to implement this deployment with Ansible in Chapter 6.

Deploying Mezzanine with Ansible

It's time to write an Ansible playbook to deploy Mezzanine to a server. We'll go through it step by step, but if you're the type of person that starts off by reading the last page of a book to see how it ends,[1] you can find the full playbook at the end of this chapter as Example 6-27. It's also available on GitHub (*http://bit.ly/19P0OAj*). Check out the README (*http://bit.ly/1Onko4u*) before trying to run it directly.

I've tried to hew as closely as possible to the original Fabric scripts that Mezzanine author Stephen McDonald wrote.[2]

Listing Tasks in a Playbook

Before we dive into the guts of our playbook, let's get a high-level view. The `ansible-playbook` command-line tool supports a flag called `--list-tasks`. This flag will print out the names of all of the tasks in a playbook. It's a handy way to summarize what a playbook is going to do. Here's how you use it:

```
$ ansible-playbook --list-tasks mezzanine.yml
```

Example 6-1 shows the output for the *mezzanine.yml* playbook in Example 6-27.

Example 6-1. List of tasks in Mezzanine playbook

```
playbook: mezzanine.yml

  play #1 (Deploy mezzanine on vagrant):
    install apt packages
```

---

1 My wife, Stacy, is notorious for doing this.

2 You can find the Fabric scripts that ship with Mezzanine on GitHub (*http://bit.ly/19P0T73*).

```
check out the repository on the host
install required python packages
install requirements.txt
create a user
create the database
generate the settings file
sync the database, apply migrations, collect static content
set the site id
set the admin password
set the gunicorn config file
set the supervisor config file
set the nginx config file
enable the nginx config file
remove the default nginx config file
ensure config path exists
create tls certificates
install poll twitter cron job
```

Organization of Deployed Files

As we discussed earlier, Mezzanine is built atop Django. In Django, a web app is called a *project*. We get to choose what to name our project, and I've chosen to name it *mezzanine-example*.

Our playbook deploys into a Vagrant machine, and will deploy the files into the home directory of the Vagrant user's account.

/home/vagrant/mezzanine-example is the top-level directory we'll deploy into. It also serves as the virtualenv directory, which means that we're going to install all of the Python packages into that directory.

home/vagrant/mezzanine-example/project will contain the source code that will be cloned from a source code repository on GitHub.

Variables and Secret Variables

As you can see from Example 6-2, this playbook defines quite a few variables.

Example 6-2. Defining the variables

```
vars:
  user: "{{ ansible_ssh_user }}"
  proj_name: mezzanine-example
  venv_home: "{{ ansible_env.HOME }}"
  venv_path: "{{ venv_home }}/{{ proj_name }}"
  proj_dirname: project
  proj_path: "{{ venv_path }}/{{ proj_dirname }}"
  reqs_path: requirements.txt
  manage: "{{ python }} {{ proj_path }}/manage.py"
```

```
  live_hostname: 192.168.33.10.xip.io
  domains:
    - 192.168.33.10.xip.io
    - www.192.168.33.10.xip.io
  repo_url: git@github.com:lorin/mezzanine-example.git
  gunicorn_port: 8000
  locale: en_US.UTF-8
  # Variables below don't appear in Mezzanine's fabfile.py
  # but I've added them for convenience
  conf_path: /etc/nginx/conf
  tls_enabled: True
  python: "{{ venv_path }}/bin/python"
  database_name: "{{ proj_name }}"
  database_user: "{{ proj_name }}"
  database_host: localhost
  database_port: 5432
  gunicorn_proc_name: mezzanine
vars_files:
  - secrets.yml
```

I've tried for the most part to use the same variable names that the Mezzanine Fabric script uses. I've also added some extra variables to make things a little clearer. For example, the Fabric scripts directly use proj_name as the database name and database username. I prefer to define intermediate variables named database_name and data base_user and define these in terms of proj_name.

A couple of things to note here. First of all, note how we can define one variable in terms of another. For example, we define venv_path in terms of venv_home and proj_name.

Also, note how we can reference Ansible facts in these variables. For example, venv_home is defined in terms of the ansible_env fact that is collected from each host.

Finally, note how we have specified some of our variables in a separate file, called *secrets.yml*, by doing this:

```
vars_files:
  - secrets.yml
```

This file contains credentials such as passwords and tokens that need to remain private. Note that my repository on GitHub does not actually contain this file. Instead, it contains a file called *secrets.yml.example* that looks like this:

```
db_pass: e79c9761d0b54698a83ff3f93769e309
admin_pass: 46041386be534591ad24902bf72071B
secret_key: b495a05c396843b6b47ac944a72c92ed
nevercache_key: b5d87bb4e17c483093296fa321056bdc
# You need to create a Twitter application at https://dev.twitter.com
# in order to get the credentials required for Mezzanine's
# twitter integration.
```

```
#
# See http://mezzanine.jupo.org/docs/twitter-integration.html
# for details on Twitter integration
twitter_access_token_key: 80b557a3a8d14cb7a2b91d60398fb8ce
twitter_access_token_secret: 1974cf8419114bdd9d4ea3db7a210d90
twitter_consumer_key: 1f1c627530b34bb58701ac81ac3fad51
twitter_consumer_secret: 36515c2b60ee4ffb9d33d972a7ec350a
```

To use this repo, you need to copy *secrets.yml.example* to *secrets.yml* and edit it so that it contains the credentials specific to your site. Also note that *secrets.yml* is included in the *.gitignore* file in the Git repository to prevent someone from accidentally committing these credentials.

It's best to avoid committing unencrypted credentials into your version control repository because of the security risks involved. This is just one possible strategy for maintaining secret credentials. We also could have passed them as environment variables. Another option, which we will describe in Chapter 7, is to commit an encrypted version of the *secrets.yml* file using Ansible's `vault` functionality.

Using Iteration (with_items) to Install Multiple Packages

We're going to need to install two different types of packages for our Mezzanine deployment. We need to install some system-level packages, and because we're going to deploy on Ubuntu, we're going to use `apt` as our package manager for the system packages. We also need to install some Python packages, and we'll use `pip` for the Python packages.

System-level packages are generally easier to deal with than Python packages, because system-level packages are designed specifically to work with the operating system. However, the system package repositories often don't have the newest versions of the Python libraries we need, so we turn to the Python packages to install those. It's a trade-off between stability versus running the latest and greatest.

Example 6-3 shows the task we'll use to install the system packages.

Example 6-3. Installing system packages

```
- name: install apt packages
  apt: pkg={{ item }} update_cache=yes cache_valid_time=3600
  sudo: True
  with_items:
    - git
    - libjpeg-dev
    - libpq-dev
    - memcached
    - nginx
    - postgresql
    - python-dev
```

```
  - python-pip
  - python-psycopg2
  - python-setuptools
  - python-virtualenv
  - supervisor
```

There's a lot to unpack here. Because we're installing multiple packages, we use Ansible's iteration functionality, the `with_items` clause. We could have installed the packages one at a time, like this:

```
- name: install git
  apt: pkg=git

- name: install libjpeg-dev
  apt: pkg=libjpeg-dev
...
```

However, it's much simpler to write and read if we group all of the packages together in a list. When we invoke the `apt` module, we pass it `{{ item }}`. This is a placeholder variable that will be populated by each of the elements in the list of the `with_items` clause.

 Ansible always uses `item` as the name of the loop iteration variable.

In addition, in the case of the `apt` module, it's more efficient to install multiple packages using the `with_items` clause. That's because Ansible will pass the entire list of packages to the `apt` module, and the module will invoke the `apt` program only once, passing it the entire list of packages to be installed. Some modules, like `apt`, have been designed to handle lists intelligently like this. If a module doesn't have native support for lists, then Ansible will simply invoke the module multiple times, once for each element of the list.

You can tell that the `apt` module is intelligent enough to handle multiple packages at once, because the output looks like this:

```
TASK: [install apt packages] ************************************************
ok: [web] => (item=git,libjpeg-dev,libpq-dev,memcached,nginx,postgresql,
python-dev,python-pip,python-psycopg2,python-setuptools,python-virtualenv,
supervisor)
```

On the other hand, the `pip` module does not handle lists intelligently, so Ansible must invoke it once for each element of the list, and the output looks like this:

```
TASK: [install other python packages] **************************************
ok: [web] => (item=gunicorn)
```

```
ok: [web] => (item=setproctitle)
ok: [web] => (item=south)
ok: [web] => (item=psycopg2)
ok: [web] => (item=django-compressor)
ok: [web] => (item=python-memcached)
```

Adding the Sudo Clause to a Task

In the playbook examples of Chapter 2, we wanted the whole playbook to run as root, so we added the sudo: True clause to the play.

When we deploy Mezzanine, most of the tasks will be run as the user who is SSHing to the host, rather than root. Therefore, we don't want to run as sudo the entire play, just select tasks.

We can accomplish this by adding sudo: True to the tasks that do need to run as root, such as Example 6-3.

Updating the Apt Cache

 All of the example commands in this subsection are run on the (Ubuntu) remote host, not the control machine.

Ubuntu maintains a cache with the names of all of the *Apt* packages that are available in the Ubuntu package archive. Let's say you try to install the package named *libssl-dev*. We can use the apt-cache program to query the local cache to see what version it knows about:

```
$ apt-cache policy libssl-dev
```

The output is shown in Example 6-4.

Example 6-4. apt cache output

```
libssl-dev:
  Installed: (none)
  Candidate: 1.0.1f-1ubuntu2.5
  Version table:
     1.0.1f-1ubuntu2.5 0
        500 http://archive.ubuntu.com/ubuntu/ trusty-updates/main amd64 Packages
        500 http://security.ubuntu.com/ubuntu/ trusty-security/main amd64
Packages
     1.0.1f-1ubuntu2 0
        500 http://archive.ubuntu.com/ubuntu/ trusty/main amd64 Packages
```

As we can see, this package is not installed locally. According to the local cache, the latest version is 1.0.1f-ubuntu2.5. We also see some information about the location of the package archive.

In some cases, when the Ubuntu project releases a new version of a package, it removes the old version from the package archive. If the local `apt` cache of an Ubuntu server hasn't been updated, then it will attempt to install a package that doesn't exist in the package archive.

To continue with our example, let's say we were to attempt to install the `libssl-dev` package:

```
$ apt-get install libssl-dev
```

If version 1.0.1f-ubuntu2.5 were no longer available in the package archive, we'd see the following error:

```
Err http://archive.ubuntu.com/ubuntu/ trusty-updates/main libssl-dev amd64
1.0.1f-1ubuntu2.5
  404  Not Found [IP: 91.189.88.153 80]
Err http://security.ubuntu.com/ubuntu/ trusty-security/main libssl-dev amd64
1.0.1f-1ubuntu2.5
  404  Not Found [IP: 91.189.88.149 80]
Err http://security.ubuntu.com/ubuntu/ trusty-security/main libssl-doc all
1.0.1f-1ubuntu2.5
  404  Not Found [IP: 91.189.88.149 80]
E: Failed to fetch
http://security.ubuntu.com/ubuntu/pool/main/o/openssl/libssl-dev_1.0.1f-1ubuntu2.
5_amd64.deb
404  Not Found [IP: 91.189.88.149 80]

E: Failed to fetch
http://security.ubuntu.com/ubuntu/pool/main/o/openssl/libssl-doc_1.0.1f-1ubuntu2.
5_all.deb
404  Not Found [IP: 91.189.88.149 80]

E: Unable to fetch some archives, maybe run apt-get update or try with
--fix-missing?
```

On the command line, the way to bring the local `apt` cache up-to-date is to run `apt-get update`. When using the `apt` Ansible module, the way to bring the local `apt` cache up-to-date is to pass the `update_cache=yes` argument when invoking the module, as shown in Example 6-3.

Because updating the cache takes some additional time, and because we might be running a playbook multiple times in quick succession in order to debug it, we can avoid paying the cache update penalty by using the `cache_valid_time` argument to the module. This instructs to update the cache only if it's older than some threshold. The example in Example 6-3 uses `cache_valid_time=3600`, which updates the cache only if it's older than 3,600 seconds (1 hour).

Checking Out the Project Using Git

Although Mezzanine can be used without writing any custom code, one of its strengths is that it is written on top of the Django platform, and Django's a great web application platform if you know Python. If you just wanted a CMS, you'd likely just use something like WordPress. But if you're writing a custom application that incorporates CMS functionality, Mezzanine is a good way to go.

As part of the deployment, you need to check out the Git repository that contains your Django applications. In Django terminology, this repository must contain a *project*. I've created a repository on GitHub (*https://github.com/lorin/mezzanine-example*) that contains a Django project with the expected files. That's the project that gets deployed in this playbook.

I created these files using the `mezzanine-project` program that ships with Mezzanine, like this:

```
$ mezzanine-project mezzanine-example
```

Note that I don't have any custom Django applications in my repository, just the files that are required for the project. In a real Django deployment, this repository would contain subdirectories that contain additional Django applications.

Example 6-5 shows how we use the `git` module to check out a Git repository onto a remote host.

Example 6-5. Checking out the Git repository

```
- name: check out the repository on the host
  git: repo={{ repo_url }} dest={{ proj_path }} accept_hostkey=yes
```

I've made the project repository public so that readers can access it, but in general, you'll be checking out private Git repositories over SSH. For this reason, I've set the `repo_url` variable to use the scheme that will clone the repository over SSH:

```
repo_url: git@github.com:lorin/mezzanine-example.git
```

If you're following along at home, to run this playbook you must:

1. Have a GitHub account.
2. Have a public SSH key associated with your GitHub account.
3. Have an SSH agent running on your control machine with agent forwarding enabled.

To enable agent forwarding, add the following to your *ansible.cfg*:

```
[ssh_connection]
ssh_args = -o ControlMaster=auto -o ControlPersist=60s -o ForwardAgent=yes
```

In addition to specifying the repository URL with the `repo` parameter and the destination path of the repository as the `dest` parameter, we also pass an additional parameter, `accept_hostkey`, which is related to *host key checking*. We discuss SSH agent forwarding and host key checking in more detail in Appendix A.

Installing Mezzanine and Other Packages into a virtualenv

As mentioned earlier in this chapter, we're going to install some of the packages as Python packages because we can get more recent versions of those than if we installed the equivalent apt package.

We can install Python packages systemwide as the root user, but it's better practice to install these packages in an isolated environment to avoid polluting the system-level Python packages. In Python, these types of isolated package environments are called *virtualenvs*. A user can create multiple virtualenvs, and can install Python packages into a virtualenv without needing root access.

Ansible's `pip` module has support for installing packages into a virtualenv and for creating the virtualenv if it is not available. Example 6-6 shows the two tasks that we use to install Python packages into the virtualenv, both of which use the `pip` module, although in different ways.

Example 6-6. Install Python packages

```
- name: install required python packages
  pip: name={{ item }} virtualenv={{ venv_path }}
  with_items:
    - gunicorn
    - setproctitle
    - south
    - psycopg2
    - django-compressor
    - python-memcached

- name: install requirements.txt
  pip: requirements={{ proj_path }}/{{ reqs_path }} virtualenv={{ venv_path }}
```

A common pattern in Python projects is to specify the package dependencies in a file called *requirements.txt*. And, indeed, the repository in our Mezzanine example contains a *requirements.txt* file. It looks like Example 6-7.

Example 6-7. requirements.txt

```
Mezzanine==3.1.10
```

The *requirements.txt* file is missing several other Python packages that we need for the deployment, so we explicitly specify these as a separate task.

Note that the Mezzanine Python package in *requirements.txt* is pinned to a specific version (3.1.10), where the other packages aren't pinned; we just grab the latest versions of those. If we did not want to pin Mezzanine, we simply could have added Mezzanine to the list of packages, like this:

```
- name: install python packages
  pip: name={{ item }} virtualenv={{ venv_path }}
  with_items:
    - mezzanine
    - gunicorn
    - setproctitle
    - south
    - psycopg2
    - django-compressor
    - python-memcached
```

Alternately, if we wanted to pin all of the packages, we have several options. We could have created a *requirements.txt* file. This file contains information about the packages and the dependencies. An example file looks like Example 6-8.

Example 6-8. Example requirements.txt

```
Django==1.6.8
Mezzanine==3.1.10
Pillow==2.6.1
South==1.0.1
argparse==1.2.1
beautifulsoup4==4.1.3
bleach==1.4
django-appconf==0.6
django-compressor==1.4
filebrowser-safe==0.3.6
future==0.9.0
grappelli-safe==0.3.13
gunicorn==19.1.1
html5lib==0.999
oauthlib==0.7.2
psycopg2==2.5.4
python-memcached==1.53
pytz==2014.10
requests==2.4.3
requests-oauthlib==0.4.2
setproctitle==1.1.8
six==1.8.0
tzlocal==1.0
wsgiref==0.1.2
```

If you have an existing virtualenv with the packages installed, you can use the `pip freeze` command to print out a list of installed packages. For example, if your virtualenv is in *~/mezzanine_example*, you can activate your virtualenv and print out the packages in the virtualenv like this:

```
$ source ~/mezzanine_example/bin/activate
$ pip freeze > requirements.txt
```

Example 6-9 shows how we could have installed the packages using a *requirements.txt* file if we had one.

Example 6-9. Installing from requirements.txt

```
- name: copy requirements.txt file
  copy: src=files/requirements.txt dest=~/requirements.txt
- name: install packages
  pip: requirements=~/requirements.txt virtualenv={{ venv_path }}
```

Alternatively, we could have specified both the package names and their versions in the list, as shown in Example 6-10. We pass a list of dictionaries, and dereference the elements with `item.name` and `item.version`.

Example 6-10. Specifying package names and version

```
- name: python packages
  pip: name={{ item.name }} version={{ item.version }} virtualenv={{ venv_path }}
  with_items:
    - {name: mezzanine, version: 3.1.10 }
    - {name: gunicorn, version: 19.1.1 }
    - {name: setproctitle, version: 1.1.8 }
    - {name: south, version: 1.0.1 }
    - {name: psycopg2, version: 2.5.4 }
    - {name: django-compressor, version: 1.4 }
    - {name: python-memcached, version: 1.53 }
```

Complex Arguments in Tasks: A Brief Digression

Up until this point in the book, every time we have invoked a module, we have passed the argument as a string. Taking the `pip` example from Example 6-10, we passed the `pip` module a string as an argument:

```
- name: install package with pip
  pip: name={{ item.name }} version={{ item.version }} virtualenv={{ venv_path }}
```

If we don't like long lines in our files, we could have broken up the argument string across multiple lines using YAML's line folding, which we originally wrote about in "Line Folding" on page 30:

```
- name: install package with pip
  pip: >
    name={{ item.name }}
    version={{ item.version }}
    virtualenv={{ venv_path }}
```

Ansible also provides us with another option for breaking up a module invocation across multiple lines. Instead of passing a string, we can pass a dictionary where the keys are the variable names. This means we could have invoked Example 6-10 like this instead:

```
- name: install package with pip
  pip:
    name: "{{ item.name }}"
    version: "{{ item.version }}"
    virtualenv: "{{ venv_path }}"
```

The dictionary-based approach to passing arguments is also useful when invoking modules that take *complex arguments*. A complex argument is an argument to a module that is a list or a dictionary. The `ec2` module, which creates new servers on Amazon EC2 cloud, is a good example of a module that takes complex arguments. Example 6-11 shows how to call a module that takes a list as an argument for the `group` parameter, and a dictionary as an argument to the `instance_tags` parameter. We'll cover this module in more detail in Chapter 12.

Example 6-11. Calling a module with complex arguments

```
- name: create an ec2 instance
  ec2:
    image: ami-8caa1ce4
    instance_type: m3.medium
    key_name: mykey
    group:
      - web
      - ssh
    instance_tags:
      type: web
      env: production
```

You can even mix it up by passing some arguments as a string and others as a dictionary, by using the `args` clause to specify some of the variables as a dictionary. We could rewrite our preceding example as:

```
- name: create an ec2 instance
  ec2: image=ami-8caa1ce4 instance_type=m3.medium key_name=mykey
  args:
    group:
      - web
      - ssh
    instance_tags:
```

```
    type: web
    env: production
```

If you're using the local_action clause (we'll cover this in more detail in Chapter 7), then the syntax for complex args changes slightly. You need to add module: <module name> as shown below:

```
- name: create an ec2 instance
  local_action:
    module: ec2
    image: ami-8caa1ce4
    instance_type: m3.medium
    key_name: mykey
    group:
      - web
      - ssh
    instance_tags:
      type: web
      env: production
```

You can also mix simple arguments and complex arguments when using local_action:

```
- name: create an ec2 instance
  local_action: ec2 image=ami-8caa1ce4 instance_type=m3.medium key_name=mykey
  args:
    image: ami-8caa1ce4
    instance_type: m3.medium
    key_name: mykey
    group:
      - web
      - ssh
    instance_tags:
      type: web
      env: production
```

Ansible allows you to specify file permissions, which are used by several modules, including file, copy, and template. If you are specifying an octal value as a complex argument, it must either start the value with a 0 or quote it as a string.

For example, note how the mode argument starts with a +0:

```
- name: copy index.html
  copy:
    src: files/index.html
    dest: /usr/share/nginx/html/index.html
    mode: "0644"
```

If you do not start the mode argument with a 0 or quote it as a string, Ansible will interpret the value as a decimal number instead of an octal, and will not set the file permissions the way you expect. For details, see GitHub (*http://bit.ly/1GASfbl*).

If you want to break your arguments across multiple lines, and you aren't passing complex arguments, which form you choose is a matter of taste. I generally prefer dictionaries to multiline strings, but in this book I use both forms.

Creating the Database and Database User

When Django runs in development mode, it uses the SQLite backend. This backend will create the database file if the file does not exist.

When using a database management system like Postgres, we need to first create the database inside of Postgres and then create the user account that owns the database. Later on, we will configure Mezzanine with the credentials of this user.

Ansible ships with the `postgresql_user` and `postgresql_db` modules for creating users and databases inside of Postgres. Example 6-12 shows how we invoke these modules in our playbook.

Example 6-12. Creating the database and database user

```
- name: create a user
  postgresql_user:
    name: "{{ database_user }}"
    password: "{{ db_pass }}"
  sudo: True
  sudo_user: postgres

- name: create the database
  postgresql_db:
    name: "{{ database_name }}"
    owner: "{{ database_user }}"
    encoding: UTF8
    lc_ctype: "{{ locale }}"
    lc_collate: "{{ locale }}"
    template: template0
  sudo: True
  sudo_user: postgres
```

Note the use of `sudo: True` and `sudo_user: postgres` on each of these tasks. When you install Postgres on Ubuntu, the installation process creates a user named *postgres* that has administrative privileges for the Postgres installation. Note that the root account does not have administrative privileges in Postgres by default, so in the playbook, we need to `sudo` to the Postgres user in order to perform administrative tasks, such as creating users and databases.

When we create the database, we set the encoding (UTF8) and locale categories (LC_CTYPE, LC_COLLATE) associated with the database. Because we are setting locale information, we use *template0* as the template.[3]

Generating the local_settings.py File from a Template

Django expects to find project-specific settings in a file called *settings.py*. Mezzanine follows the common Django idiom of breaking up these settings into two groups:

- Settings that are the same for all deployments (*settings.py*)
- Settings that vary by deployment (*local_settings.py*)

We define the settings that are the same for all deployments in the *settings.py* file in our project repository. You can find that file on GitHub (*http://bit.ly/1F5B7cY*).

As shown in Example 6-13, the *settings.py* file contains a Python snippet that loads a *local_settings.py* file. Django will raise an exception if the *local_settings.py* file does not exist.

Example 6-13. Loading the local settings

```
try:
    from local_settings import *
except ImportError as e:
    if "local_settings" not in str(e):
        raise e
```

In addition, the *.gitignore* file is configured to ignore the *local_settings.py* file, since developers will commonly create this file and configure it for local development.

As part of our deployment, we need to create a *local_settings.py* file and upload it to the remote host. Example 6-14 shows the Jinja2 template that we use.

Example 6-14. local_settings.py.j2

```
from __future__ import unicode_literals

SECRET_KEY = "{{ secret_key }}"
NEVERCACHE_KEY = "{{ nevercache_key }}"
ALLOWED_HOSTS = [{% for domain in domains %}"{{ domain }}",{% endfor %}]

DATABASES = {
    "default": {
        # Ends with "postgresql_psycopg2", "mysql", "sqlite3" or "oracle".
```

---

3 See the Postgres documentation (*http://bit.ly/1F5AYpN*) for more details about template databases.

```
        "ENGINE": "django.db.backends.postgresql_psycopg2",
        # DB name or path to database file if using sqlite3.
        "NAME": "{{ proj_name }}",
        # Not used with sqlite3.
        "USER": "{{ proj_name }}",
        # Not used with sqlite3.
        "PASSWORD": "{{ db_pass }}",
        # Set to empty string for localhost. Not used with sqlite3.
        "HOST": "127.0.0.1",
        # Set to empty string for default. Not used with sqlite3.
        "PORT": "",
    }
}

SECURE_PROXY_SSL_HEADER = ("HTTP_X_FORWARDED_PROTOCOL", "https")

CACHE_MIDDLEWARE_SECONDS = 60

CACHE_MIDDLEWARE_KEY_PREFIX = "{{ proj_name }}"

CACHES = {
    "default": {
        "BACKEND": "django.core.cache.backends.memcached.MemcachedCache",
        "LOCATION": "127.0.0.1:11211",
    }
}

SESSION_ENGINE = "django.contrib.sessions.backends.cache"
```

Most of this template is straightforward; it uses the `{{ variable }}` syntax to insert the values of variables such as `secret_key`, `nevercache_key`, `proj_name`, and `db_pass`. The only non-trivial bit of logic is the line shown in Example 6-15:

Example 6-15. Using a for loop in a Jinja2 template

```
ALLOWED_HOSTS = [{% for domain in domains %}"{{ domain }}",{% endfor %}]
```

If we look back at our variable definition, we have a variable called `domains` that's defined like this:

```
domains:
  - 192.168.33.10.xip.io
  - www.192.168.33.10.xip.io
```

Our Mezzanine app is going to respond only to requests that are for one of the hostnames listed in the `domains` variable: *http://192.168.33.10.xip.io* or *http://www.192.168.33.10.xip.io* in our case. If a request reaches Mezzanine but the host header is something other than those two domains, the site will return "Bad Request (400)."

We want this line in the generated file to look like this:

```
ALLOWED_HOSTS = ["192.168.33.10.xip.io", "www.192.168.33.10.xip.io"]
```

We can achieve this by using a for loop, as shown in Example 6-15. Note that it doesn't do exactly what we want. Instead, it will have a trailing comma, like this:

```
ALLOWED_HOSTS = ["192.168.33.10.xip.io", "www.192.168.33.10.xip.io",]
```

However, Python is perfectly happy with trailing commas in lists, so we can leave it like this.

What's xip.io?

You might have noticed that the domains we are using look a little strange: *192.168.33.10.xip.io* and *www.192.168.33.10.xip.io*. They are domain names, but they have the IP address embedded within them.

When you access a website, you pretty much always point your browser to a domain name such as *http://www.ansiblebook.com*, instead of an IP address like *http://54.225.155.135*.

When we write our playbook to deploy Mezzanine to Vagrant, we want to configure the application with the domain name or names that it should be accessible by.

The problem is that we don't have a DNS record that maps to the IP address of our Vagrant box. In this case, that's *192.168.33.10*. There's nothing stopping us from setting up a DNS entry for this. For example, I could create a DNS entry from *mezzanine-internal.ansiblebook.com* that points to *192.168.33.10*.

However, if we want to create a DNS name that resolves to a particular IP address, there's a convenient service called *xip.io*, provided free of charge by Basecamp, that we can use so that we don't have to avoid creating our own DNS records. If *AAA.BBB.CCC.DDD* is an IP address, then the DNS entry *AAA.BBB.CCC.DDD.xip.io* will resolve to *AAA.BBB.CCC.DDD*. For example, *192.168.33.10.xip.io* resolves to *192.168.33.10*. In addition, *www.192.168.33.10.xip.io* also resolves to *192.168.33.10*.

I find *xip.io* to be a great tool when I'm deploying web applications to private IP addresses for testing purposes.

Alternatively, you can simply add entries to the */etc/hosts* file on your local machine, which also works when you're offline.

Let's examine the Jinja2 for loop syntax. To make things a little easier to read, we'll break it up across multiple lines, like this:

```
ALLOWED_HOSTS = [
{% for domain in domains %}
                "{{ domain }}",
{% endfor %}
                ]
```

The generated config file would look like this, which is still valid Python.

```
ALLOWED_HOSTS = [
                "192.168.33.10.xip.io",
                "www.192.168.33.10.xip.io",
                ]
```

Note that the for loop has to be terminated by an {% endfor %} statement. Also note that the for statement and the endfor statement are surrounded by {% %} delimiters, which are different from the {{ }} delimiters that we use for variable substitution.

All variables and facts that have been defined in a playbook are available inside of Jinja2 templates, so we never need to explicitly pass variables to templates.

Running django-manage Commands

Django applications use a special script called *manage.py* (*http://bit.ly/1FvJwnp*) that performs administrative actions for Django applications such as:

- creating database tables
- applying database migrations
- loading fixtures from files into the database
- dumping fixtures from the database to files
- copying static assets to the appropriate directory

In addition to the built-in commands that *manage.py* supports, Django applications can add custom commands, and Mezzanine adds a custom command called crea tedb that is used to initialize the database and copy the static assets to the appropriate place. The official Fabric scripts do the equivalent of:

```
$ manage.py createdb --noinput --nodata
```

Ansible ships with a django_manage module that invokes manage.py commands. We could invoke it like this:

```
- name: initialize the database
  django_manage:
    command: createdb --noinput --nodata
    app_path: "{{ proj_path }}"
    virtualenv: "{{ venv_path }}"
```

Unfortunately, the custom createdb command that Mezzanine adds isn't idempotent. If invoked a second time, it will fail like this:

```
TASK: [initialize the database] **********************************************
failed: [web] => {"cmd": "python manage.py createdb --noinput --nodata", "failed"
: true, "path": "/home/vagrant/mezzanine_example/bin:/usr/local/sbin:/usr/local/b
in:/usr/sbin: /usr/bin:/sbin:/bin:/usr/games:/usr/local/games", "state": "absent"
```

```
, "syspath": ["", "/usr/lib/python2.7", "/usr/lib/python2.7/plat-x86_64-linux-gnu
", "/usr/lib/python2.7/lib-tk", "/usr/lib/python2.7/lib-old", "/usr/lib/python2.7
/lib-dynload", "/usr/local/lib/python2.7/dist-packages", "/usr/lib/python2.7/dist
-packages"]}
msg:
:stderr: CommandError: Database already created, you probably want the syncdb or
migrate command
```

Fortunately, the custom `createdb` command is effectively equivalent to three idempotent built-in `manage.py` commands:

syncdb

> Create database tables for Django models that are not versioned with South (*http://south.readthedocs.org*), a library that implements database migrations for Django.

migrate

> Create and update database tables for Django models that are versioned with South.

collectstatic

> Copy the static assets to the appropriate directories.

By invoking these commands, we get an idempotent task:

```
- name: sync the database, apply migrations, collect static content
  django_manage:
    command: "{{ item }}"
    app_path: "{{ proj_path }}"
    virtualenv: "{{ venv_path }}"
  with_items:
    - syncdb
    - migrate
    - collectstatic
```

Running Custom Python Scripts in the Context of the Application

To initialize our application, we need to make two changes to our database.

1. We need to create a Site (*http://bit.ly/1FvJFaz*) model object that contains the domain name of our site (in our case, that's *192.168.33.10.xip.io*).

2. We need to set the administrator username and password.

While we could make these changes with raw SQL commands, typically you'd do this by writing Python code, and that's how the Mezzanine Fabric scripts do it, so that's how we're going to do it.

There are two tricky parts here. The Python scripts need to run in the context of the virtualenv that we've created, and the Python environment needs to be set up properly so that the script will import the *settings.py* file that's in *~/mezzanine_example/ project*.

In most cases, if I needed some custom Python code, I'd write a custom Ansible module. However, as far as I know, Ansible doesn't let you execute a module in the context of a virtualenv, so that's out.

I used the `script` module instead. This will copy over a custom script and execute it. I wrote two scripts, one to set the Site record, and the other to set the admin username and password.

You can pass command-line arguments to `script` modules and parse them out, but I decided to pass the arguments as environment variables instead. I didn't want to pass passwords via command-line argument (those show up in the process list when you run the `ps` command), and it's easier to parse out environment variables in the scripts than it is to parse command-line arguments.

Passing Environment Variables to Ansible Tasks

Ansible allows you to set environment variables by adding an `envi ronment` clause to a task, passing it a dictionary that contains the environment variable names and values. You can add an `environ ment` clause to any task; it doesn't have to be a `script`.

In order to run these scripts in the context of the virtualenv, I also needed to set the `path` variable so that the first Python executable in the `path` would be the one inside of the virtualenv. Example 6-16 shows how I invoked the two scripts.

Example 6-16. Using the script module to invoke custom Python code

```
- name: set the site id
  script: scripts/setsite.py
  environment:
    PATH: "{{ venv_path }}/bin"
    PROJECT_DIR: "{{ proj_path }}"
    WEBSITE_DOMAIN: "{{ live_hostname }}"

- name: set the admin password
  script: scripts/setadmin.py
  environment:
    PATH: "{{ venv_path }}/bin"
    PROJECT_DIR: "{{ proj_path }}"
    ADMIN_PASSWORD: "{{ admin_pass }}"
```

The scripts themselves are shown in Examples 6-17 and 6-18. I put these in a *scripts* subdirectory.

Example 6-17. scripts/setsite.py

```
#!/usr/bin/env python
# A script to set the site domain
# Assumes two environment variables
#
# PROJECT_DIR: the project directory (e.g., ~/projname)
# WEBSITE_DOMAIN: the domain of the site (e.g., www.example.com)

import os
import sys

# Add the project directory to system path
proj_dir = os.path.expanduser(os.environ['PROJECT_DIR'])
sys.path.append(proj_dir)

os.environ['DJANGO_SETTINGS_MODULE'] = 'settings'
from django.conf import settings
from django.contrib.sites.models import Site

domain = os.environ['WEBSITE_DOMAIN']
Site.objects.filter(id=settings.SITE_ID).update(domain=domain)
Site.objects.get_or_create(domain=domain)
```

Example 6-18. scripts/setadmin.py

```
#!/usr/bin/env python
# A script to set the admin credentials
# Assumes two environment variables
#
# PROJECT_DIR: the project directory (e.g., ~/projname)
# ADMIN_PASSWORD: admin user's password

import os
import sys

# Add the project directory to system path
proj_dir = os.path.expanduser(os.environ['PROJECT_DIR'])
sys.path.append(proj_dir)

os.environ['DJANGO_SETTINGS_MODULE'] = 'settings'


from mezzanine.utils.models import get_user_model
User = get_user_model()
u, _ = User.objects.get_or_create(username='admin')
u.is_staff = u.is_superuser = True
```

```
u.set_password(os.environ['ADMIN_PASSWORD'])
u.save()
```

Setting Service Configuration Files

Next, we set the configuration file for Gunicorn (our application server), nginx (our web server), and Supervisor (our process manager), as shown in Example 6-19. The template for the Gunicorn configuration file is shown in Example 6-21.

Example 6-19. Setting configuration files

```
- name: set the gunicorn config file
  template: src=templates/gunicorn.conf.py.j2 dest={{ proj_path }}/gunicorn.conf.py

- name: set the supervisor config file
  template: src=templates/supervisor.conf.j2
        dest=/etc/supervisor/conf.d/mezzanine.conf
  sudo: True
  notify: restart supervisor

- name: set the nginx config file
  template: src=templates/nginx.conf.j2
        dest=/etc/nginx/sites-available/mezzanine.conf
  notify: restart nginx
  sudo: True
```

In all three cases, we generate the config files using templates. The Supervisor and nginx processes are started by root (although they drop down to non-root users when running), so we need to sudo so that we have the appropriate permissions to write their configuration files.

If the supervisor configuration file changes, then Ansible will fire the restart super visor handler. If the nginx configuration file changes, then Ansible will fire the restart nginx handler, as shown in Example 6-20.

Example 6-20. Handlers

```
handlers:
  - name: restart supervisor
    supervisorctl: name=gunicorn_mezzanine state=restarted
    sudo: True

  - name: restart nginx
    service: name=nginx state=restarted
    sudo: True
```

Example 6-21. templates/gunicorn.conf.py.j2

```
from __future__ import unicode_literals
import multiprocessing

bind = "127.0.0.1:{{ gunicorn_port }}"
workers = multiprocessing.cpu_count() * 2 + 1
loglevel = "error"
proc_name = "{{ proj_name }}"
```

Example 6-22. templates/supervisor.conf.j2

```
[group: {{ proj_name }}]
programs=gunicorn_{{ proj_name }}

[program:gunicorn_{{ proj_name }}]
command={{ venv_path }}/bin/gunicorn_django -c gunicorn.conf.py -p gunicorn.pid
directory={{ proj_path }}
user={{ user }}
autostart=true
autorestart=true
redirect_stderr=true
environment=LANG="{{ locale }}",LC_ALL="{{ locale }}",LC_LANG="{{ locale }}"
```

The only template that has any template logic (other than variable substitution) is
Example 6-23. It has conditional logic to enable TLS if the `tls_enabled` variable is set
to true. You'll see some `if` statements scattered about the templates that look like this:

```
{% if tls_enabled %}
...
{% endif %}
```

It also uses the `join` Jinja2 filter here:

```
server_name {{ domains|join(", ") }};
```

This code snippet expects the variable `domains` to be a list. It will generate a string
with the elements of `domains` connected together, separated by commas. Recall that in
our case, the `domains` list is defined as:

```
domains:
  - 192.168.33.10.xip.io
  - www.192.168.33.10.xip.io
```

When the template renders, the line looks like this:

```
server_name 192.168.33.10.xip.io, www.192.168.33.10.xip.io;
```

Example 6-23. templates/nginx.conf.j2

```
upstream {{ proj_name }} {
    server 127.0.0.1:{{ gunicorn_port }};
```

```
}

server {

    listen 80;

    {% if tls_enabled %}
    listen 443 ssl;
    {% endif %}
    server_name {{ domains|join(", ") }};
    client_max_body_size 10M;
    keepalive_timeout    15;

    {% if tls_enabled %}
    ssl_certificate       conf/{{ proj_name }}.crt;
    ssl_certificate_key   conf/{{ proj_name }}.key;
    ssl_session_cache     shared:SSL:10m;
    ssl_session_timeout   10m;
    # ssl_ciphers entry is too long to show in this book
    # See https://github.com/lorin/ansiblebook
    #     ch06/playbooks/templates/nginx.conf.j2
    ssl_prefer_server_ciphers on;
    {% endif %}

    location / {
        proxy_redirect      off;
        proxy_set_header    Host                    $host;
        proxy_set_header    X-Real-IP               $remote_addr;
        proxy_set_header    X-Forwarded-For         $proxy_add_x_forwarded_for;
        proxy_set_header    X-Forwarded-Protocol    $scheme;
        proxy_pass          http://{{ proj_name }};
    }

    location /static/ {
        root            {{ proj_path }};
        access_log      off;
        log_not_found   off;
    }

    location /robots.txt {
        root            {{ proj_path }}/static;
        access_log      off;
        log_not_found   off;
    }

    location /favicon.ico {
        root            {{ proj_path }}/static/img;
        access_log      off;
        log_not_found   off;
    }
}
```

Enabling the Nginx Configuration

The convention with nginx configuration files is to put your configuration files in */etc/nginx/sites-available* and enable them by symlinking them into */etc/nginx/sites-enabled*.

The Mezzanine Fabric scripts just copy the configuration file directly into *sites-enabled*, but I'm going to deviate from how Mezzanine does it because it gives me an excuse to use the `file` module to create a symlink. We also need to remove the default configuration file that the nginx package sets up in */etc/nginx/sites-enabled/ default*.

Example 6-24. Enabling nginx configuration

```
- name: enable the nginx config file
  file:
    src: /etc/nginx/sites-available/mezzanine.conf
    dest: /etc/nginx/sites-enabled/mezzanine.conf
    state: link
  notify: restart nginx
  sudo: True

- name: remove the default nginx config file
  file: path=/etc/nginx/sites-enabled/default state=absent
  notify: restart nginx
  sudo: True
```

As shown in Example 6-24, we use the `file` module to create the symlink and to remove the default config file. This module is useful for creating directories, symlinks, and empty files; deleting files, directories, and symlinks; and setting properties such as permissions and ownership.

Installing TLS Certificates

Our playbook defines a variable named `tls_enabled`. If this variable is set to `true`, then the playbook will install TLS certificates. In our example, we use self-signed certificates, so the playbook will create the certificate if it doesn't exist.

In a production deployment, you would copy an existing TLS certificate that you obtained from a certificate authority.

Example 6-25. Installing TLS certificates

```
- name: ensure config path exists
  file: path={{ conf_path }} state=directory
  sudo: True
  when: tls_enabled
```

```
- name: create tls certificates
  command: >
    openssl req -new -x509 -nodes -out {{ proj_name }}.crt
    -keyout {{ proj_name }}.key -subj '/CN={{ domains[0] }}' -days 3650
    chdir={{ conf_path }}
    creates={{ conf_path }}/{{ proj_name }}.crt
  sudo: True
  when: tls_enabled
  notify: restart nginx
```

Example 6-25 shows the two tasks involved in configuring for TLS certificates. We use the `file` module to ensure that the directory that will house the TLS certificates exists.

Note how both tasks contain the clause:

```
when: tls_enabled
```

If `tls_enabled` evaluates to `false`, then Ansible will skip the task.

Ansible doesn't ship with modules for creating TLS certificates, so we need to use the `command` module to invoke the `openssl` command in order to create the self-signed certificate. Since the command is very long, we use YAML line folding syntax (see "Line Folding" on page 30) so that we can break the command across multiple lines.

These two lines at the end of the command are additional parameters that are passed to the module; they are not passed to the command line. The `chdir` parameter changes directory before running the command. The `creates` parameter implements idempotence: Ansible will first check to see if the file `{{ conf_path }}/{{ proj_name }}.crt` exists on the host. If it already exists, then Ansible will skip this task.

```
chdir={{ conf_path }}
creates={{ conf_path }}/{{ proj_name }}.crt
```

Installing Twitter Cron Job

If you run `manage.py poll_twitter`, then Mezzanine will retrieve tweets associated with the configured accounts and show them on the home page.

The Fabric scripts that ship with Mezzanine keep these tweets up-to-date by installing a cron job that runs every five minutes.

If we followed the Fabric scripts exactly, we'd copy a cron script into the */etc/cron.d* directory that had the cron job. We could use the `template` module to do this. However, Ansible ships with a `cron` module that allows us to create or delete cron jobs, which I find more elegant. Example 6-26 shows the task that installs the cron job.

Example 6-26. Installing cron job for polling twitter

```
- name: install poll twitter cron job
  cron: name="poll twitter" minute="*/5" user={{ user }} job="{{ manage }} poll_twitter"
```

If you manually SSH to the box, you can see the cron job that gets installed by doing `crontab -l` to list the jobs. Here's what it looks like for me when I deploy as the Vagrant user:

```
#Ansible: poll twitter
*/5 * * * * /home/vagrant/mezzanine-example/bin/python /home/vagrant/mezzanine-
example/project/manage.py poll_twitter
```

Notice the comment at the first line. That's how the Ansible module supports deleting cron jobs by name. If you were to do:

```
- name: remove cron job
  cron: name="poll twitter" state=absent
```

The `cron` module would look for the comment line that matches the name and delete the job associated with that comment.

The Full Playbook

Example 6-27 shows the complete playbook in all its glory.

Example 6-27. mezzanine.yml: the complete playbook

```
---
- name: Deploy mezzanine
  hosts: web
  vars:
    user: "{{ ansible_ssh_user }}"
    proj_name: mezzanine-example
    venv_home: "{{ ansible_env.HOME }}"
    venv_path: "{{ venv_home }}/{{ proj_name }}"
    proj_dirname: project
    proj_path: "{{ venv_path }}/{{ proj_dirname }}"
    reqs_path: requirements.txt
    manage: "{{ python }} {{ proj_path }}/manage.py"
    live_hostname: 192.168.33.10.xip.io
    domains:
      - 192.168.33.10.xip.io
      - www.192.168.33.10.xip.io
    repo_url: git@github.com:lorin/mezzanine-example.git
    gunicorn_port: 8000
    locale: en_US.UTF-8
    # Variables below don't appear in Mezzanine's fabfile.py
    # but I've added them for convenience
    conf_path: /etc/nginx/conf
    tls_enabled: True
```

```
      python: "{{ venv_path }}/bin/python"
      database_name: "{{ proj_name }}"
      database_user: "{{ proj_name }}"
      database_host: localhost
      database_port: 5432
      gunicorn_proc_name: mezzanine
  vars_files:
    - secrets.yml
  tasks:
    - name: install apt packages
      apt: pkg={{ item }} update_cache=yes cache_valid_time=3600
      sudo: True
      with_items:
        - git
        - libjpeg-dev
        - libpq-dev
        - memcached
        - nginx
        - postgresql
        - python-dev
        - python-pip
        - python-psycopg2
        - python-setuptools
        - python-virtualenv
        - supervisor

    - name: check out the repository on the host
      git: repo={{ repo_url }} dest={{ proj_path }} accept_hostkey=yes

    - name: install required python packages
      pip: name={{ item }} virtualenv={{ venv_path }}
      with_items:
        - gunicorn
        - setproctitle
        - south
        - psycopg2
        - django-compressor
        - python-memcached
    - name: install requirements.txt
      pip: requirements={{ proj_path }}/{{ reqs_path }} virtualenv={{ venv_path }}

    - name: create a user
      postgresql_user:
        name: "{{ database_user }}"
        password: "{{ db_pass }}"
      sudo: True
      sudo_user: postgres

    - name: create the database
      postgresql_db:
        name: "{{ database_name }}"
        owner: "{{ database_user }}"
```

```
      encoding: UTF8
      lc_ctype: "{{ locale }}"
      lc_collate: "{{ locale }}"
      template: template0
    sudo: True
    sudo_user: postgres

  - name: generate the settings file
    template:
      src: templates/local_settings.py.j2
      dest: "{{ proj_path }}/local_settings.py"

  - name: sync the database, apply migrations, collect static content
    django_manage:
      command: "{{ item }}"
      app_path: "{{ proj_path }}"
      virtualenv: "{{ venv_path }}"
    with_items:
      - syncdb
      - migrate
      - collectstatic

  - name: set the site id
    script: scripts/setsite.py
    environment:
      PATH: "{{ venv_path }}/bin"
      PROJECT_DIR: "{{ proj_path }}"
      WEBSITE_DOMAIN: "{{ live_hostname }}"

  - name: set the admin password
    script: scripts/setadmin.py
    environment:
      PATH: "{{ venv_path }}/bin"
      PROJECT_DIR: "{{ proj_path }}"
      ADMIN_PASSWORD: "{{ admin_pass }}"

  - name: set the gunicorn config file
    template:
      src: templates/gunicorn.conf.py.j2
      dest: "{{ proj_path }}/gunicorn.conf.py"

  - name: set the supervisor config file
    template:
      src: templates/supervisor.conf.j2
      dest: /etc/supervisor/conf.d/mezzanine.conf
    sudo: True
    notify: restart supervisor

  - name: set the nginx config file
    template:
      src: templates/nginx.conf.j2
      dest: /etc/nginx/sites-available/mezzanine.conf
```

```
    notify: restart nginx
    sudo: True

  - name: enable the nginx config file
    file:
      src: /etc/nginx/sites-available/mezzanine.conf
      dest: /etc/nginx/sites-enabled/mezzanine.conf
      state: link
    notify: restart nginx
    sudo: True

  - name: remove the default nginx config file
    file: path=/etc/nginx/sites-enabled/default state=absent
    notify: restart nginx
    sudo: True

  - name: ensure config path exists
    file: path={{ conf_path }} state=directory
    sudo: True
    when: tls_enabled

  - name: create tls certificates
    command: >
      openssl req -new -x509 -nodes -out {{ proj_name }}.crt
      -keyout {{ proj_name }}.key -subj '/CN={{ domains[0] }}' -days 3650
      chdir={{ conf_path }}
      creates={{ conf_path }}/{{ proj_name }}.crt
    sudo: True
    when: tls_enabled
    notify: restart nginx

  - name: install poll twitter cron job
    cron: name="poll twitter" minute="*/5" user={{ user }}
      job="{{ manage }} poll_twitter"

handlers:
  - name: restart supervisor
    supervisorctl: name=gunicorn_mezzanine state=restarted
    sudo: True

  - name: restart nginx
    service: name=nginx state=restarted
    sudo: True
```

Running the Playbook Against a Vagrant Machine

The live_hostname and domains variables in our playbook assume that the host we
are going to deploy to is accessible at *192.168.33.10*. The Vagrantfile shown in
Example 6-28 will configure a Vagrant machine with that IP address.

Example 6-28. Vagrantfile

```
VAGRANTFILE_API_VERSION = "2"

Vagrant.configure(VAGRANTFILE_API_VERSION) do |config|
  config.vm.box = "ubuntu/trusty64"
  config.vm.network "private_network", ip: "192.168.33.10"
end
```

Deploy Mezzanine into the Vagrant machine:

```
$ ansible-playbook mezzanine.yml
```

You can then reach your newly deployed Mezzanine site at any of the following URLs:

- *http://192.168.33.10.xip.io*
- *https://192.168.33.10.xip.io*
- *http://www.192.168.33.10.xip.io*
- *https://www.192.168.33.10.xip.io*

Deploying Mezzanine on Multiple Machines

In this scenario, we've deployed Mezzanine entirely on a single machine. However, it's common to deploy the database service on a separate host from the web service. In Chapter 8, we'll show a playbook that deploys across the database and web services on separate hosts.

You've now seen what it's like to deploy a real application with Mezzanine. In the next chapter, we'll cover some more advanced features of Ansible that didn't come up in our example.

## CHAPTER 7

Complex Playbooks

In the last chapter, we went over a fully functional Ansible playbook for deploying the Mezzanine CMS. That example exercised a number of common Ansible features, but it didn't cover all of them. This chapter touches on those additional features, which makes it a bit of a grab bag.

Running a Task on the Control Machine

Sometimes you want to run a particular task on the control machine instead of on the remote host. Ansible provides the `local_action` clause for tasks to support this.

Imagine that the server we wanted to install Mezzanine onto had just booted, so that if we ran our playbook too soon, it would error out because the server hadn't fully started up yet.

We could start off our playbook by invoking the `wait_for` module to wait until the SSH server was ready to accept connections before we executed the rest of the playbook. In this case, we want this module to execute on our laptop, not on the remote host.

The first task of our playbook would have to start off like this:

```
- name: wait for ssh server to be running
  local_action: wait_for port=22 host="{{ inventory_hostname }}"
    search_regex=OpenSSH
```

Note how we're referencing `inventory_hostname` in this task, which evaluates to the name of the remote host, not localhost. That's because the scope of these variables is still the remote host, even though the task is executing locally.

If your play involves multiple hosts, and you use `local_action`, the task will be executed multiple times, one for each host. You can restrict this using `run_once`, as described in "Running on One Host at a Time" on page 123.

Running a Task on a Machine Other Than the Host

Sometimes you want to run a task that's associated with a host, but you want to execute the task on a different server. You can use the `delegate_to` clause to run the task on a different host.

Two common use cases are:

- Enabling host-based alerts with an alerting system such as Nagios
- Adding a host to a load balancer such as HAProxy

For example, imagine we want to enable Nagios alerts for all of the hosts in our `web` group. Assume we have an entry in our inventory named *nagios.example.com* that is running Nagios. Example 7-1 shows an example that uses `delegate_to`.

Example 7-1. Using delegate_to with Nagios

```
- name: enable alerts for web servers
  hosts: web
  tasks:
    - name: enable alerts
      nagios: action=enable_alerts service=web host={{ inventory_hostname }}
      delegate_to: nagios.example.com
```

In this example, Ansible would execute the `nagios` task on *nagios.example.com*, but the `inventory_hostname` variable referenced in the play would evaluate to the web host.

For a more detailed example that uses `delegate_to`, see the *lamp_haproxy/rolling_update.yml* example in the Ansible project's examples GitHub repo (*https://github.com/ansible/ansible-examples*).

Manually Gathering Facts

If it was possible that the SSH server wasn't yet running when we started our playbook, we need to turn off explicit fact gathering; otherwise, Ansible will try to SSH to the host to gather facts before running the first tasks. Since we still need access to facts (recall that we use the `ansible_env` fact in our playbook), we can explicitly invoke the `setup` module to get Ansible to gather our facts, as shown in Example 7-2.

Example 7-2. Waiting for ssh server to come up

```
- name: Deploy mezzanine
  hosts: web
  gather_facts: False
  # vars & vars_files section not shown here
  tasks:
    - name: wait for ssh server to be running
      local_action: wait_for port=22 host="{{ inventory_hostname }}"
        search_regex=OpenSSH

    - name: gather facts
      setup:
  # The rest of the tasks go here
```

Running on One Host at a Time

By default, Ansible runs each task in parallel across all hosts. Sometimes you want to run your task on one host at a time. The canonical example is when upgrading application servers that are behind a load balancer. Typically, you take the application server out of the load balancer, upgrade it, and put it back. But you don't want to take all of your application servers out of the load balancer, or your service will become unavailable.

You can use the `serial` clause on a play to tell Ansible to restrict the number of hosts that a play runs on. Example 7-3 shows an example that removes hosts one at a time from an Amazon EC2 elastic load balancer, upgrades the system packages, and then puts them back into the load balancer. (We cover Amazon EC2 in more detail in Chapter 12.)

Example 7-3. Removing hosts from load balancer and upgrading packages

```
- name: upgrade packages on servers behind load balancer
  hosts: myhosts
  serial: 1
  tasks:

    - name: get the ec2 instance id and elastic load balancer id
      ec2_facts:

    - name: take the host out of the elastic load balancer
      local_action: ec2_elb
      args:
        instance_id: "{{ ansible_ec2_instance_id }}"
        state: absent

    - name: upgrade packages
      apt: update_cache=yes upgrade=yes
```

```
- name: put the host back in the elastic load balancer
  local_action: ec2_elb
  args:
    instance_id: "{{ ansible_ec2_instance_id }}"
    state: present
    ec2_elbs: "{{ item }}"
  with_items: ec2_elbs
```

In our example, we passed 1 as the argument to the `serial` clause, telling Ansible to run on only one host at a time. If we had passed 2, then Ansible would have run two hosts at a time.

Normally, when a task fails, Ansible stops running tasks against the host that fails, but continues to run against other hosts. In the load-balancing scenario, you might want Ansible to fail the entire play before all hosts have failed a task. Otherwise, you might end up with the situation where you have taken each host out of the load balancer, and have it fail, leaving no hosts left inside of your load balancer.

You can use a `max_fail_percentage` clause along with the `serial` clause to specify the maximum percentage of failed hosts before Ansible fails the entire play. For example, assume that we specify a maximum fail percentage of 25%, as shown here:

```
- name: upgrade packages on servers behind load balancer
  hosts: myhosts
  serial: 1
  max_fail_percentage: 25
  tasks:
    # tasks go here
```

If we had four hosts behind the load balancer, and one of the hosts failed a task, then Ansible would keep executing the play, because this would not exceed the 25% threshold. However, if a second host failed a task, Ansible would fail the entire play, because then 50% of the hosts would have failed a task, exceeding the 25% threshold. If you want Ansible to fail if any of the hosts fail a task, set the `max_fail_percentage` to 0.

Running Only Once

Sometimes you might want a task to run only once, even if there are multiple hosts. For example, perhaps you have multiple application servers running behind the load balancer, and you want to run a database migration, but you only need to run the migration on one application server.

You can use the `run_once` clause to tell Ansible to run the command only once.

```
- name: run the database migrations
  command: /opt/run_migrations
  run_once: true
```

Using `run_once` can be particularly useful when using `local_action` if your playbook involves multiple hosts, and you want to run the local task only once:

```
- name: run the task locally, only once
  local_action: command /opt/my-custom-command
  run_once: true
```

Dealing with Badly Behaved Commands: changed_when and failed_when

Recall that in Chapter 6, we avoided invoking the custom `createdb manage.py` command, shown in Example 7-4, because the call wasn't idempotent.

Example 7-4. Calling django manage.py createdb

```
- name: initialize the database
  django_manage:
    command: createdb --noinput --nodata
    app_path: "{{ proj_path }}"
    virtualenv: "{{ venv_path }}"
```

We got around this problem by invoking several `django manage.py` commands that were idempotent, and that did the equivalent of `createdb`. But what if we didn't have a module that could invoke equivalent commands? The answer is to use `changed_when` and `failed_when` clauses to change how Ansible identifies that a task has changed state or failed.

First, we need to understand what the output of this command is the first time it's run, and what the output is when it's run the second time.

Recall from Chapter 4 that to capture the output of a failed task, you add a `register` clause to save the output to a variable and a `failed_when: False` clause so that the execution doesn't stop even if the module returns failure. Then add a `debug` task to print out the variable, and finally a `fail` clause so that the playbook stops executing, as shown in Example 7-5.

Example 7-5. Viewing the output of a task

```
- name: initialize the database
  django_manage:
    command: createdb --noinput --nodata
    app_path: "{{ proj_path }}"
    virtualenv: "{{ venv_path }}"
  failed_when: False
  register: result

- debug: var=result
```

```
- fail:
```

The output of the playbook when invoked the second time is Example 7-6.

Example 7-6. Returned values when database has already been created

```
TASK: [debug var=result] ****************************************************
ok: [default] => {
    "result": {
        "cmd": "python manage.py createdb --noinput --nodata",
        "failed": false,
        "failed_when_result": false,
        "invocation": {
            "module_args": '',
            "module_name": "django_manage"
        },
        "msg": "\n:stderr: CommandError: Database already created, you probably
want the syncdb or migrate command\n",
        "path":
"/home/vagrant/mezzanine_example/bin:/usr/local/sbin:/usr/local/bin:/usr/sbin:/usr/bi
n:/sbin:/bin:/usr/games:/usr/local/games",
        "state": "absent",
        "syspath": [
            `` ,
            "/usr/lib/python2.7",
            "/usr/lib/python2.7/plat-x86_64-linux-gnu",
            "/usr/lib/python2.7/lib-tk",
            "/usr/lib/python2.7/lib-old",
            "/usr/lib/python2.7/lib-dynload",
            "/usr/local/lib/python2.7/dist-packages",
            "/usr/lib/python2.7/dist-packages"
        ]
    }
}
```

This is what happens when the task has been run multiple times. To see what happens the first time, delete the database and then have the playbook recreate it. The simplest way to do that is to run an Ansible ad-hoc task that deletes the database:

```
$ ansible default --sudo --sudo-user postgres -m postgresql_db -a \
"name=mezzanine_example state=absent"
```

Now when I run the playbook again, the output is Example 7-7.

Example 7-7. Returned values when invoked the first time

```
ASK: [debug var=result] ****************************************************
ok: [default] => {
    "result": {
        "app_path": "/home/vagrant/mezzanine_example/project",
```

```
        "changed": false,
        "cmd": "python manage.py createdb --noinput --nodata",
        "failed": false,
        "failed_when_result": false,
        "invocation": {
            "module_args": '',
            "module_name": "django_manage"
        },
        "out": "Creating tables ...\nCreating table auth_permission\nCreating
table auth_group_permissions\nCreating table auth_group\nCreating table
auth_user_groups\nCreating table auth_user_user_permissions\nCreating table
auth_user\nCreating table django_content_type\nCreating table
django_redirect\nCreating table django_session\nCreating table
django_site\nCreating table conf_setting\nCreating table
core_sitepermission_sites\nCreating table core_sitepermission\nCreating table
generic_threadedcomment\nCreating table generic_keyword\nCreating table
generic_assignedkeyword\nCreating table generic_rating\nCreating table
blog_blogpost_related_posts\nCreating table blog_blogpost_categories\nCreating
table blog_blogpost\nCreating table blog_blogcategory\nCreating table
forms_form\nCreating table forms_field\nCreating table forms_formentry\nCreating
table forms_fieldentry\nCreating table pages_page\nCreating table
pages_richtextpage\nCreating table pages_link\nCreating table
galleries_gallery\nCreating table galleries_galleryimage\nCreating table
twitter_query\nCreating table twitter_tweet\nCreating table
south_migrationhistory\nCreating table django_admin_log\nCreating table
django_comments\nCreating table django_comment_flags\n\nCreating default site
record: vagrant-ubuntu-trusty-64 ... \n\nInstalled 2 object(s) from 1
fixture(s)\nInstalling custom SQL ...\nInstalling indexes ...\nInstalled 0
object(s) from 0 fixture(s)\n\nFaking initial migrations ...\n\n",
        "pythonpath": null,
        "settings": null,
        "virtualenv": "/home/vagrant/mezzanine_example"
    }
}
```

Note that changed is set to false even though it did, indeed, change the state of the
database. That's because the django_manage module always returns changed=false
when it runs commands that the module doesn't know about.

We can add a changed_when clause that looks for "Creating tables" in the out
return value, as shown in Example 7-8.

Example 7-8. First attempt at adding changed_when

```
- name: initialize the database
  django_manage:
    command: createdb --noinput --nodata
    app_path: "{{ proj_path }}"
    virtualenv: "{{ venv_path }}"
  register: result
  changed_when: '"Creating tables" in result.out'
```

The problem with this approach is that, if we look back at Example 7-6, we see that there is no out variable. Instead, there's a msg variable. This means that if we executed the playbook, we'd get the following (not terribly helpful) error the second time:

```
TASK: [initialize the database] **********************************************
fatal: [default] => error while evaluating conditional: "Creating tables" in
result.out
```

Instead, we need to ensure that Ansible evaluates result.out only if that variable is defined. One way is to explicitly check to see if the variable is defined:

```
changed_when: result.out is defined and "Creating tables" not in result.out
```

Alternatively, we could also provide a default value for result.out if it doesn't exist by using the Jinja2 default filter:

```
changed_when: '"Creating tables" not in result.out|default("")'
```

Or we could simply check for failed to be false:

```
changed_when: not result.failed and "Creating tables" not in result.out
```

We also need to change the failure behavior, since we don't want Ansible to consider the task as failed just because createdb has been invoked already:

```
failed_when: result.failed and "Database already created" not in result.msg
```

Here the failed check serves as a guard for the existence of the msg variable. The final idempotent task is shown in Example 7-9.

Example 7-9. Idempotent manage.py createdb

```
- name: initialize the database
  django_manage:
    command: createdb --noinput --nodata
    app_path: "{{ proj_path }}"
    virtualenv: "{{ venv_path }}"
  register: result
  changed_when: not result.failed and "Creating tables" in result.out
  failed_when: result.failed and "Database already created" not in result.msg
```

Retrieving the IP Address from the Host

In our playbook, several of the hostnames we use are derived from the IP address of the web server.

```
live_hostname: 192.168.33.10.xip.io
domains:
  - 192.168.33.10.xip.io
  - www.192.168.33.10.xip.io
```

What if we wanted to use the same scheme but not hardcode the IP addresses into the variables? That way, if the IP address of the web server changes, we wouldn't have to modify our playbook.

Ansible retrieves the IP address of each host and stores it as a fact. Each network interface has an associated Ansible fact. For example, details about network interface eth0 are stored in the `ansible_eth0` fact, an example of which is shown in Example 7-10.

Example 7-10. ansible_eth0 fact

```
"ansible_eth0": {
    "active": true,
    "device": "eth0",
    "ipv4": {
        "address": "10.0.2.15",
        "netmask": "255.255.255.0",
        "network": "10.0.2.0"
    },
    "ipv6": [
        {
            "address": "fe80::a00:27ff:fefe:1e4d",
            "prefix": "64",
            "scope": "link"
        }
    ],
    "macaddress": "08:00:27:fe:1e:4d",
    "module": "e1000",
    "mtu": 1500,
    "promisc": false,
    "type": "ether"
}
```

Our Vagrant box has two interfaces, eth0 and eth1. The eth0 interface is a private interface whose IP address (*10.0.2.15*) we cannot reach. The eth1 interface is the one that has the IP address we've assigned in our Vagrantfile (*192.168.33.10*).

We can define our variables like this:

```
live_hostname: "{{ ansible_eth1.ipv4.address }}.xip.io"
domains:
  - ansible_eth1.ipv4.address.xip.io
  - www.ansible_eth1.ipv4.address.xip.io
```

Encrypting Sensitive Data with Vault

Our Mezzanine playbook required access to some sensitive information, such as database and administrator passwords. We dealt with this in Chapter 6 by putting all of the sensitive information in a separate file called *secrets.yml* and making sure that we didn't check this file into our version control repository.

Ansible provides an alternative solution: instead of keeping the *secrets.yml* file out of version control, we can commit an encrypted version. That way, even if our version control repository were compromised, the attacker would not have access to the contents of the *secrets.yml* file unless he also had the password used for the encryption.

The `ansible-vault` command-line tool allows you to create and edit an encrypted file that `ansible-playbook` will recognize and decrypt automatically, given the password.

We can encrypt an existing file like this:

```
$ ansible-vault encrypt secrets.yml
```

Alternately, we can create a new encrypted *secrets.yml* file by doing:

```
$ ansible-vault create secrets.yml
```

You will be prompted for a password, and then `ansible-vault` will launch a text editor so that you can populate the file. It launches the editor specified in the `$EDITOR` environment variable. If that variable is not defined, it defaults to `vim`.

Example 7-11 shows an example of the contents of a file encrypted using `ansible-vault`.

Example 7-11. Contents of file encrypted with ansible-vault

```
$ANSIBLE_VAULT;1.1;AES256
34306434353230663665633539363736353836333936383931316434343030316366653331363262
66306333663831353862663330303939363430366461366123500a6238376634623930316262333376232
31613735376632333232316266166376662623933373835653239316230386339303330366383530
...
62346633343464313330383832646531623338633334383336465323166626335623639383363643438
64636665366538343038383303165646161366566326563306639643833316565336
```

You can use the `vars_files` section of a play to reference a file encrypted with `ansible-vault` the same way you would access a regular file: we would not need to modify Example 6-27 at all if we encrypted the `secrets.yml` file.

We do need to tell `ansible-playbook` to prompt us for the password of the encrypted file, or it will simply error out. Do so by using the `--ask-vault-pass` argument:

```
$ ansible-playbook mezzanine.yml --ask-vault-pass
```

You can also store the password in a text file and tell `ansible-playbook` the location of this password file using the `--vault-password-file` flag:

```
$ ansible-playbook mezzanine --vault-password-file ~/password.txt
```

If the argument to `--vault-password-file` has the executable bit set, Ansible will execute it and use the contents of standard out as the vault password. This allows you to use a script to provide the password to Ansible.

Table 7-1 shows the available `ansible-vault` commands.

Table 7-1. ansible-vault commands

Command	Description
ansible-vault encrypt *file.yml*	Encrypt the plaintext *file.yml* file
ansible-vault decrypt *file.yml*	Decrypt the encrypted *file.yml* file
ansible-vault view *file.yml*	Print the contents of the encrypted *file.yml* file
ansible-vault create *file.yml*	Create a new encrypted *file.yml* file
ansible-vault edit *file.yml*	Edit an encrypted *file.yml* file
ansible-vault rekey *file.yml*	Change the password on an encrypted *file.yml* file

Patterns for Specifying Hosts

So far, the host parameter in our plays has specified a single host or group, like this:

```
hosts: web
```

Instead of specifying a single host or group, you can specify a *pattern*. So far, we've seen the all pattern, which lets will run a play against all known hosts:

```
hosts: all
```

You can specify a union of two groups with a colon. To specify all dev and staging machines:

```
hosts: dev:staging
```

You can specify an intersection using colon ampersand. For example, to specify all of the database servers in your staging environment, you might do:

```
hosts: staging:&database
```

Table 7-2 shows the patterns that Ansible supports. Note that the regular expression pattern always starts with a tilde.

Table 7-2. Supported patterns

Action	Example usage
All hosts	`all`
All hosts	`*`
Union	`dev:staging`
Intersection	`staging:&database`
Exclusion	`dev:!queue`
Wildcard	`*.example.com`
Range of numbered servers	`web[5:10]`
Regular expression	`~web\d\.example\.(com`

Ansible supports multiple combinations of patterns—for example:

```
hosts: dev:staging:&database:!queue
```

Limiting Which Hosts Run

Use the `-l hosts` or `--limit hosts` flag to tell Ansible to limit the hosts to run the playbook against the specified list of hosts, as shown in Example 7-12.

Example 7-12. Limiting which hosts run

```
$ ansible-playbook -l hosts playbook.yml
$ ansible-playbook --limit hosts playbook.yml
```

You can use the pattern syntax just described to specify arbitrary combinations of hosts. For example:

```
$ ansible-playbook -l 'staging:&database' playbook.yml
```

Filters

Filters are a feature of the Jinja2 templating engine. Since Ansible uses Jinja2 for evaluating variables, as well as for templates, you can use filters inside of `{{ braces }}` in your playbooks, as well as inside of your template files. Using filters resembles using Unix pipes, where a variable is piped through a filter. Jinja2 ships with a set of built-in filters (*http://bit.ly/1FvOGzI*). In addition, Ansible ships with its own filters to augment the Jinja2 filters (*http://bit.ly/1FvOIrj*).

We'll cover a few sample filters here, but check out the official Jinja2 and Ansible docs for a complete list of the available filters.

The Default Filter

The default filter is a useful one. Here's an example of this filter in action:

```
"HOST": "{{ database_host | default('localhost') }}",
```

If the variable database_host is defined, then the braces will evaluate to the value of that variable. If the variable database_host is not defined, then the braces will evaluate to the string localhost. Some filters take arguments, and some don't.

Filters for Registered Variables

Let's say we want to run a task and print out its output, even if the task fails. However, if the task did fail, we want Ansible to fail for that host after printing the output. Example 7-13 shows how we would use the failed filter in the argument to the failed_when clause.

Example 7-13. Using the failed filter

```
- name: Run myprog
  command: /opt/myprog
  register: result
  ignore_errors: True

- debug: var=result

- debug: msg="Stop running the playbook if myprog failed"
  failed_when: result|failed
# more tasks here
```

Table 7-3 shows a list of filters you can use on registered variables to check the status.

Table 7-3. Task return value filters

Name	Description
failed	True if a registered value is a task that failed
changed	True if a registered value is a task that changed
success	True if a registered value is a task that succeeded
skipped	True if a registered value is a task that was skipped

Filters That Apply to File Paths

Table 7-4 shows a number of filters that are useful when a variable contains the path to a variable on the control machine's filesystem.

Table 7-4. File path filters

basename	basename of file path
dirname	Directory of file path
expanduser	File path with ~ replaced by home directory
realpath	Canonical path of file path, resolves symbolic links

Consider this playbook fragment:

```
vars:
  homepage: /usr/share/nginx/html/index.html
tasks:
- name: copy home page
  copy: src=files/index.html dest={{ homepage }}
```

Note how it references *index.html* twice, once in the definition of the homepage variable, and a second time to specify the path to the file on the control machine.

The basename filter will let us extract the *index.html* part of the filename from the full path, allowing us to write the playbook without repeating the filename:[1]

```
vars:
  homepage: /usr/share/nginx/html/index.html
tasks:
- name: copy home page
  copy: src=files/{{ homepage | basename }} dest={{ homepage }}
```

Writing Your Own Filter

Recall that in our Mezzanine example, we generated the *local_settings.py* file from a template, where there is a line in the generated file that looks like what is shown in Example 7-14.

Example 7-14. Line from local_settings.py generated by template

```
ALLOWED_HOSTS = ["www.example.com", "example.com"]
```

---

1 Thanks to John Jarvis for this tip.

We had a variable named *domains* that contained a list of the hostnames. We originally used a for loop in our template to generate this line, but a filter would be an even more elegant approach.

There is a built-in Jinja2 filter called join, that will join a list of strings with a delimiter such as a column. Unfortunately, it doesn't quite give us what we want. If we did this in the template:

```
ALLOWED_HOSTS = [{{ domains|join(", ") }}]
```

Then we would end up with the strings unquoted in our file, as shown in Example 7-15.

Example 7-15. Strings incorrectly unquoted

```
ALLOWED_HOSTS = [www.example.com, example.com]
```

If we had a Jinja2 filter that quoted the strings in the list, as shown in Example 7-16, then the template would generate the output depicted in Example 7-14.

Example 7-16. Using a filter to quote the strings in the list

```
ALLOWED_HOSTS = [{{ domains|surround_by_quote|join(", ") }}]
```

Unfortunately, there's no existing surround_by_quote filter that does what we want. However, we can write it ourselves. (In fact, Hanfei Sun on Stack Overflow covered (*http://stackoverflow.com/questions/15514365/*) this very topic.)

Ansible will look for custom filters in the filter_plugins directory, relative to the directory where your playbooks are.

Example 7-17 shows what the filter implementation looks like.

Example 7-17. filter_plugins/surround_by_quotes.py

```
# From http://stackoverflow.com/a/15515929/742

def surround_by_quote(a_list):
    return ['"%s"' % an_element for an_element in a_list]


class FilterModule(object):
    def filters(self):
        return {'surround_by_quote': surround_by_quote}
```

The surround_by_quote function defines the Jinja2 filter. The FilterModule class defines a *filters* method that returns a dictionary with the name of the filter function and the function itself. The `FilterModule` class is Ansible-specific code that makes the Jinja2 filter available to Ansible.

You can also place filter plug-ins in the */usr/share/ansible_plugins/filter_plugins* directory, or you can specify the directory by setting the `ANSIBLE_FILTER_PLUGINS` environment variable to the directory where your plug-ins are located. These paths are also documented in Appendix B.

Lookups

In an ideal world, all of your configuration information would be stored as Ansible variables, in the various places that Ansible lets you define variables (e.g., the *vars* section of your playbooks, files loaded by *vars_files*, files in the *host_vars* or *group_vars* directory that we discussed in Chapter 3).

Alas, the world is a messy place, and sometimes a piece of configuration data you need lives somewhere else. Maybe it's in a text file or a *.csv* file, and you don't want to just copy the data into an Ansible variable file because now you have to maintain two copies of the same data, and you believe in the DRY[2] principle. Or maybe the data isn't maintained as a file at all; it's maintained in a key-value storage service such as *etcd*.[3] Ansible has a feature called *lookups* that allows you to read in configuration data from various sources and then use that data in your playbooks and template.

Ansible supports a collection of lookups for retrieving data from different sources, as shown in Table 7-5.

Table 7-5. Lookups

Name	Description
file	Contents of a file
password	Randomly generate a password
pipe	Output of locally executed command
env	Environment variable
template	Jinja2 template after evaluation
csvfile	Entry in a .csv file

---

2 Don't Repeat Yourself, a term popularized by *The Pragmatic Programmer: From Journeyman to Master*, which is a fantastic book.

3 etcd is a distributed key-value store, and is maintained by the CoreOS project (*https://coreos.com/docs/etcd/*).

Name	Description
dnstxt	DNS TXT record
redis_kv	Redis key lookup
etcd	etcd key lookup

You invoke lookups by calling the lookup function with two arguments. The first is a string with the name of the lookup, and the second is a string that contains one or more arguments to pass to the lookup. For example, we call the file lookup like this:

```
lookup('file', '/path/to/file.txt')
```

You can invoke lookups in your playbooks in between {{ braces }}, or you can put them in templates.

In this section, I provided only a brief overview of what lookups are available. The Ansible documentation provide more details (*http://docs.ansible.com/playbooks_lookups.html*) on how to use these lookups.

 All Ansible lookup plug-ins execute on the control machine, not the remote host.

file

Let's say that you have a text file on your control machine that contains a public SSH key that you want to copy to a remote server. Example 7-18 shows how you can use the file lookup to read the contents of a file and pass that as a parameter to a module.

Example 7-18. Using the file lookup

```
- name: Add my public key as an EC2 key
  ec2_key: name=mykey key_material="{{ lookup('file', \
  '/Users/lorinhochstein/.ssh/id_rsa.pub') }}"
```

You can invoke lookups in templates as well. If we wanted to use the same technique to create an *authorized_keys* file that contained the contents of a public key file, we could create a Jinja2 template that invokes the lookup, as shown in Example 7-19, and then call the template module in our playbook, as shown in Example 7-20.

Example 7-19. authorized_keys.j2

```
{{ lookup('file', '/Users/lorinhochstein/.ssh/id_rsa.pub') }}
```

Example 7-20. Task to generate authorized_keys

```
- name: copy authorized_host file
  template: src=authorized_keys.j2 dest=/home/deploy/.ssh/authorized_keys
```

pipe

The `pipe` lookup invokes an external program on the control machine and evaluates to the program's output on standard out.

For example, if our playbooks are version controlled using git, and we wanted to get the SHA-1 value of the most recent `git commit`,[4] we could use the `pipe` lookup:

```
- name: get SHA of most recent commit
  debug: msg="{{ lookup('pipe', 'git rev-parse HEAD') }}"
```

The output would look something like this:

```
TASK: [get the sha of the current commit] ************************************
ok: [myserver] => {
    "msg": "e7748af0f040d58d61de1917980a210df419eae9"
}
```

env

The `env` lookup retrieves the value of an environment variable set on the control machine. For example, we could use the lookup like this:

```
- name: get the current shell
  debug: msg="{{ lookup('env', 'SHELL') }}"
```

Since I use Zsh as my shell, the output looks like this when I run it:

```
TASK: [get the current shell] ************************************************
ok: [myserver] => {
    "msg": "/bin/zsh"
}
```

password

The `password` lookup evaluates to a random password, and it will also write the password to a file specified in the argument. For example, if we wanted to create a Post-

---

[4] If this sounds like gibberish, don't worry about it; it's just an example of running a command.

gres user named *deploy* with a random password and write that password to *deploy-password.txt* on the control machine, we could do:

```
- name: create deploy postgres user
  postgresql_user:
    name: deploy
    password: "{{ lookup('password', 'deploy-password.txt') }}"
```

template

The `template` lookup lets you specify a Jinja2 template file, and then returns the result of evaluating the template. If we had a template that looked like Example 7-21:

Example 7-21. message.j2

```
This host runs {{ ansible_distribution }}
```

And we defined a task like this:

```
- name: output message from template
  debug: msg="{{ lookup('template', 'message.j2') }}"
```

Then we'd see output that looks like this:

```
TASK: [output message from template] ****************************************
ok: [myserver] => {
    "msg": "This host runs Ubuntu\n"
}
```

csvfile

The `csvfile` lookup reads an entry from a *.csv* file. Assume we had a *.csv* file that looked like Example 7-22.

Example 7-22. users.csv

```
username,email
lorin,lorin@ansiblebook.com
john,john@example.com
sue,sue@example.org
```

If we wanted to extract Sue's email address using the `csvfile` lookup plug-in, we would invoke the lookup plug-in like this:

```
lookup('csvfile', 'sue file=users.csv delimiter=, col=1')
```

The `csvfile` lookup is a good example of a lookup that takes multiple arguments. Here, there are four arguments being passed to the plug-in:

- sue
- file=users.csv
- delimiter=,
- col=1

You don't specify a name for the first argument to a lookup plug-in, but you do specify names for the additional arguments. In the case of `csvfile`, the first argument is an entry that must appear exactly once in column 0 (the first column, 0-indexed) of the table.

The other arguments specify the name of the *.csv* file, the delimiter, and which column should be returned. In our example, we want to look in the file named *users.csv* and locate where the fields are delimited by commas; look up the row where the value in the first column is *sue*; and return the value in the second column (column 1, indexed by 0). This will evaluate to *sue@example.org*.

If the user name we wanted to look up was stored in a variable named `username`, we could construct the argument string by using the + sign to concatenate the `username` string with the rest of the argument string:

```
lookup('csvfile', username + ' file=users.csv delimiter=, col=1')
```

dnstxt

The `dnstxt` module requires that you install the *dnspython* Python package on the control machine.

If you're reading this book, you're probably aware of what the domain name system (DNS) does, but just in case you aren't, DNS is the service that translates hostnames such as *ansiblebook.com* to IP addresses such as *64.99.80.30*.

DNS works by associating one or more records with a hostname. The most commonly used types of DNS records are *A* records and *CNAME* records, which associate a hostname with an IP address (A record) or specify that a hostname is an alias for another hostname (CNAME record).

The DNS protocol supports another type of record that you can associate with a hostname, called a *TXT* record. A TXT record is just an arbitrary string that you can attach to a hostname. Once you've associated a TXT record with a hostname, anybody can retrieve the text using a DNS client.

For example, I own the *ansiblebook.com* domain, so I can create TXT records associated with any hostnames in that domain.[5] I associated a TXT record with the *ansiblebook.com* hostname that contains the ISBN number for this book. You can look up the TXT record using the `dig` command-line tool, as shown in Example 7-23.

Example 7-23. Using the dig tool to look up a TXT record

```
$ dig +short ansiblebook.com TXT
"isbn=978-1491915325"
```

The `dnstxt` lookup queries the DNS server for the TXT record associated with the host. If we created a task like this in a playbook:

```
- name: look up TXT record
  debug: msg="{{ lookup('dnstxt', 'ansiblebook.com') }}"
```

The output would look like this:

```
TASK: [look up TXT record] ****************************************************
ok: [myserver] => {
    "msg": "isbn=978-1491915325"
}
```

If there are multiple TXT records associated with a host, then the module will concatenate them together, and it might do this in a different order each time it is called. For example, if there were a second TXT record on *ansiblebook.com* with the text:

```
author=lorin
```

Then the *dnstxt* lookup will randomly return one of the two:

- `isbn=978-1491915325author=lorin`
- `author=lorinisbn=978-1491915325`

redis_kv

The `redis_kv` module requires that you install the *redis* Python package on the control machine.

---

5 DNS service providers typically have web interfaces to let you perform DNS-related tasks such as creating TXT records.

Redis is a popular key-value store, commonly used as a cache, as well as a data store for job queue services such as Sidekiq. You can use the `redis_kv` lookup to retrieve the value of a key. The key must be a string, as the module does the equivalent of calling the Redis *GET* command.

For example, let's say that we had a Redis server running on our control machine, and we had set the key `weather` to the value `sunny`, by doing something like this:

```
$ redis-cli SET weather sunny
```

If we defined a task in our playbook that invoked the Redis lookup:

```
- name: look up value in Redis
  debug: msg="{{ lookup('redis_kv', 'redis://localhost:6379,weather') }}"
```

The output would look like this:

```
TASK: [look up value in Redis] ************************************************
ok: [myserver] => {
    "msg": "sunny"
}
```

The module will default to *redis://localhost:6379* if the URL isn't specified, so we could have invoked the module like this instead (note the comma before the key):

```
lookup('redis_kv', ',weather')
```

etcd

Etcd is a distributed key-value store, commonly used for keeping configuration data and for implementing service discovery. You can use the `etcd` lookup to retrieve the value of a key.

For example, let's say that we had an `etcd` server running on our control machine, and we had set the key `weather` to the value `cloudy` by doing something like this:

```
$ curl -L http://127.0.0.1:4001/v2/keys/weather -XPUT -d value=cloudy
```

If we defined a task in our playbook that invoked the `etcd` plug-in:

```
- name: look up value in etcd
  debug: msg="{{ lookup('etcd', 'weather') }}"
```

The output would look like this:

```
TASK: [look up value in etcd] ************************************************
ok: [localhost] => {
    "msg": "cloudy"
}
```

By default, the `etcd` lookup will look for the etcd server at *http://127.0.0.1:4001*, but you can change this by setting the `ANSIBLE_ETCD_URL` environment variable before invoking *ansible-playbook*.

Writing Your Own Lookup Plug-in

You can also write your own lookup plug-in if you need functionality not provided by the existing plug-ins. Writing a custom lookup plug-in is out of scope for this book, but if you're really interested, I suggest that you take a look at the source code for the lookup plug-ins that ship with Ansible (*http://bit.ly/1F6jTMz*).

Once you've written your lookup plug-in, place it in one of the following directories:

- The *lookup_plugins* directory next to your playbook
- */usr/share/ansible_plugins/lookup_plugins*
- The directory specified in your `ANSIBLE_LOOKUP_PLUGINS` environment variable

More Complicated Loops

Up until this point, whenever we've written a task that iterates over a list of items, we've used the `with_items` clause to specify a list of items. Although this is the most common way to do loops, Ansible supports other mechanisms for doing iteration. Table 7-6 provides a summary of the constructs that are available.

Table 7-6. Looping constructs

Name	Input	Looping strategy
with_items	list	Loop over list elements
with_lines	command to execute	Loop over lines in command output
with_fileglob	glob	Loop over filenames
with_first_found	list of paths	First file in input that exists
with_dict	dictionary	Loop over dictionary elements
with_flattened	list of lists	Loop over flattened list
with_indexed_items	list	Single iteration
with_nested	list	Nested loop
with_random_choice	list	Single iteration
with_sequence	sequence of integers	Loop over sequence
with_subelements	list of dictionaries	Nested loop

Name	Input	Looping strategy
with_together	list of lists	Loop over zipped list
with_inventory_hostnames	host pattern	Loop over matching hosts

The official documentation (*http://bit.ly/1F6kfCP*) covers these quite thoroughly, so I'll just show examples from a few of them to give you a sense of how they work.

with_lines

The `with_lines` looping construct lets you run an arbitrary command on your control machine and iterate over the output, one line at a time.

Imagine you have a file that contains a list of names, and you want to send a Slack message for each name, something like this:

```
Leslie Lamport
Silvio Micali
Shafi Goldwasser
Judea Pearl
```

Example 7-24 shows how you can use `with_lines` to read a file and iterate over its contents line by line.

Example 7-24. Using with_lines as a loop

```
- name: Send out a slack message
  slack:
    domain: example.slack.com
    token: "{{ slack_token }}"
    msg: "{{ item }} was in the list"
  with_lines:
    - cat files/turing.txt
```

with_fileglob

The `with_fileglob` construct is useful for iterating over a set of files on the control machine.

Example 7-25 shows how to iterate over files that end in *.pub* in the */var/keys* directory, as well as a *keys* directory next to your playbook. It then uses the file lookup plug-in to extract the contents of the file, which are passed to the `authorized_key` module.

Example 7-25. Using with_fileglob to add keys

```
- name: add public keys to account
  authorized_key: user=deploy key="{{ lookup('file', item) }}"
  with_fileglob:
    - /var/keys/*.pub
    - keys/*.pub
```

with_dict

The with_dict lets you iterate over a dictionary instead of a list. When you use this looping construct, the item loop variable is a dictionary with two keys:

key

> One of the keys in the dictionary

value

> The value in the dictionary that corresponds to *key*

For example, if your host has an eth0 interface, then there will be an Ansible fact named ansible_eth0, with a key named *ipv4* that contains a dictionary that looks something like this:

```
{
 "address": "10.0.2.15",
 "netmask": "255.255.255.0",
 "network": "10.0.2.0"
}
```

We could iterate over this dictionary and print out the entries one at a time by doing:

```
- name: iterate over ansible_eth0
  debug: msg={{ item.key }}={{ item.value }}
  with_dict: ansible_eth0.ipv4
```

The output would look like this:

```
TASK: [iterate over ansible_eth0] ********************************************
ok: [myserver] => (item={'key': u'netmask', 'value': u'255.255.255.0'}) => {
    "item": {
        "key": "netmask",
        "value": "255.255.255.0"
    },
    "msg": "netmask=255.255.255.0"
}
ok: [myserver] => (item={'key': u'network', 'value': u'10.0.2.0'}) => {
    "item": {
        "key": "network",
        "value": "10.0.2.0"
    },
    "msg": "network=10.0.2.0"
}
```

```
ok: [myserver] => (item={'key': u'address', 'value': u'10.0.2.15'}) => {
    "item": {
        "key": "address",
        "value": "10.0.2.15"
    },
    "msg": "address=10.0.2.15"
}
```

Looping Constructs as Lookup Plug-ins

Ansible implements looping constructs as lookup plug-ins. You just slap a `with` at the beginning of a lookup plug-in to use it in its loop form. For example, we can rewrite Example 7-18 using the `with_file` form in Example 7-26.

Example 7-26. Using the file lookup as a loop

```
- name: Add my public key as an EC2 key
  ec2_key: name=mykey key_material="{{ item }}"
  with_file: /Users/lorinhochstein/.ssh/id_rsa.pub
```

Typically, you'd only use a lookup plug-in as a looping construct if it returns a list, which is how I was able to separate out the plug-ins into Table 7-5 (return strings) and Table 7-6 (return lists).

We covered a lot of ground in this chapter. In the next one, we'll discuss *roles*, a convenient mechanism for organizing your playbooks.

## CHAPTER 8

Roles: Scaling Up Your Playbooks

One of the things I like about Ansible is how it scales both up and down. I'm not referring to the number of hosts you're managing, but rather the complexity of the jobs you're trying to automate.

Ansible scales down well because simple tasks are easy to implement. It scales up well because it provides mechanisms for decomposing complex jobs into smaller pieces.

In Ansible, the *role* is the primary mechanism for breaking apart a playbook into multiple files. This simplifies writing complex playbooks, and it also makes them easier to reuse. Think of a role as something you assign to one or more hosts. For example, you'd assign a *database* role to the hosts that will act as database servers.

Basic Structure of a Role

An Ansible role has a name, such as "database." Files associated with the database role go in the *roles/database* directory, which contains the following files and directories.

roles/database/tasks/main.yml
>Tasks

roles/database/files/
>Holds files to be uploaded to hosts

roles/database/templates/
>Holds Jinja2 template files

roles/database/handlers/main.yml
>Handlers

roles/database/vars/main.yml
>Variables that shouldn't be overridden

roles/database/defaults/main.yml
> Default variables that can be overridden

roles/database/meta/main.yml
> Dependency information about a role

Each individual file is optional; if your role doesn't have any handlers, there's no need to have an empty *handlers/main.yml* file.

Where Does Ansible Look for My Roles?

Ansible will look for roles in the *roles* directory alongside your . playbooks. It will also look for systemwide roles in */etc/ansible/roles*. You can customize the system-wide location of roles by setting the *roles_path* setting in the defaults section of your *ansible.cfg* file, as shown in Example 8-1.

Example 8-1. ansible.cfg: overriding default roles path

```
[defaults]
roles_path = ~/ansible_roles
```

You can also override this by setting the ANSIBLE_ROLES_PATH environment variable, as described in Appendix B.

Example: Database and Mezzanine Roles

Let's take our Mezzanine playbook and implement it with Ansible roles. We could create a single role called "mezzanine," but instead I'm going to break out the deployment of the Postgres database into a separate role called "database." This will make it easier to eventually deploy the database on a host separate from the Mezzanine application.

Using Roles in Your Playbooks

Before we get into the details of how to define roles, let's go over how to assign roles to hosts in a playbook.

Example 8-2 shows what our playbook looks like for deploying Mezzanine onto a single host, once we have database and Mezzanine roles defined.

Example 8-2. mezzanine-single-host.yml

```
- name: deploy mezzanine on vagrant
  hosts: web
  vars_files:
```

```
      - secrets.yml

  roles:
    - role: database
      database_name: "{{ mezzanine_proj_name }}"
      database_user: "{{ mezzanine_proj_name }}"

    - role: mezzanine
      live_hostname: 192.168.33.10.xip.io
      domains:
        - 192.168.33.10.xip.io
        - www.192.168.33.10.xip.io
```

When we use roles, we have a roles section in our playbook. The roles section expects a list of roles. In our example, our list contains two roles, database and mezzanine.

Note how we can pass in variables when invoking the roles. In our example, we pass the `database_name` and `database_user` variables for the database role. If these variables have already been defined in the role (either in *vars/main.yml* or *defaults/main.yml*), then the values will be overridden with the variables that were passed in.

If you aren't passing in variables to roles, you can simply specify the names of the roles, like this:

```
  roles:
    - database
    - mezzanine
```

With database and mezzanine roles defined, writing a playbook that deploys the web application and database services to multiple hosts becomes much simpler. Example 8-3 shows a playbook that deploys the database on the db host and the web service on the web host. Note that this playbook contains two separate plays.

Example 8-3. mezzanine-across-hosts.yml

```
- name: deploy postgres on vagrant
  hosts: db
  vars_files:
    - secrets.yml
  roles:
    - role: database
      database_name: "{{ mezzanine_proj_name }}"
      database_user: "{{ mezzanine_proj_name }}"

- name: deploy mezzanine on vagrant
  hosts: web
  vars_files:
    - secrets.yml
  roles:
    - role: mezzanine
```

```
    database_host: "{{ hostvars.db.ansible_eth1.ipv4.address }}"
    live_hostname: 192.168.33.10.xip.io
    domains:
      - 192.168.33.10.xip.io
      - www.192.168.33.10.xip.io
```

Pre-Tasks and Post-Tasks

Sometimes you want to run some tasks before or after you invoke your roles. Let's say you wanted to update the apt cache before you deployed Mezzanine, and you wanted to send a notification to Slack channel after you deployed.

Ansible allows you to define a list of tasks that execute before the roles with a `pre_tasks` section, and a list of tasks that executes after the roles with a `post_tasks` section. Example 8-4 shows an example of these in action.

Example 8-4. Using pre-tasks and post-tasks

```
- name: deploy mezzanine on vagrant
  hosts: web
  vars_files:
    - secrets.yml
  pre_tasks:
    - name: update the apt cache
      apt: update_cache=yes
  roles:
    - role: mezzanine
      database_host: "{{ hostvars.db.ansible_eth1.ipv4.address }}"
      live_hostname: 192.168.33.10.xip.io
      domains:
        - 192.168.33.10.xip.io
        - www.192.168.33.10.xip.io
  post_tasks:
    - name: notify Slack that the servers have been updated
      local_action: >
        slack
        domain=acme.slack.com
        token={{ slack_token }}
        msg="web server {{ inventory_hostname }} configured"
```

But enough about using roles; let's talk about writing them.

A "Database" Role for Deploying the Database

The job of our "database" role will be to install Postgres and create the required database and database user.

Our database role involves the following files:

- *roles/database/tasks/main.yml*
- *roles/database/defaults/main.yml*
- *roles/database/handlers/main.yml*
- *roles/database/files/pg_hba.conf*
- *roles/database/files/postgresql.conf*

This role includes two customized Postgres configuration files.

postgresql.conf

> Modifies the default `listen_addresses` configuration option so that Postgres will accept connections on any network interface. The default for Postgres is to accept connections only from localhost, which doesn't work for us if we want our database to run on a separate host from our web application.

pg_hba.conf

> Configures Postgres to authenticate connections over the network using username and password.

I don't show these files here because they are quite large. You can find them in the code samples on GitHub (*https://github.com/lorin/ansiblebook*) in the ch08 directory.

Example 8-5 shows the tasks involved in deploying Postgres.

Example 8-5. roles/database/tasks/main.yml

```
- name: install apt packages
  apt: pkg={{ item }} update_cache=yes cache_valid_time=3600
  sudo: True
  with_items:
    - libpq-dev
    - postgresql
    - python-psycopg2

- name: copy configuration file
  copy: >
    src=postgresql.conf dest=/etc/postgresql/9.3/main/postgresql.conf
    owner=postgres group=postgres mode=0644
  sudo: True
  notify: restart postgres

- name: copy client authentication configuration file
  copy: >
    src=pg_hba.conf dest=/etc/postgresql/9.3/main/pg_hba.conf
```

```
      owner=postgres group=postgres mode=0640
    sudo: True
    notify: restart postgres

- name: create a user
  postgresql_user:
    name: "{{ database_user }}"
    password: "{{ db_pass }}"
  sudo: True
  sudo_user: postgres

- name: create the database
  postgresql_db:
    name: "{{ database_name }}"
    owner: "{{ database_user }}"
    encoding: UTF8
    lc_ctype: "{{ locale }}"
    lc_collate: "{{ locale }}"
    template: template0
  sudo: True
  sudo_user: postgres
```

Example 8-6 shows the handlers file.

Example 8-6. roles/database/handlers/main.yml

```
- name: restart postgres
  service: name=postgresql state=restarted
  sudo: True
```

The only default variable we are going to specify is the database port, shown in Example 8-7.

Example 8-7. roles/database/defaults/main.yml

```
database_port: 5432
```

Note that our list of tasks refers to several variables that we haven't defined anywhere in the role:

- database_name
- database_user
- db_pass
- locale

In Example 8-2 and Example 8-3, we pass in database_name and database_user when we invoke the role. I'm assuming that db_pass is defined in the *secrets.yml* file, which is included in the *vars_files* section. The `locale` variable is likely something that would be the same for every host, and might be used by multiple roles or playbooks, so I defined it in the *group_vars/all* file in the code samples that accompany this book.

Why Are There Two Ways to Define Variables in Roles?

When Ansible first introduced support for roles, there was only one place to define role variables, in *vars/main.yml*. Variables defined in this location have a higher precedence than variables defined in the *vars* section of a play, which meant that you couldn't override the variable unless you explicitly passed it as an argument to the role.

Ansible later introduced the notion of default role variables that go in *defaults/main.yml*. This type of variable is defined in a role, but has a low precedence, so it will be overridden if another variable with the same name is defined in the playbook.

If you think you might want to change the value of a variable in a role, use a default variable. If you don't want it to change, then use a regular variable.

A "Mezzanine" Role for Deploying Mezzanine

The job of our "mezzanine" role will be to install Mezzanine. This includes installing *nginx* as the reverse proxy and *supervisor* as the process monitor.

Here are the files that are involved:

- *roles/mezzanine/defaults/main.yml*
- *roles/mezzanine/handlers/main.yml*
- *roles/mezzanine/tasks/django.yml*
- *roles/mezzanine/tasks/main.yml*
- *roles/mezzanine/tasks/nginx.yml*
- *roles/mezzanine/templates/gunicorn.conf.py.j2*
- *roles/mezzanine/templates/local_settings.py.filters.j2*
- *roles/mezzanine/templates/local_settings.py.j2*
- *roles/mezzanine/templates/nginx.conf.j2*
- *roles/mezzanine/templates/supervisor.conf.j2*
- *roles/mezzanine/vars/main.yml*

Example 8-8 shows the variables we've defined for this role. Note that we've changed the name of the variables so that they all start with *mezzanine*. It's good practice to do this with role variables because Ansible doesn't have any notion of namespace across roles. This means that variables that are defined in other roles, or elsewhere in a playbook, will be accessible everywhere. This can cause some unexpected behavior if you accidentally use the same variable name in two different roles.

Example 8-8. roles/mezzanine/vars/main.yml

```
# vars file for mezzanine
mezzanine_user: "{{ ansible_ssh_user }}"
mezzanine_venv_home: "{{ ansible_env.HOME }}"
mezzanine_venv_path: "{{ mezzanine_venv_home }}/{{ mezzanine_proj_name }}"
mezzanine_repo_url: git@github.com:lorin/mezzanine-example.git
mezzanine_proj_dirname: project
mezzanine_proj_path: "{{ mezzanine_venv_path }}/{{ mezzanine_proj_dirname }}"
mezzanine_reqs_path: requirements.txt
mezzanine_conf_path: /etc/nginx/conf
mezzanine_python: "{{ mezzanine_venv_path }}/bin/python"
mezzanine_manage: "{{ mezzanine_python }} {{ mezzanine_proj_path }}/manage.py"
mezzanine_gunicorn_port: 8000
```

Example 8-9 shows the default variables defined on our mezzanine role. In this case, we have only a single variable. When I write default variables, I'm less likely to prefix them because I might intentionally want to override them elsewhere.

Example 8-9. roles/mezzanine/defaults/main.yml

```
tls_enabled: True
```

Because the task list is pretty long, I've decided to break it up across several files. Example 8-10 shows the top-level task file for the mezzanine role. It installs the apt packages, and then it uses `include` statements to invoke two other task files that are in the same directory, shown in Examples 8-11 and 8-12.

Example 8-10. roles/mezzanine/tasks/main.yml

```
- name: install apt packages
  apt: pkg={{ item }} update_cache=yes cache_valid_time=3600
  sudo: True
  with_items:
    - git
    - libjpeg-dev
    - libpq-dev
    - memcached
    - nginx
    - python-dev
    - python-pip
    - python-psycopg2
    - python-setuptools
```

```
        - python-virtualenv
        - supervisor

  - include: django.yml

  - include: nginx.yml
```

Example 8-11. roles/mezzanine/tasks/django.yml

```
- name: check out the repository on the host
  git:
    repo: "{{ mezzanine_repo_url }}"
    dest: "{{ mezzanine_proj_path }}"
    accept_hostkey: yes

- name: install required python packages
  pip: name={{ item }} virtualenv={{ mezzanine_venv_path }}
  with_items:
    - gunicorn
    - setproctitle
    - south
    - psycopg2
    - django-compressor
    - python-memcached

- name: install requirements.txt
  pip: >
    requirements={{ mezzanine_proj_path }}/{{ mezzanine_reqs_path }}
    virtualenv={{ mezzanine_venv_path }}

- name: generate the settings file
  template: src=local_settings.py.j2 dest={{ mezzanine_proj_path }}/local_settings.py

- name: sync the database, apply migrations, collect static content
  django_manage:
    command: "{{ item }}"
    app_path: "{{ mezzanine_proj_path }}"
    virtualenv: "{{ mezzanine_venv_path }}"
  with_items:
    - syncdb
    - migrate
    - collectstatic

- name: set the site id
  script: scripts/setsite.py
  environment:
    PATH: "{{ mezzanine_venv_path }}/bin"
    PROJECT_DIR: "{{ mezzanine_proj_path }}"
    WEBSITE_DOMAIN: "{{ live_hostname }}"

- name: set the admin password
  script: scripts/setadmin.py
```

```
  environment:
    PATH: "{{ mezzanine_venv_path }}/bin"
    PROJECT_DIR: "{{ mezzanine_proj_path }}"
    ADMIN_PASSWORD: "{{ admin_pass }}"

- name: set the gunicorn config file
  template: src=gunicorn.conf.py.j2 dest={{ mezzanine_proj_path }}/gunicorn.conf.py

- name: set the supervisor config file
  template: src=supervisor.conf.j2 dest=/etc/supervisor/conf.d/mezzanine.conf
  sudo: True
  notify: restart supervisor

- name: ensure config path exists
  file: path={{ mezzanine_conf_path }} state=directory
  sudo: True
  when: tls_enabled

- name: install poll twitter cron job
  cron: >
    name="poll twitter" minute="*/5" user={{ mezzanine_user }}
    job="{{ mezzanine_manage }} poll_twitter"
```

Example 8-12. roles/mezzanine/tasks/nginx.yml

```
- name: set the nginx config file
  template: src=nginx.conf.j2 dest=/etc/nginx/sites-available/mezzanine.conf
  notify: restart nginx
  sudo: True

- name: enable the nginx config file
  file:
    src: /etc/nginx/sites-available/mezzanine.conf
    dest: /etc/nginx/sites-enabled/mezzanine.conf
    state: link
  notify: restart nginx
  sudo: True

- name: remove the default nginx config file
  file: path=/etc/nginx/sites-enabled/default state=absent
  notify: restart nginx
  sudo: True

- name: create tls certificates
  command: >
    openssl req -new -x509 -nodes -out {{ mezzanine_proj_name }}.crt
    -keyout {{ mezzanine_proj_name }}.key -subj '/CN={{ domains[0] }}' -days 3650
    chdir={{ mezzanine_conf_path }}
    creates={{ mezzanine_conf_path }}/{{ mezzanine_proj_name }}.crt
  sudo: True
  when: tls_enabled
  notify: restart nginx
```

There's one important difference between tasks defined in a role and tasks defined in a regular playbook, and that's when using the `copy` or `template` modules.

When invoking `copy` in a task defined in a role, Ansible will first check the *rolename/files/* directory for the location of the file to copy. Similarly, when invoking `template` in a task defined in a role, Ansible will first check the *rolename/templates* directory for the location of the template to use.

This means that a task that used to look like this in a playbook:

```
- name: set the nginx config file
  template: src=templates/nginx.conf.j2 \
    dest=/etc/nginx/sites-available/mezzanine.conf
```

Now looks like this when invoked from inside the role (note the change of the `src` parameter):

```
- name: set the nginx config file
  template: src=nginx.conf.j2 dest=/etc/nginx/sites-available/mezzanine.conf
  notify: restart nginx
```

Example 8-13 shows the handlers file.

Example 8-13. roles/mezzanine/handlers/main.yml

```
- name: restart supervisor
  supervisorctl: name=gunicorn_mezzanine state=restarted
  sudo: True

- name: restart nginx
  service: name=nginx state=restarted
  sudo: True
```

I won't show the template files here, since they're basically the same as in the previous chapter, although some of the variable names have changed. Check out the accompanying code samples for details.

Creating Role Files and Directories with ansible-galaxy

Ansible ships with another command-line tool we haven't talked about yet, *ansible-galaxy*. Its primary purpose is to download roles that have been shared by the Ansible community (more on that later in the chapter). But it can also be used to generate *scaffolding*, an initial set of files and directories involved in a role:

```
$ ansible-galaxy init -p playbooks/roles web
```

The `-p` flag tells ansible-galaxy where your roles directory is. If you don't specify it, then the role files will be created in your current directory.

Running the command creates the following files and directories:

- *playbooks/roles/web/tasks/main.yml*
- *playbooks/roles/web/handlers/main.yml*
- *playbooks/roles/web/vars/main.yml*
- *playbooks/roles/web/defaults/main.yml*
- *playbooks/roles/web/meta/main.yml*
- *playbooks/roles/web/files/*
- *playbooks/roles/web/templates/*
- *playbooks/roles/web/README.md*

Dependent Roles

Imagine that we had two roles, web and database, that both required an NTP[1] server to be installed on the host. We could specify the installation of the NTP server in both the web and database roles, but that would result in duplication. We could create a separate ntp role, but then we would have to remember that whenever we apply the web or database role to a host, we have to apply the ntp role as well. This would avoid the duplication, but it's error-prone because we might forget to specify the ntp role. What we really want is to have an ntp role that is always applied to a host whenever we apply the web role or the database role.

Ansible supports a feature called *dependent roles* to deal with this scenario. When you define a role, you can specify that it depends on one or more other roles. Ansible will ensure that roles that are specified as dependencies are executed first.

Continuing with our example, let's say that we created an ntp role that configures a host to synchronize its time with an NTP server. Ansible allows us to pass parameters to dependent roles, so let's also assume that we can pass the NTP server as a parameter to that role.

We'd specify that the web role depends on the ntp role by creating a *roles/web/meta/main.yml* file and listing it as a role, with a parameter, as shown in Example 8-14.

Example 8-14. roles/web/meta/main.yml

```
dependencies:
    - { role: ntp, ntp_server=ntp.ubuntu.com }
```

---

1 NTP stands for Network Time Protocol, used for synchronizing clocks.

We can also specify multiple dependent roles. For example, if we had a *django* role for setting up a Django web server, and we wanted to specify *nginx* and *memcached* as dependent roles, then the role metadata file might look like Example 8-15.

Example 8-15. roles/django/meta/main.yml

```
dependencies:
    - { role: web }
    - { role: memcached }
```

For details on how Ansible evaluates the role dependencies, check out the official Ansible documentation on role dependencies (*http://bit.ly/1F6tH9a*).

Ansible Galaxy

If you need to deploy an open source software system onto your hosts, chances are somebody has already written an Ansible role to do it. Although Ansible does make it easier to write scripts for deploying software, some systems are just plain tricky to deploy.

Whether you want to reuse a role somebody has already written, or you just want to see how someone else solved the problem you're working on, *Ansible Galaxy* can help you out. Ansible Galaxy is an open source repository of Ansible roles contributed by the Ansible community. The roles themselves are stored on GitHub.

Web Interface

You can explore the available roles on the Ansible Galaxy site (*http://galaxy.ansible.com*). Galaxy supports freetext searching and browsing by category or contributor.

Command-Line Interface

The ansible-galaxy command-line tool allows you to download roles from Ansible Galaxy.

Installing a role

Let's say I want to install the role named *ntp*, written by GitHub user bennojoy. This is a role that will configure a host to synchronize its clock with an NTP server.

Install the role with the install command.

```
$ ansible-galaxy install -p ./roles bennojoy.ntp
```

The ansible-galaxy program will install roles to your systemwide location by default (see "Where Does Ansible Look for My Roles?" on page 148), which we overrode in the preceding example with the -p flag.

The output should look like this:

```
downloading role 'ntp', owned by bennojoy
no version specified, installing master
- downloading role from https://github.com/bennojoy/ntp/archive/master.tar.gz
- extracting bennojoy.ntp to ./roles/bennojoy.ntp
write_galaxy_install_info!
bennojoy.ntp was installed successfully
```

The ansible-galaxy tool will install the role files to *roles/bennojoy.ntp*.

Ansible will install some metadata about the installation to the *./roles/bennojoy.ntp/ meta/.galaxy_install_info* file. On my machine, that file contains:

```
{install_date: 'Sat Oct  4 20:12:58 2014', version: master}
```

 The bennojoy.ntp role does not have a specific version number, so the version is simply listed as "master." Some roles will have a specific version number, such as 1.2.

List installed roles

You can list installed roles by doing:

```
$ ansible-galaxy list
```

Output should look like this:

```
bennojoy.ntp, master
```

Uninstall a role

Remove a role with the `remove` command:

```
$ ansible-galaxy remove bennojoy.ntp
```

Contributing Your Own Role

See "How To Share Roles You've Written" on the Ansible Galaxy website (*https:// galaxy.ansible.com/intro*) for details on how to contribute a role to the community. Because the roles are hosted on GitHub, you'll need to have a GitHub account to contribute.

At this point, you should now have an understanding of how to use roles, how to write your own roles, and how to download roles written by others. Roles are a great way to organize your playbooks. I use them all the time, and I highly recommend them.

## CHAPTER 9

Making Ansible Go Even Faster

In this chapter, we will discuss strategies for reducing the time it takes Ansible to execute playbooks.

SSH Multiplexing and ControlPersist

If you've made it this far in the book, you know that Ansible uses SSH as its primary transport mechanism for communicating with servers. In particular, Ansible will use the system SSH program by default.

Because the SSH protocol runs on top of the TCP protocol, when you make a connection to a remote machine with SSH, you need to make a new TCP connection. The client and server have to negotiate this connection before you can actually start doing useful work. The negotiation takes a small amount of time.

When Ansible runs a playbook, it will make many SSH connections, in order to do things such as copy over files and run commands. Each time Ansible makes a new SSH connection to a host, it has to pay this negotiation penalty.

OpenSSH is the most common implementation of SSH and is almost certainly the SSH client you have installed on your local machine if you are on Linux or Mac OS X. OpenSSH supports an optimization called *SSH multiplexing*, which is also referred to as *ControlPersist*. When you use SSH multiplexing, then multiple SSH sessions to the same host will share the same TCP connection, so the TCP connection negotiation only happens the first time.

When you enable multiplexing:

- The first time you try to SSH to a host, OpenSSH starts a master connection.

- OpenSSH creates a Unix domain socket (known as the *control socket*) that is associated with the remote host.
- The next time you try to SSH to a host, OpenSSH will use the control socket to communicate with the host instead of making a new TCP connection.

The master connection stays open for a user-configurable amount of time, and then the *SSH* client will terminate the connection. Ansible uses a default of 60 seconds.

Manually Enabling SSH Multiplexing

Ansible automatically enables SSH multiplexing, but to give you a sense of what's going on behind the scenes, let's work through the steps of manually enabling SSH multiplexing and using it to SSH to a remote machine.

Example 9-1 shows an example of an entry in the *~/.ssh/config* file for *myserver.example.com*, which is configured to use SSH multiplexing.

Example 9-1. ssh/config for enabling ssh multiplexing

```
Host myserver.example.com
  ControlMaster auto
  ControlPath /tmp/%r@%h:%p
  ControlPersist 10m
```

The `ControlMaster auto` line enables SSH multiplexing, and it tells SSH to create the master connection and the control socket if it does not exist yet.

The `ControlPath /tmp/%r@%h:%p` line tells SSH where to put the control Unix domain socket file on the file system. `%h` is the target host name, `%r` is the remote login username, and `%p` is the port. If we SSH as the Ubuntu user:

```
$ ssh ubuntu@myserver.example.com
```

Then SSH will create the control socket at */tmp/ubuntu@myserver.example.com:22* the first time you SSH to the server.

The `ControlPersist 10m` line tells SSH to close the master connection if there have been no SSH connections for 10 minutes.

You can check if a master connection is open using the `-O check` flag:

```
$ ssh -O check ubuntu@myserver.example.com
```

It will return output like this if the control master is running:

```
Master running (pid=4388)
```

Here's what the control master process looks like if you do `ps 4388`:

```
    PID  TT  STAT      TIME COMMAND
   4388  ??  Ss     0:00.00 ssh: /tmp/ubuntu@myserver.example.com:22 [mux]
```

You can also terminate the master connection using the -O exit flag, like this:

```
$ ssh -O exit ubuntu@myserver.example.com
```

You can see more details about these settings on the *ssh_config* man page.

I tested out the speed of making an SSH connection like this:

```
$ time ssh ubuntu@myserver.example.com /bin/true
```

This will time how long it takes to indicate an SSH connection to the server and run the */bin/true* program, which simply exits with a 0 return code.

The first time I ran it, the timing part of the output looked like this:[1]

```
0.01s user 0.01s system 2% cpu 0.913 total
```

The time we really care about is the total time: `0.913 total`. This tells us it took 0.913 seconds to execute the whole command. (Total time is also sometimes called *wall-clock time*, since it's how much time elapsed if we were measuring the time on the clock on the wall.)

The second time, the output looked like this:

```
0.00s user 0.00s system 8% cpu 0.063 total
```

The total time went down to 0.063s, for a savings of about 0.85s for each SSH connection after the first one. Recall that Ansible uses at least two SSH sessions to execute each task: one session to copy the module file to the host, and another session to execute the host.[2] This means that SSH multiplexing should save you on the order of one or two seconds for each task that runs in your playbook.

SSH Multiplexing Options in Ansible

Ansible uses the options for SSH multiplexing shown in Table 9-1.

---

1 The output format may look different depending on your shell and OS. I'm running zsh on Mac OS X.

2 One of these steps can be optimized away using pipelining, described later in this chapter.

Table 9-1. Ansible's SSH multiplexing options

Option	Value
ControlMaster	auto
ControlPath	$HOME/.ansible/cp/ansible-ssh-%h-%p-%r
ControlPersist	60s

I've never needed to change Ansible's default `ControlMaster` or `ControlPersist` values. However, I have needed to change the value for the `ControlPath` option. That's because the operating system sets a maximum length on the path of a Unix domain socket, and if the `ControlPath` string is too long, then multiplexing won't work. Unfortunately, Ansible won't tell you if the `ControlPath` string is too long; it will simply run without using SSH multiplexing.

You can test it out on your control machine by manually trying to SSH using the same `ControlPath` that Ansible would use:

```
$ CP=~/.ansible/cp/ansible-ssh-%h-%p-%r
$ ssh -o ControlMaster=auto -o ControlPersist=60s \
-o ControlPath=$CP \
ubuntu@ec2-203-0-113-12.compute-1.amazonaws.com \
/bin/true
```

If the `ControlPath` is too long, you'll see an error that looks like Example 9-2.

Example 9-2. ControlPath too long

```
ControlPath
"/Users/lorinhochstein/.ansible/cp/ansible-ssh-ec2-203-0-113-12.compute-1.amazonaws.
com-22-ubuntu.KIwEKEsRzCKFABch"
too long for Unix domain socket
```

This is a common occurrence when connecting to Amazon EC2 instances, because EC2 uses long hostnames.

The workaround is to configure Ansible to use a shorter `ControlPath`. The official documentation (*http://bit.ly/1F6y4Bn*) recommends setting this option in your *ansible.cfg* file:

```
[ssh_connection]
control_path = %(directory)s/%%h-%%r
```

Ansible sets `%(directory)s` to `$HOME/.ansible.cp`, and the double percent signs (`%%`) are needed to escape these characters because percent signs are special characters for files in *.ini* format.

If you have SSH multiplexing enabled, and you change a configuration of your SSH connection, say by modifying the ssh_args configuration option, this change won't take effect if the control socket is still open from a previous connection.

Pipelining

Recall how Ansible executes a task:

1. It generates a Python script based on the module being invoked.
2. Then it copies the Python script to the host.
3. Finally, it executes the Python script.

Ansible supports an optimization called *pipelining*, where it will execute the Python script by piping it to the SSH session instead of copying it. This saves time because it tells Ansible to use one SSH session instead of two.

Enabling Pipelining

Pipelining is off by default because it can require some configuration on your remote hosts, but I like to enable it because it speeds up execution. To enable it, modify your *ansible.cfg* file as shown in Example 9-3.

Example 9-3. ansible.cfg Enable pipelining

```
[defaults]
pipelining = True
```

Configuring Hosts for Pipelining

For pipelining to work, you need to make sure that the requiretty is not enabled in your */etc/sudoers* file on your hosts. Otherwise, you'll get errors that look like Example 9-4 when you run your playbook.

Example 9-4. Error when requiretty is enabled

```
failed: [vagrant1] => {"failed": true, "parsed": false}
invalid output was: sudo: sorry, you must have a tty to run sudo
```

If sudo on your hosts is configured to read files from the */etc/sudoers.d*, then the simplest way to resolve this is to add a sudoers config file that disables the requiretty restriction for the user you use to SSH with.

If the /etc/sudoers.d directory is present, then your hosts should support adding sudoers config files in that directory. You can use the `ansible` command-line tool to check if it's there:

```
$ ansible vagrant -a "file /etc/sudoers.d"
```

If the directory is present, the output will look like this:

```
vagrant1 | success | rc=0 >>
/etc/sudoers.d: directory

vagrant3 | success | rc=0 >>
/etc/sudoers.d: directory

vagrant2 | success | rc=0 >>
/etc/sudoers.d: directory
```

If the directory is not present, the output will look like this:

```
vagrant3 | FAILED | rc=1 >>
/etc/sudoers.d: ERROR: cannot open `/etc/sudoers.d' (No such file or
directory)

vagrant2 | FAILED | rc=1 >>
/etc/sudoers.d: ERROR: cannot open `/etc/sudoers.d' (No such file or
directory)

vagrant1 | FAILED | rc=1 >>
/etc/sudoers.d: ERROR: cannot open `/etc/sudoers.d' (No such file or
directory)
```

If the directory is present, create a template file that looks like Example 9-5.

Example 9-5. templates/disable-requiretty.j2

```
Defaults:{{ ansible_ssh_user }} !requiretty
```

Then run the playbook shown in Example 9-6, replacing `myhosts` with your hosts. Don't forget to disable pipelining before you do this, or the playbook will fail with an error.

Example 9-6. disable-requiretty.yml

```
- name: do not require tty for ssh-ing user
  hosts: myhosts
  sudo: True
  tasks:
    - name: Set a sudoers file to disable tty
      template: >
        src=templates/disable-requiretty.j2
        dest=/etc/sudoers.d/disable-requiretty
```

```
owner=root group=root mode=0440
validate="visudo -cf %s"
```

Note the use of `validate="visudo -cf %s"`. See "Validating Files" on page 277 for a discussion of why it's a good idea to use validation when modifying sudoers files.

Fact Caching

If your play doesn't reference any Ansible facts, you can turn off fact gathering for that play. Recall that you can disable fact gathering with the `gather_facts` clause in a play, for example:

```
- name: an example play that doesn't need facts
  hosts: myhosts
  gather_facts: False
  tasks:
     # tasks go here:
```

You can disable fact gathering by default by adding the following to your *ansible.cfg* file:

```
[defaults]
gathering = explicit
```

If you write plays that do reference facts, you can use fact caching so that Ansible gathers facts for a host only once, even if you rerun the playbook or run a different playbook that connects to the same host.

If fact caching is enabled, Ansible will store facts in a cache the first time it connects to hosts. For subsequent playbook runs, Ansible will look up the facts in the cache instead of fetching them from the remote host, until the cache expires.

Example 9-7 shows the lines you must add to your *ansible.cfg* file to enable fact caching. The `fact_caching_timeout` value is in seconds, and the example uses a 24-hour (86,400 second) timeout.

As with all caching-based solutions, there's always the danger of the cached data becoming stale. Some facts, such as the CPU architecture (stored in the *ansible_architecture* fact), are unlikely to change often. Others, such as the date and time reported by the machine (stored in the *ansible_date_time* fact), are guaranteed to change often.

If you decide to enable fact caching, make sure you know how quickly the facts used in your playbook are likely to change, and set an appropriate fact caching timeout value. If you want to clear the fact cache before running a playbook, pass the `--flush-cache` flag to *ansible-playbook*.

Example 9-7. ansible.cfg Enable fact caching

```
[defaults]
gathering = smart
# 24-hour timeout, adjust if needed
fact_caching_timeout = 86400

# You must specify a fact caching implementation
fact_caching = ...
```

Setting the `gathering` configuration option to "smart" in *ansible.cfg* tells Ansible to use *smart gathering*. This means that Ansible will only gather facts if they are not present in the cache or if the cache has expired.

 If you want to use fact caching, make sure your playbooks do **not** explicitly specify `gather_facts: True` or `gather_facts: False`. With smart gathering enabled in the configuration file, Ansible will gather facts only if they are not present in the cache.

You must explicitly specify a `fact_caching` implementation in *ansible.cfg*, or Ansible will not cache facts between playbook runs.

As of this writing, there are three fact-caching implementations:

- JSON files
- Redis
- Memcached

JSON File Fact-Caching Backend

With the JSON file fact-caching backend, Ansible will write the facts it gathers to files on your control machine. If the files are present on your system, it will use those files instead of connecting to the host and gathering facts.

To enable the JSON fact-caching backend, add the settings in Example 9-8 to your *ansible.cfg* file.

Example 9-8. ansible.cfg with JSON fact caching

```
[defaults]
gathering = smart

# 24-hour timeout, adjust if needed
fact_caching_timeout = 86400
```

```
# JSON file implementation
fact_caching = jsonfile
fact_caching_connection = /tmp/ansible_fact_cache
```

Use the `fact_caching_connection` configuration option to specify a directory where Ansible should write the JSON files that contain the facts. If the directory does not exist, Ansible will create it.

Ansible uses the file modification time to determine whether the fact-caching timeout has occurred yet.

Redis Fact Caching Backend

Redis is a popular key-value data store that is often used as a cache. To enable fact caching using the Redis backend, you need to:

1. Install Redis on your control machine.
2. Ensure the Redis service is running on the control machine.
3. Install the Python Redis package.
4. Modify *ansible.cfg* to enable fact caching with Redis.

Example 9-9 shows how to configure *ansible.cfg* to use Redis as the cache backend.

Example 9-9. ansible.cfg with Redis fact caching

```
[defaults]
gathering = smart

# 24-hour timeout, adjust if needed
fact_caching_timeout = 86400

fact_caching = redis
```

Ansible needs the Python Redis package on the control machine, which you can install using pip:[3]

```
$ pip install redis
```

You must also install Redis and ensure that it is running on your control machine. If you are using OS X, you can install Redis using Homebrew. If you are using Linux, install Redis using your native package manager.

---

[3] You may need to sudo or activate a virtualenv, depending on how you installed Ansible on your control machine

Memcached Fact Caching Backend

Memcached is another popular key-value data store that is often used as a cache. To enable fact caching using the Memcached backend, you need to:

1. Install Memcached on your control machine.
2. Ensure the Memcached service is running on the control machine.
3. Install the Python Memcached Python package.
4. Modify *ansible.cfg* to enable fact caching with Memcached.

Example 9-10 shows how to configure *ansible.cfg* to use Memcached as the cache backend.

Example 9-10. ansible.cfg with Memcached fact caching

```
[defaults]
gathering = smart

# 24-hour timeout, adjust if needed
fact_caching_timeout = 86400

fact_caching = memcached
```

Ansible needs the Python Memcached package on the control machine, which you can install using pip. You might need to sudo or activate a virtualenv, depending on how you installed Ansible on your control machine.

```
$ pip install python-memcached
```

You must also install Memcached and ensure that it is running on your control machine. If you are using OS X, you can install Memcached using Homebrew. If you are using Linux, install Memcached using your native package manager.

For more information on fact caching, check out the official documentation (*http://bit.ly/1F6BHap*).

Parallelism

For each task, Ansible will connect to the hosts in parallel to execute the tasks. But Ansible doesn't necessarily connect to *all* of the hosts in parallel. Instead, the level of parallelism is controlled by a parameter, which defaults to 5. You can change this default parameter in one of two ways.

You can set the ANSIBLE_FORKS environment variable, as shown in Example 9-11.

Example 9-11. Setting ANSIBLE_FORKS

```
$ export ANSIBLE_FORKS=20
$ ansible-playbook playbook.yml
```

You can modify the Ansible configuration file (*ansible.cfg*) by setting a `forks` option in the defaults section, as shown in Example 9-12.

Example 9-12. ansible.cfg Configuring number of forks

```
[defaults]
forks = 20
```

Accelerated Mode

Ansible supports a connection mode called *accelerated mode*. This feature is older than pipelining, and the official documentation recommends using pipelining instead of accelerated mode, unless your environment prevents you from enabling pipelining. For more details on accelerated mode, see the official documentation (*http://bit.ly/1F6CWpS*).

Fireball Mode

Fireball mode is a deprecated Ansible feature that was previously used to improve performance. It was replaced by *accelerated mode*.

You should now know how to configure SSH multiplexing, pipelining, fact caching, and parallelism in order to get your playbooks to run more quickly. Next, we'll discuss writing your own Ansible modules.

## CHAPTER 10

Custom Modules

Sometimes you want to perform a task that is too complex for the `command` or `shell` modules, and there is no existing module that does what you want. In that case, you might want to write your own module.

In the past, I've written custom modules to retrieve my public IP address when I'm behind a network address translation (NAT) getaway, and to initialize the databases in an OpenStack deployment. I've thought about writing a custom module for generating self-signed TLS certificates, though I've never gotten around to it.

Another common use for custom modules is if you want to interact with some third-party service over a REST API. For example, GitHub offers what it calls Releases, which let you attach binary assets to repositories, and these are exposed via GitHub's API. If your deployment required you to download a binary asset attached to a private GitHub repository, this would be a good candidate for implementing inside of a custom module.

Example: Checking That We Can Reach a Remote Server

Let's say we want to check that we can connect to a remote server on a particular port. If we can't, we want Ansible to treat that as an error and stop running the play.

> The custom module we will develop in this chapter is basically a simpler version of the `wait_for` module.

Using the Script Module Instead of Writing Your Own

Recall in Example 6-16 how we used the `script` module to execute custom scripts on remote hosts. Sometimes it's simpler to just use the `script` module rather than write a full-blown Ansible module.

I like putting these types of scripts in a *scripts* folder along with my playbooks. For example, we could create a script file called *playbooks/scripts/can_reach.sh* that accepts as arguments the name of a host, the port to connect to, and how long it should try to connect before timing out.

```
can_reach.sh www.example.com 80 1
```

We can create a script as shown in Example 10-1.

Example 10-1. can_reach.sh

```
#!/bin/bash
host=$1
port=$2
timeout=$3

nc -z -w $timeout $host $port
```

We can then invoke this by doing:

```
- name: run my custom script
  script: scripts/can_reach.sh www.example.com 80 1
```

Keep in mind that your script will execute on the remote hosts, just like Ansible modules do. Therefore, any programs your script requires must have been installed previously on the remote hosts. For example, you can write your script in Ruby, as long as Ruby has been installed on the remote hosts, and the first line of the script invokes the Ruby interpreter, such as:

```
#!/usr/bin/ruby
```

can_reach as a Module

Next, let's implement `can_reach` as a proper Ansible module, which we will be able to invoke like this:

```
- name: check if host can reach the database server
  can_reach: host=db.example.com port=5432 timeout=1
```

This will check if the host can make a TCP connection to *db.example.com* on port 5432. It will time out after one second if it fails to make a connection.

We'll use this example throughout the rest of this chapter.

Where to Put Custom Modules

Ansible will look in the *library* directory relative to the playbook. In our example, we put our playbooks in the *playbooks* directory, so we will put our custom module at *playbooks/library/can_reach*.

How Ansible Invokes Modules

Before we actually implement the module, let's go over how Ansible invokes them. Ansible will:

1. Generate a standalone Python script with the arguments (Python modules only).
2. Copy the module to the host.
3. Create an arguments file on the host (nonPython modules only).
4. Invoke the module on the host, passing the arguments file as an argument.
5. Parse the standard output of the module.

Let's look at each of these steps in more detail.

Generate a Standalone Python Script with the Arguments (Python Only)

If the module is written in Python and uses the helper code that Ansible provides (described later), then Ansible will generate a self-contained Python script that injects helper code, as well as the module arguments.

Copy the Module to the Host

Ansible will copy the generated Python script (for Python-based modules) or the local file *playbooks/library/can_reach* (for non-Python-based modules) to a temporary directory on the remote host. If you are accessing the remote host as the *ubuntu* user, Ansible will copy the file to a path that looks like the following:

/home/ubuntu/.ansible/tmp/ansible-tmp-1412459504.14-47728545618200/can_reach

Create an Arguments File on the Host (Non-Python Only)

If the module is not written in Python, Ansible will create a file on the remote host with a name like this:

/home/ubuntu/.ansible/tmp/ansible-tmp-1412459504.14-47728545618200/arguments

If we invoke the module like this:

```
- name: check if host can reach the database server
  can_reach: host=db.example.com port=5432 timeout=1
```

Then the arguments file will have the following contents:

```
host=db.example.com port=5432 timeout=1
```

We can tell Ansible to generate the arguments file for the module as JSON, by adding the following line to *playbooks/library/can_reach*:

```
# WANT_JSON
```

If our module is configured for JSON input, the arguments file will look like this:

```
{"host": "www.example.com", "port": "80", "timeout": "1"}
```

Invoke the Module

Ansible will call the module and pass the argument file as arguments. If it's a Python-based module, Ansible executes the equivalent of the following (with */path/to/* replaced by the actual path):

```
/path/to/can_reach
```

If it's a non-Python-based module, Ansible will look at the first line of the module to determine the interpreter and execute the equivalent of:

```
/path/to/interpreter /path/to/can_reach /path/to/arguments
```

Assuming the `can_reach` module is implemented as a Bash script and starts with:

```
#!/bin/bash
```

Then Ansible will do something like:

```
/bin/bash /path/to/can_reach /path/to/arguments
```

But even this isn't strictly true. What Ansible actually does is:

```
/bin/sh -c 'LANG=en_US.UTF-8 LC_CTYPE=en_US.UTF-8 /bin/bash /path/to/can_reach \
/path/to/arguments; rm -rf /path/to/ >/dev/null 2>&1'
```

You can see the exact command that Ansible invokes by passing -vvv to `ansible-playbook`.

Expected Outputs

Ansible expects modules to output JSON. For example:

```
{'changed': false, 'failed': true, 'msg': 'could not reach the host'}
```

Prior to version 1.8, Ansible supported a shorthand output format, also known as *baby JSON*, that looked like key=value. Ansible dropped support for this format in 1.8. As we'll see later, if you write your modules in Python, Ansible provides some helper methods that make it easy to generate JSON output.

Output Variables Ansible Expects

Your module can return whatever variables you like, but Ansible has special treatment for certain returned variables:

changed

All Ansible modules should return a changed variable. The changed variable is a Boolean that indicates whether the module execution caused the host to change state. When Ansible runs, it will show in the output whether a state change has happened. If a task has a notify clause to notify a handler, the notification will fire only if changed is true.

failed

If the module failed to complete, it should return failed=true. Ansible will treat this task execution as a failure and will not run any further tasks against the host that failed, unless the task has an ignore_errors or failed_when clause.

If the module succeeds, you can either return failed=false or you can simply leave out the variable.

msg

Use the msg variable to add a descriptive message that describes the reason why a module failed.

If a task fails, and the module returns a msg variable, then Ansible will output that variable slightly differently than it does the other variables. For example, if a module returns:

```
{"failed": true, "msg": "could not reach www.example.com:81"}
```

Then Ansible will output the following lines when executing this task:

```
failed: [vagrant1] => {"failed": true}
msg: could not reach www.example.com:81
```

Implementing Modules in Python

If you implement your custom module in Python, Ansible provides the `AnsibleModule` Python class that makes it easier to:

- Parse the inputs
- Return outputs in JSON format
- Invoke external programs

In fact, when writing a Python module, Ansible will inject the arguments directly into the generated Python file rather than require you to parse a separate arguments file. We'll discuss how that works later in this chapter.

We'll create our module in Python by creating a *can_reach* file. I'll start with the implementation and then break it down (see Example 10-2).

Example 10-2. can_reach

```python
#!/usr/bin/python

def can_reach(module, host, port, timeout):
    nc_path = module.get_bin_path('nc', required=True)  ❶
    args = [nc_path, "-z", "-w", str(timeout),
            host, str(port)]
    (rc, stdout, stderr) = module.run_command(args)  ❷
    return rc == 0

def main():
    module = AnsibleModule(  ❸
        argument_spec=dict(  ❹
            host=dict(required=True),  ❺
            port=dict(required=True, type='int'),
            timeout=dict(required=False, type='int', default=3)  ❻
        ),
        supports_check_mode=True  ❼
    )

    # In check mode, we take no action
    # Since this module never changes system state, we just
    # return changed=False
    if module.check_mode:  ❽
        module.exit_json(changed=False)  ❾

    host = module.params['host']  ❿
    port = module.params['port']
    timeout = module.params['timeout']

    if can_reach(module, host, port, timeout):
```

```
        module.exit_json(changed=False)
    else:
        msg = "Could not reach %s:%s" % (host, port)
        module.fail_json(msg=msg)  ⓫

from ansible.module_utils.basic import *  ⓬
main()
```

❶ Gets the path of an external program

❷ Invokes an external program

❸ Instantiates the `AnsibleModule` helper class

❹ Specifies the permitted set of arguments

❺ A required argument

❻ An optional argument with a default value

❼ Specify that this module supports check mode

❽ Test to see if module is running in check mode

❾ Exit successfully, passing a return value

❿ Extract an argument

⓫ Exit with failure, passing an error message

⓬ "Imports" the `AnsibleModule` helper class

Parsing Arguments

It's easier to understand the way `AnsibleModule` handles argument parsing by looking at an example. Recall that our module is invoked like this:

```
- name: check if host can reach the database server
  can_reach: host=db.example.com port=5432 timeout=1
```

Let's assume that the `host` and `port` parameters are required, and `timeout` is an optional parameter with a default value of 3 seconds.

You instantiate an `AnsibleModule` object by passing it an `argument_spec`, which is a dictionary where the keys are parameter names and the values are dictionaries that contain information about the parameters.

```
module = AnsibleModule(
    argument_spec=dict(
        ...
```

In our example, we declare a required argument named host. Ansible will report an error if this argument isn't passed to the module when we use it in a task.

```
host=dict(required=True),
```

The variable named timeout is optional. Ansible assumes that arguments are strings unless specified otherwise. Our timeout variable is an integer, so we specify the type as int so that Ansible will automatically convert it into a Python number. If timeout is not specified, then the module will assume it has a value of 3:

```
timeout=dict(required=False, type='int', default=3)
```

The AnsibleModule constructor takes arguments other than argument_spec. In the preceding example, we added this argument:

```
supports_check_mode = True
```

This indicates that our module supports check mode. We'll explain that a little later in this chapter.

Accessing Parameters

Once you've declared an AnsibleModule object, you can access the values of the arguments through the params dictionary, like this:

```
module = AnsibleModule(...)

host = module.params["host"]
port = module.params["port"]
timeout = module.params["timeout"]
```

Importing the AnsibleModule Helper Class

Near the bottom of the module, you'll see this import statement:

```
from ansible.module_utils.basic import *
```

If you've written Python scripts before, you're probably used to seeing an import at the top, rather than the bottom. However, this is really a pseudo import statement. It looks like a traditional Python import, but behaves differently.

Import statements behave differently in modules because Ansible copies only a single Python file to the remote host to execute it. Ansible simulates the behavior of a traditional Python import by including the imported code directly into the generated Python file (similar to how an #include statement works in C or C++).

Because Ansible will replace the import statement with code, the line numbers in the module as written will be different than the line numbers of the generated Python file. By putting the import statement at the bottom of the file, all of the line numbers above it are the same in the module and the generated file, which makes life much easier when interpreting Python tracebacks that contain line numbers.

Because this import statement behaves differently from a traditional Python import, you shouldn't import classes explicitly, as shown in Example 10-3, even though explicit imports traditionally are considered good form in Python:

Example 10-3. Explicit imports (don't do this)

```
from ansible.module_utils.basic import AnsibleModule
```

If you import explicitly, you won't be able to use the Ansible module debugging scripts. That's because these debugging scripts look for the specific string that includes the * and will fail with an error if they don't find it.

> Earlier versions of Ansible used this line instead of an import statement to mark the location of where Ansible should insert the generated helper code.
>
> ```
> #<<INCLUDE_ANSIBLE_MODULE_COMMON>>
> ```

Argument Options

For each argument to an Ansible module, you can specify several options:

Table 10-1. Argument options

Option	Description
required	If True, argument is required
default	Default value if argument is not required
choices	A list of possible values for the argument
aliases	Other names you can use as an alias for this argument
type	Argument type. Allowed values: `'str'`, `'list'`, `'dict'`, `'bool'`, `'int'`, `'float'`

required

The `required` option is the only option that you should always specify. If it is true, then Ansible will return an error if the user failed to specify the argument.

In our `can_reach` module example, host and port are required, and timeout is not required.

default

For arguments that have `required=False` set, you should generally specify a default value for that option. In our example:

```
timeout=dict(required=False, type='int', default=3)
```

If the user invokes the module like this:

```
can_reach: host=www.example.com port=443
```

Then `module.params["timeout"]` will contain the value 3.

choices

The `choices` option allows you to restrict the allowed arguments to a predefined list.

Consider the `distros` argument in the following example:

```
distro=dict(required=True, choices=['ubuntu', 'centos', 'fedora'])
```

If the user were to pass an argument that was not in the list, for example:

```
distro=suse
```

This would cause Ansible to throw an error.

aliases

The `aliases` option allows you to use different names to refer to the same argument. For example, consider the `package` argument in the `apt` module:

```
module = AnsibleModule(
    argument_spec=dict(
        ...
        package = dict(default=None, aliases=['pkg', 'name'], type='list'),
    )
)
```

Since `pkg` and `name` are aliases for the `package` argument, these invocations are all equivalent:

```
- apt: package=vim
- apt: name=vim
- apt: pkg=vim
```

type

The `type` option enables you to specify the type of an argument. By default, Ansible assumes all arguments are strings.

However, you can specify a type for the argument, and Ansible will convert the argument to the desired type. The types supported are:

- *str*
- *list*
- *dict*
- *bool*
- *int*
- *float*

In our example, we specified the `port` argument as an `int`:

```
port=dict(required=True, type='int'),
```

When we access it from the `params` dictionary, like this:

```
port = module.params['port']
```

Then the value of the `port` variable will be an integer. If we had not specified the type as `int` when declaring the `port` variable, then the `module.params['port']` value would have been a string instead of an `int`.

Lists are comma-delimited. For example, if you had a module named `foo` with a list parameter named `colors`:

```
colors=dict(required=True, type='list')
```

Then you'd pass a `list` like this:

```
foo: colors=red,green,blue
```

For dictionaries, you can either do `key=value` pairs, delimited by commas, or you can do JSON inline.

For example, if you had a module named `bar`, with a `dict` parameter named `tags`:

```
tags=dict(required=False, type='dict', default={})
```

Then you could pass this argument like this:

```
- bar: tags=env=staging,function=web
```

Or you could pass the argument like this:

```
- bar: tags={"env": "staging", "function": "web"}
```

The official Ansible documentation uses the term *complex args* to refer to lists and dictionaries that are passed to modules as arguments. See "Complex Arguments in Tasks: A Brief Digression" on page 99 for how to pass these types of arguments in playbooks.

AnsibleModule Initializer Parameters

The `AnsibleModule` initializer method takes a number of arguments. The only required argument is `argument_spec`.

Table 10-2. AnsibleModule initializer arguments

Parameter	Default	Description
argument_spec	(none)	Dictionary that contains information about arguments
bypass_checks	False	If true, don't check any of the parameter constrains
no_log	False	If true, don't log the behavior of this module
check_invalid_arguments	True	If true, return error if user passed an unknown argument
mutually_exclusive	None	List of mutually exclusive arguments
required_together	None	List of arguments that must appear together
required_one_of	None	List of arguments where at least one must be present
add_file_common_args	False	Supports the arguments of the `file` module
supports_check_mode	False	If true, indicates module supports check mode

argument_spec

This is a dictionary that contains the descriptions of the allowed arguments for the module, as described in the previous section.

no_log

When Ansible executes a module on a host, the module will log output to the syslog, which on Ubuntu is at */var/log/syslog*.

The logging output looks like this:

```
Sep 28 02:31:47 vagrant-ubuntu-trusty-64 ansible-ping: Invoked with data=None
Sep 28 02:32:18 vagrant-ubuntu-trusty-64 ansible-apt: Invoked with dpkg_options=
force-confdef,force-confold upgrade=None force=False name=nginx package=['nginx'
] purge=False state=installed update_cache=True default_release=None install_rec
ommends=True deb=None cache_valid_time=None Sep 28 02:33:01 vagrant-ubuntu-trust
y-64 ansible-file: Invoked with src=None
original_basename=None directory_mode=None force=False remote_src=None selevel=N
one seuser=None recurse=False serole=None content=None delimiter=None state=dire
ctory diff_peek=None mode=None regexp=None owner=None group=None path=/etc/nginx
/ssl backup=None validate=None setype=None
```

Sep 28 02:33:01 vagrant-ubuntu-trusty-64 ansible-copy: Invoked with src=/home/va
grant/.ansible/tmp/ansible-tmp-1411871581.19-43362494744716/source directory_mod
e=None force=True remote_src=None dest=/etc/nginx/ssl/nginx.key selevel=None seu
ser=None serole=None group=None content=NOT_LOGGING_PARAMETER setype=None origin
al_basename=nginx.key delimiter=None mode=0600 owner=root regexp=None validate=N
one backup=False
Sep 28 02:33:01 vagrant-ubuntu-trusty-64 ansible-copy: Invoked with src=/home/va
grant/.ansible/tmp/ansible-tmp-1411871581.31-95111161791436/source directory_mod
e=None force=True remote_src=None dest=/etc/nginx/ssl/nginx.crt selevel=None seu
ser=None serole=None group=None content=NOT_LOGGING_PARAMETER setype=None origin
al_basename=nginx.crt delimiter=None mode=None owner=None regexp=None validate=N
one backup=False

If a module accepts sensitive information as an argument, you might want to disable this logging.

To configure a module so that it does not write to syslog, pass the no_log=True parameter to the AnsibleModule initializer.

check_invalid_arguments

By default, Ansible will verify that all of the arguments that a user passed to a module are legal arguments. You can disable this check by passing the check_invalid_argu ments=False parameter to the AnsibleModule initializer.

mutually_exclusive

The mutually_exclusive parameter is a list of arguments that cannot be specified during the same module invocation.

For example, the lineinfile module allows you to add a line to a file. You can use the insertbefore argument to specify which line it should appear before, or the insertafter argument to specify which line it should appear after, but you can't specify both.

Therefore, this module specifies that the two arguments are mutually exclusive, like this:

```
mutually_exclusive=[['insertbefore', 'insertafter']]
```

required_one_of

The required_one_of parameter is a list of arguments where at least one must be passed to the module.

For example, the pip module, which is used for installing Python packages, can take either the name of a package or the name of a requirements file that contains a list of packages. The module specifies that one of these arguments is required like this:

```
required_one_of=[['name', 'requirements']]
```

add_file_common_args

Many modules create or modify a file. A user will often want to set some attributes on the resulting file, such as the owner, group, and file permissions.

You could invoke the `file` module to set these parameters, like this:

```
- name: download a file
  get_url: url=http://www.example.com/myfile.dat dest=/tmp/myfile.dat

- name: set the permissions
  file: path=/tmp/myfile.dat owner=ubuntu mode=0600
```

As a shortcut, Ansible allows you to specify that a module will accept all of the same arguments as the `file` module, so you can simply set the file attributes by passing the relevant arguments to the module that created or modified the file. For example:

```
- name: download a file
  get_url: url=http://www.example.com/myfile.dat dest=/tmp/myfile.dat \
  owner=ubuntu mode=0600
```

To specify that a module should support these arguments:

```
add_file_common_args=True
```

The `AnsibleModule` module provides helper methods for working with these arguments.

The `load_file_common_arguments` method takes the parameters dictionary as an argument and returns a parameters dictionary that contains all of the arguments that relate to setting file attributes.

The `set_fs_attributes_if_different` method takes a file parameters dictionary and a Boolean indicating whether a host state change has occurred yet. The method sets the file attributes as a side effect and returns `true` if there was a host state change (either the initial argument was true, or it made a change to the file as part of the side effect).

If you are using the file common arguments, do not specify the arguments explicitly. To get access to these attributes in your code, use the helper methods to extract the arguments and set the file attributes, like this:

```
module = AnsibleModule(
    argument_spec=dict(
        dest=dict(required=True),
        ...
    ),
    add_file_common_args=True
)

# "changed" is True if module caused host to change state
changed = do_module_stuff(param)
```

```
file_args = module.load_file_common_arguments(module.params)

changed = module.set_fs_attributes_if_different(file_args, changed)
module.exit_json(changed=changed, ...)
```

 Ansible assumes your module has an argument named `path` or `dest`, which contains the path to the file.

bypass_checks

Before an Ansible module executes, it first checks that all of the argument constraints are satisfied, and returns an error if they aren't. These include:

- No mutually exclusive arguments are present.
- Arguments marked with the `required` option are present.
- Arguments restricted by the `choices` option have the expected values.
- Arguments where a `type` is specified have values that are consistent with the type.
- Arguments marked as `required_together` appear together.
- At least one argument in the list of `required_one_of` is present.

You can disable all of these checks by setting `bypass_checks=True`.

Returning Success or Failure

Use the `exit_json` method to return success. You should always return `changed` as an argument, and it's good practice to return `msg` with a meaningful message:

```
module = AnsibleModule(...)
...
module.exit_json(changed=False, msg="meaningful message goes here")
```

Use the `fail_json` method to indicate failure. You should always return a `msg` parameter to explain to the user the reason for the failure:

```
module = AnsibleModule(...)
...
module.fail_json(msg="Out of disk space")
```

Invoking External Commands

The `AnsibleModule` class provides the `run_command` convenience method for calling an external program, which wraps the native Python `subprocess` module. It accepts the following arguments.

Table 10-3. run_command arguments

Argument	Type	Default	Description
args (default)	string or list of strings	(none)	The command to be executed (see the following section)
check_rc	Boolean	False	If true, will call `fail_json` if command returns a non-zero value.
close_fds	Boolean	True	Passes as `close_fds` argument to `subprocess.Popen`
executable	string (path to program)	None	Passes as `executable` argument to `subprocess.Popen`
data	string	None	Send to `stdin` if child process
binary_data	Boolean	False	If false and `data` is present, Ansible will send a newline to `stdin` after sending `data`
path_prefix	string (list of paths)	None	Colon-delimited list of paths to prepend to PATH environment variable
cwd	string (directory path)	None	If specified, Ansible will change to this directory before executing
use_unsafe_shell	Boolean	False	See the following section

If `args` is passed as a list, as shown in Example 10-4, then Ansible will invoke `subprocess.Popen` with `shell=False`.

Example 10-4. Passing args as a list

```
module = AnsibleModule(...)
...
module.run_command(['/usr/local/bin/myprog', '-i', 'myarg'])
```

If *args* is passed as a string, as shown in Example 10-5, then the behavior depends on the value of `use_unsafe_shell`. If `use_unsafe_shell` is false, Ansible will split `args` into a list and invoke `subprocess.Popen` with `shell=False`. If `use_unsafe_shell` is true, Ansible will pass `args` as a string to `subprocess.Popen` with `shell=True`.[1]

Example 10-5. Passing args as a string

```
module = AnsibleModule(...)
...
module.run_command('/usr/local/bin/myprog -i myarg')
```

Check Mode (Dry Run)

Ansible supports something called "check mode," which is enabled when passing the `-C` or `--check` flag to `ansible-playbook`. It is similar to the "dry run" mode supported by many other tools.

When Ansible runs a playbook in check mode, it will not make any changes to the hosts when it runs. Instead, it will simply report whether each task would have changed the host, returned successfully without making a change, or returned an error.

Support Check Mode

Modules must be explicitly configured to support check mode. If you're going to write your own module, I recommend you support check mode so that your module is a good Ansible citizen.

To tell Ansible that your module supports check mode, set `supports_check_mode` to `true` in the AnsibleModule initializer method, as shown in Example 10-6.

Example 10-6. Telling Ansible the module supports check mode

```
module = AnsibleModule(
    argument_spec=dict(...),
    supports_check_mode=True)
```

Your module should check that check mode has been enabled by checking the value of the `check_mode`[2] attribute of the AnsibleModule object, as shown in Example 10-7. Call the `exit_json` or `fail_json` methods as you would normally.

---

1 For more on the Python standard library `subprocess.Popen` class, see its online documentation (*http://bit.ly/1F72tiU*).

2 Phew! That was a lot of checks.

Example 10-7. Checking if check mode is enabled

```
module = AnsibleModule(...)
...
if module.check_mode:
    # check if this module would make any changes
    would_change = would_executing_this_module_change_something()
    module.exit_json(changed=would_change)
```

It is up to you, the module author, to ensure that your module does not modify the state of the host when running in check mode.

Documenting Your Module

You should document your modules according to the Ansible project standards so that HTML documentation for your module will be correctly generated and the *ansible-doc* program will display documentation for your module. Ansible uses a special YAML-based syntax for documenting modules.

Near the top of your module, define a string variable called DOCUMENTATION that contains the documentation, and a string variable called EXAMPLES that contains example usage.

Example 10-8 shows an example for the documentation section for our can_reach module.

Example 10-8. Example of module documentation

```
DOCUMENTATION = '''
---
module: can_reach
short_description: Checks server reachability
description:
 - Checks if a remote server can be reached
version_added: "1.8"
options:
  host:
    description:
      - A DNS hostname or IP address
    required: true
  port:
    description:
    - The TCP port number
    required: true
  timeout:
    description:
    - The amount of time try to connecting before giving up, in seconds
    required: false
    default: 3
```

```
  flavor:
    description:
    - This is a made-up option to show how to specify choices.
    required: false
    choices: ["chocolate", "vanilla", "strawberry"]
    aliases: ["flavour"]
    default: chocolate
requirements: [netcat]
author: Lorin Hochstein
notes:
  - This is just an example to demonstrate how to write a module.
  - You probably want to use the native M(wait_for) module instead.
'''

EXAMPLES = '''
# Check that ssh is running, with the default timeout
- can_reach: host=myhost.example.com port=22

# Check if postgres is running, with a timeout
- can_reach: host=db.example.com port=5432 timeout=1
'''
```

Ansible supports some limited markup in the documentation. Table 10-4 shows the markup syntax supported by the Ansible documentation tool with recommendations about when you should use this markup:

Table 10-4. Documentation markup

Type	Syntax with example	When to use
URL	U(*http://www.example.com*)	URLs
Module	M(apt)	Module names
Italics	I(port)	Parameter names
Constant-width	C(/bin/bash)	File and option names

The existing Ansible modules are a great source of examples for documentation.

Debugging Your Module

The Ansible repository in GitHub contains a couple of scripts that allow you to invoke your module directly on your local machine, without having to run it using the ansible or ansible-playbook commands.

Clone the Ansible repo:

```
$ git clone https://github.com/ansible/ansible.git --recursive
```

Set up your environment variables so that you can invoke the module:

```
$ source ansible/hacking/env-setup
```

Invoke your module:

```
$ ansible/hacking/test-module -m /path/to/can_reach -a "host=example.com port=81"
```

Since `example.com` doesn't have a service that listens on port 81, our module should fail with a meaningful error message. And it does:

```
* including generated source, if any, saving to:
  /Users/lorinhochstein/.ansible_module_generated
* this may offset any line numbers in tracebacks/debuggers!
***********************************
RAW OUTPUT
{"msg": "Could not reach example.com:81", "failed": true}


***********************************
PARSED OUTPUT
{
    "failed": true,
    "msg": "Could not reach example.com:81"
}
```

As the output suggests, when you run this `test-module`, Ansible will generate a Python script and copy it to *~/.ansible_module_generated*. This is a standalone script that you can execute directly if you like. The debug script will replace the following line:

```
from ansible.module_utils.basic import *
```

with the contents of the file *lib/ansible/module_utils/basic.py*, which can be found in the Ansible repository.

This file does not take any arguments; rather, Ansible inserts the arguments directly into the file:

```
MODULE_ARGS = 'host=example.com port=91'
```

Implementing the Module in Bash

If you're going to write an Ansible module, I recommend writing it in Python because, as we saw earlier in this chapter, Ansible provides helper classes for writing your modules in Python. However, you can write modules in other languages as well. Perhaps you need to write in another language because your module depends on a third-party library that's not implemented in Python. Or maybe the module is so simple that it's easiest to write it in Bash. Or, maybe, you just prefer writing your scripts in Ruby.

In this section, we'll work through an example of implementing the module as a Bash script. It's going to look quite similar to the implementation in Example 10-1. The main difference is parsing the input arguments and generating the outputs that Ansible expects.

I'm going to use the JSON format for input and use a tool called jq (*http://stedo lan.github.io/jq/*) for parsing out JSON on the command line. This means that you'll need to install jq on the host before invoking this module. Example 10-9 shows the complete Bash implementation of our module.

Example 10-9. can_reach module in Bash

```bash
#!/bin/bash
# WANT_JSON

# Read the variables form the file
host=`jq -r .host < $1`
port=`jq -r .port < $1`
timeout=`jq -r .timeout < $1`.

# Check if we can reach the host
nc -z -w $timeout $host $port

# Output based on success or failure
if [ $? -eq 0 ]; then
    echo '{"changed": false}'
else
    echo "{\"failed\": true, \"msg\": \"could not reach $host:$port\"}"
fi
```

We added `WANT_JSON` in a comment to tell Ansible that we want the input to be in JSON syntax.

Bash Modules with Shorthand Input

It's possible to implement Bash modules using the shorthand notation for input. I don't recommend doing it this way, since the simplest approach involves using the `source` built-in, which is a potential security risk. However, if you're really determined, check out the blog post, "Shell scripts as Ansible modules," (*http://bit.ly/ 1F789tb*) by Jan-Piet Mens.

Specifying an Alternaive Location for Bash

Note that our module assumes that Bash is located at */bin/bash*. However, not all systems will have the Bash executable in that location. You can tell Ansible to look elsewhere for the Bash interpreter by setting the `ansible_bash_interpreter` variable on hosts that install it elsewhere.

For example, let's say you have a FreeBSD host named *fileserver.example.com* that has Bash installed in */usr/local/bin/bash*. You can create a host variable by creating the file *host_vars/fileserver.example.com* that contains:

```
ansible_bash_interpreter: /usr/local/bin/bash
```

Then, when Ansible invokes this module on the FreeBSD host, it will use */usr/local/bin/bash* instead of */bin/bash*.

Ansible determines which interpreter to use by looking for the "she-bang" (#!) and then looking at the basename of the first element. In our example, Ansible would see this line:

```
#!/bin/bash
```

Ansible would then look for the basename of */bin/bash*, which is *bash*. It would then use the `ansible_bash_interpreter` if the user specified one.

Because of how Ansible looks for the interpreter, if your she-bang calls /usr/bin/env, for example:

```
#!/usr/bin/env bash
```

Ansible will mistakenly identify the interpreter as `env` because it will call basename on */usr/bin/env* to identify the interpreter.

The takeaway is: don't invoke `env` in she-bang. Instead, explicitly specify the location of the interpreter and override with `ansible_bash_interpreter` (or equivalent) when needed.

Example Modules

The best way to learn how to write Ansible modules is to read the source code for the modules that ship with Ansible. Check them out on GitHub: modules core (*https://github.com/ansible/ansible-modules-core*) and modules extras (*https://github.com/ansible/ansible-modules-extras*).

In this chapter, we covered how to write modules in Python, as well as other languages, and how to avoid writing your own full-blown modules using the `script` module. If you do write a module, I encourage you to propose it for inclusion in the main Ansible project.

## CHAPTER 11

Vagrant

Vagrant is a great environment for testing Ansible playbooks, which is why I've been using it all along in this book, and why I often use Vagrant for testing my own Ansible playbooks.

Vagrant isn't just for testing configuration management scripts; it was originally designed to create repeatable development environments. If you've ever joined a new software team and spent a couple of days discovering what software you had to install on your laptop so you could run a development version of an internal product, you've felt the pain that Vagrant was built to alleviate. Ansible playbooks are a great way to specify how to configure a Vagrant machine so newcomers on your team can get up and running on day one.

Vagrant has some built-in support for Ansible that we haven't been taking advantage of. In this chapter, we'll cover Vagrant's support for using Ansible to configure Vagrant machines.

A full treatment of Vagrant is out of scope of this book. For more information, check out *Vagrant: Up and Running*, authored by Mitchell Hashimoto, the creator of Vagrant.

Convenient Vagrant Configuration Options

Vagrant exposes many configuration options for virtual machines, but there are two that I find particularly useful when using Vagrant for testing: setting a specific IP address and enabling agent forwarding.

Port Forwarding and Private IP Addresses

When you create a new Vagrantfile using the vagrant init command, the default networking configuration allows you to reach the Vagrant box only via an SSH port that is forwarded from localhost. For the first Vagrant machine that you start, that's port 2222, and each subsequent Vagrant machine that you bring up will forward a different port. As a consequence, the only way to access your Vagrant machine in the default configuration is to SSH to localhost on port 2222. Vagrant forwards this to port 22 on the Vagrant machine.

This default configuration isn't very useful for testing web-based applications, since the web application will be listening on some port that we can't access.

There are two ways around this. One way is to tell Vagrant to set up another forwarded port. For example, if your web application listens on port 80 inside of your Vagrant machine, you can configure Vagrant to forward port 8000 on your local machine to port 80 on the Vagrant machine. Example 11-1 shows how you'd configure port forwarding by editing the Vagrantfile.

Example 11-1. Forwarding local port 8000 to Vagrant machine port 80

```
# Vagrantfile
VAGRANTFILE_API_VERSION = "2"

Vagrant.configure(VAGRANTFILE_API_VERSION) do |config|
  # Other config options not shown

  config.vm.network :forwarded_port, host: 8000, guest: 80
end
```

Port forwarding works, but I find it more useful to assign the Vagrant machine its own IP address. That way, interacting with it is more like interacting with a real remote server: I can connect directly to port 80 on the machine's IP rather than connecting to port 8000 on localhost.

A simpler approach is to assign the machine a private IP. Example 11-2 shows how you would assign the IP address *192.168.33.10* to the machine by editing the Vagrantfile.

Example 11-2. Assign a private IP to a Vagrant machine

```
# Vagrantfile
VAGRANTFILE_API_VERSION = "2"

Vagrant.configure(VAGRANTFILE_API_VERSION) do |config|
  # Other config options not shown
```

```
config.vm.network "private_network", ip: "192.168.33.10"
end
```

If we run a web server on port 80 of our Vagrant machine, we can access it at *http://192.168.33.10*.

This configuration uses a Vagrant "private network." This means that the machine will only be accessible from the machine that runs Vagrant. You won't be able to connect to this IP address from another physical machine, even if it's on the same network as the machine running Vagrant. However, different Vagrant machines can connect to each other.

Check out the Vagrant documentation for more details on the different networking configuration options.

Enabling Agent Forwarding

If you are checking out a remote Git repository over SSH, and you need to use agent forwarding, then you must configure your Vagrant machine so that Vagrant enables agent forwarding when it connects to the agent via SSH. See Example 11-3 for how to enable this. For more on agent forwarding, see Appendix A.

Example 11-3. Enabling agent forwarding

```
# Vagrantfile
VAGRANTFILE_API_VERSION = "2"

Vagrant.configure(VAGRANTFILE_API_VERSION) do |config|
  # Other config options not shown

  config.ssh.forward_agent = true

end
```

The Ansible Provisioner

Vagrant has a notion of *provisioners*. A provisioner is an external tool that Vagrant uses to configure a virtual machine once it has started up. In addition to Ansible, Vagrant can also provision with shell scripts, Chef, Puppet, Salt, CFengine, and even Docker.

Example 11-4 shows a `Vagrantfile` that has been configured to use Ansible as a provisioner, specifically using the *playbook.yml* playbook.

Example 11-4. Vagrantfile

```
VAGRANTFILE_API_VERSION = "2"

Vagrant.configure(VAGRANTFILE_API_VERSION) do |config|
  config.vm.box = "ubuntu/trusty64"

  config.vm.provision "ansible" do |ansible|
    ansible.playbook = "playbook.yml"
  end
end
```

When the Provisioner Runs

The first time you do `vagrant up`, Vagrant will execute the provisioner and will mark record that the provisioner was run. If you halt the virtual machine and then start it up, Vagrant remembers that it has already run the provisioner and will not run it a second time.

You can force Vagrant to run the provisioner against a running virtual machine by doing:

```
$ vagrant provision
```

You can reboot a virtual machine and run the provisioner after reboot by invoking:

```
$ vagrant reload --provision
```

Similarly, you can start up a halted virtual machine and have Vagrant run the provisioner by doing:

```
$ vagrant up --provision
```

Inventory Generated by Vagrant

When Vagrant runs, it generates an Ansible inventory file named *.vagrant/provisioners/ansible/inventory/vagrant_ansible_inventory*. Example 11-5 shows what this file looks like for our example:

Example 11-5. vagrant_ansible_inventory

```
# Generated by Vagrant

default ansible_ssh_host=127.0.0.1 ansible_ssh_port=2202
```

Note how it uses `default` as the inventory hostname. When writing playbooks for the Vagrant provisioner, specify `hosts: default` or `hosts: all`.

More interesting is the case where you have a multi-machine Vagrant environment, where the `Vagrantfile` specifies multiple virtual machines. For example, see Example 11-6.

Example 11-6. Vagrantfile (multi-machine)

```
VAGRANTFILE_API_VERSION = "2"

Vagrant.configure(VAGRANTFILE_API_VERSION) do |config|
  config.vm.define "vagrant1" do |vagrant1|
    vagrant1.vm.box = "ubuntu/trusty64"
    vagrant1.vm.provision "ansible" do |ansible|
      ansible.playbook = "playbook.yml"
    end
  end
  config.vm.define "vagrant2" do |vagrant2|
    vagrant2.vm.box = "ubuntu/trusty64"
    vagrant2.vm.provision "ansible" do |ansible|
      ansible.playbook = "playbook.yml"
    end
  end
  config.vm.define "vagrant3" do |vagrant3|
    vagrant3.vm.box = "ubuntu/trusty64"
    vagrant3.vm.provision "ansible" do |ansible|
      ansible.playbook = "playbook.yml"
    end
  end
end
```

The generated inventory file will look like Example 11-7. Note how the Ansible aliases (`vagrant1`, `vagrant2`, `vagrant3`) match the names assigned to the machines in the `Vagrantfile`.

Example 11-7. vagrant_ansible_inventory (multi-machine)

```
# Generated by Vagrant

vagrant1 ansible_ssh_host=127.0.0.1 ansible_ssh_port=2222
vagrant2 ansible_ssh_host=127.0.0.1 ansible_ssh_port=2200
vagrant3 ansible_ssh_host=127.0.0.1 ansible_ssh_port=2201
```

Provisioning in Parallel

In Example 11-6, Vagrant is shown running `ansible-playbook` once for each virtual machine, and it uses the `--limit` flag so that the provisioner only runs against a single virtual machine at a time.

Alas, running Ansible this way doesn't take advantage of Ansible's ability to execute tasks in parallel across the hosts. We can work around this by configuring our Vagrantfile to run the provisioner only when the last virtual machine is brought up, and to tell Vagrant not to pass the --limit flag to Ansible. See Example 11-8 for the modified playbook.

Example 11-8. Vagrantfile (multi-machine with parallel provisioning)

```
VAGRANTFILE_API_VERSION = "2"

Vagrant.configure(VAGRANTFILE_API_VERSION) do |config|
  # Use the same key for each machine
  config.ssh.insert_key = false

  config.vm.define "vagrant1" do |vagrant1|
    vagrant1.vm.box = "ubuntu/trusty64"
  end
  config.vm.define "vagrant2" do |vagrant2|
    vagrant2.vm.box = "ubuntu/trusty64"
  end
  config.vm.define "vagrant3" do |vagrant3|
    vagrant3.vm.box = "ubuntu/trusty64"
    vagrant3.vm.provision "ansible" do |ansible|
      ansible.limit = 'all'
      ansible.playbook = "playbook.yml"
    end
  end
end
```

Now, when you run vagrant up the first time, it will run the Ansible provisioner only after all three virtual machines have started up.

From Vagrant's perspective, only the last virtual machine, vagrant3, has a provisioner, so doing vagrant provision vagrant1 or vagrant provision vagrant2 will have no effect.

As we discussed in "Preliminaries: Multiple Vagrant Machines" on page 46, Vagrant 1.7+ defaults to using a different SSH key for each host. If we want to provision in parallel, we need to configure the Vagrant machines so that they all use the same SSH key, which is why Example 11-8 includes the line:

```
config.ssh.insert_key = false
```

Specifying Groups

It can be useful to assign groups to Vagrant virtual machines, especially if you are reusing playbooks that reference existing groups. Example 11-9 shows how to assign vagrant1 to the web group, vagrant2 to the task group, and vagrant3 to the redis group:

Example 11-9. Vagrantfile (multi-machine with groups)

```
VAGRANTFILE_API_VERSION = "2"

Vagrant.configure(VAGRANTFILE_API_VERSION) do |config|
  # Use the same key for each machine
  config.ssh.insert_key = false

  config.vm.define "vagrant1" do |vagrant1|
    vagrant1.vm.box = "ubuntu/trusty64"
  end
  config.vm.define "vagrant2" do |vagrant2|
    vagrant2.vm.box = "ubuntu/trusty64"
  end
  config.vm.define "vagrant3" do |vagrant3|
    vagrant3.vm.box = "ubuntu/trusty64"
    vagrant3.vm.provision "ansible" do |ansible|
      ansible.limit = 'all'
      ansible.playbook = "playbook.yml"
      ansible.groups = {
        "web"   => ["vagrant1"],
        "task"  => ["vagrant2"],
        "redis" => ["vagrant3"]
      }
    end
  end
end
```

Example 11-10 shows the resulting inventory file generated by Vagrant.

Example 11-10. vagrant_ansible_inventory (multi-machine, with groups)

```
# Generated by Vagrant

vagrant1 ansible_ssh_host=127.0.0.1 ansible_ssh_port=2222
vagrant2 ansible_ssh_host=127.0.0.1 ansible_ssh_port=2200
vagrant3 ansible_ssh_host=127.0.0.1 ansible_ssh_port=2201

[web]
vagrant1

[task]
vagrant2

[redis]
vagrant3
```

This chapter was a quick—but I hope useful—overview on how to get the most out of combining Vagrant and Ansible. Vagrant's Ansible provisioner supports many other options to Ansible that aren't covered in this chapter. For more details, see the official Vagrant documentation on the Ansible provisioner (*http://bit.ly/1F7ekxp*).

## CHAPTER 12

Amazon EC2

Ansible has a number of features that make working with infrastructure-as-a-service (IaaS) clouds much easier. This chapter focuses on Amazon EC2 because it's the most popular IaaS cloud and the one I know best. However, many of the concepts should transfer to other clouds supported by Ansible.

The two ways Ansible supports EC2 are:

- A dynamic inventory plug-in for automatically populating your Ansible inventory instead of manually specifying your servers
- Modules that perform actions on EC2 such as creating new servers

In this chapter, we'll discuss both the EC2 dynamic inventory plug-in, as well as the EC2 modules.

What Is an IaaS Cloud?

You've probably heard so many references to "the cloud" in the technical press that you're suffering from buzzword overload.[1] I'll be precise about what I mean by an infrastructure-as-a-service (IaaS) cloud.

To start, here's a typical user interaction with an IaaS cloud:

User
> I want five new servers, each one with two CPUs, 4 GB of memory, and 100 GB of storage, running Ubuntu 14.04.

---

[1] The National Institute of Standards and Technology (NIST) has a pretty good definition of cloud computing *The NIST Definition of Cloud Computing*.

Service

    Request received. Your request number is 432789.

User

    What's the current status of request 432789?

Service

    Your servers are ready to go, at IP addresses *203.0.113.5*, *203.0.113.13*, *203.0.113.49*, *203.0.113.124*, *203.0.113.209*.

User

    I'm done with the servers associated with request 432789.

Service

    Request received, the servers will be terminated.

An IaaS cloud is a service that enables a user to *provision* (create) new servers. All IaaS clouds are *self-serve*, meaning that the user interacts directly with a software service rather than, say, filing a ticket with the IT department. Most IaaS clouds offer three different types of interfaces to allow users to interact with the system:

- Web interface
- Command-line interface
- REST API

In the case of EC2, the web interface is called the AWS Management Console (*https://console.aws.amazon.com*), and the command-line interface is called (unimaginatively) the AWS Command-Line Interface (*http://aws.amazon.com/cli/*). The REST API is documented at Amazon (*http://amzn.to/1F7g6yA*).

IaaS clouds typically use virtual machines to implement the servers, although you can build an IaaS cloud using bare metal servers (i.e., users run directly on the hardware rather than inside of a virtual machine) or containers. The SoftLayer and Rackspace clouds have bare metal offerings, and Amazon Elastic Compute Cloud, Google Compute Engine, and Joyent clouds offer containers.

Most IaaS clouds let you do more than than just start up and tear down servers. In particular, they typically give you provision storage so you can attach and detach disks to your servers. This type of storage is commonly referred to as *block storage*. They also provide networking features, so you can define network topologies that describe how your servers are interconnected, and you can define firewall rules that restrict networking access to your servers.

Amazon EC2 is the most popular public IaaS cloud provider, but there are a number of other IaaS clouds out there. In addition to EC2, Ansible ships with modules for Microsoft Azure, Digital Ocean, Google Compute Engine, Linode, and Rackspace, as well as clouds built using OpenStack and VMWare vSphere.

Terminology

EC2 exposes many different concepts. I'll explain these concepts as they come up in this chapter, but there are two terms I'd like to cover up front.

Instance

EC2's documentation uses the term *instance* to refer to a virtual machine, and I use that terminology in this chapter. Keep in mind that an EC2 instance is a *host* from Ansible's perspective.

EC2 documentation (*http://amzn.to/1Fw5S8l*) interchangeably uses the terms *creating instances*, *launching instances*, and *running instances* to describe the process of bringing up a new instance. However, *starting instances* means something different—starting up an instance that had previously been put in the stopped state.

Amazon Machine Image

An Amazon machine image (AMI) is a virtual machine image, which contains a filesystem with an installed operating system on it. When you create an instance on EC2, you choose which operating system you want your instance to run by specifying the AMI that EC2 will use to create the instance.

Each AMI has an associated identifier string, called an *AMI ID*, which starts with "ami-" and then contains eight hexadecimal characters; for example, `ami-12345abc`.

Tags

EC2 lets you annotate your instances[2] with custom metadata that it calls *tags*. Tags are just key-value pairs of strings. For example, we could annotate an instance with the following tags:

```
Name=Staging database
env=staging
type=database
```

If you've ever given your EC2 instance a name in the AWS Management Console, you've used tags without even knowing it. EC2 implements instance names as tags where the key is `Name` and the value is whatever name you gave the instance. Other than that, there's nothing special about the `Name` tag, and you can configure the management console to show the value of other tags in addition to the `Name` tag.

---

2 You can add tags to entities other than instances, such as AMIs, volumes, and security groups.

Tags don't have to be unique, so you can have 100 instances that all have the same tag. Because Ansible's EC2 modules make heavy use of tags, they will come up several times in this chapter.

Specifying Credentials

When you make requests against Amazon EC2, you need to specify credentials. If you've used the Amazon web console, you've used your username and password to log in. However, all of the bits of Ansible that interact with EC2 talk to the EC2 API. The API does not use username and password for credentials. Instead, it uses two strings: an *access key ID* and a *secret access key*.

These strings typically look like this:

- Sample EC2 access key ID: `AKIAIOSFODNN7EXAMPLE`
- Sample EC2 secret access key: `wJalrXUtnFEMI/K7MDENG/bPxRfiCYEXAMPLEKEY`

When you are calling EC2-related modules, you can pass these strings as module arguments. For the dynamic inventory plug-in, you can specify the credentials in the *ec2.ini* file (discussed in the next section). However, both the EC2 modules and the dynamic inventory plug-in also allow you to specify these credentials as environment variables. You can also use something called *identity and access management* (IAM) roles if your control machine is itself an Amazon EC2 instance, which is covered in Appendix C.

Environment Variables

Although Ansible does allow you to pass credentials explicitly as arguments to modules, it also supports setting EC2 credentials as environment variables. Example 12-1 shows how you would set these environment variables.

Example 12-1. Setting EC2 environment variables

```
# Don't forget to replace these values with your actual credentials!
export AWS_ACCESS_KEY_ID=AKIAIOSFODNN7EXAMPLE
export AWS_SECRET_ACCESS_KEY=wJalrXUtnFEMI/K7MDENG/bPxRfiCYEXAMPLEKEY
export AWS_REGION=us-east-1
```

Not all of Ansible's EC2 modules respect the `AWS_REGION` environment variable, so I recommend that you always explicitly pass the EC2 region as an argument when invoking your modules. All of the examples in this chapter explicitly pass the region as an argument.

I recommend using environment variables because it allows you to use EC2-related modules and inventory plug-ins without putting your credentials in any of your Ansible-related files. I put these in a dotfile that runs when my session starts. I use Zsh, so in my case that file is *~/.zshrc*. If you're running Bash, you might want to put it in your *~/.profile* file.[3] If you're using a shell other than Bash or Zsh, you're probably knowledgeable enough to know which dotfile to modify to set these environment variables.

Once you have set these credentials in your environment variables, you can invoke the Ansible EC2 modules on your control machine, as well as use the dynamic inventory.

Configuration Files

An alternative to using environment variables is to place your EC2 credentials in a configuration file. As discussed in the next section, Ansible uses the Python Boto library, so it supports Boto's conventions for maintaining credentials in a Boto configuration file. I don't cover the format here; for more information, check out the Boto config documentation (*http://bit.ly/1Fw66MM*).

Prerequisite: Boto Python Library

All of the Ansible EC2 functionality requires you to install the Python Boto library as a Python system package on the control machine. To do so:[4]

```
$ pip install boto
```

If you already have instances running on EC2, you can verify that Boto is installed properly and that your credentials are correct by interacting with the Python command line, as shown in Example 12-2.

Example 12-2. Testing out Boto and credentials

```
$ python
Python 2.7.6 (default, Sep  9 2014, 15:04:36)
[GCC 4.2.1 Compatible Apple LLVM 6.0 (clang-600.0.39)] on darwin
Type "help", "copyright", "credits" or "license" for more information.
>>> import boto.ec2
>>> conn = boto.ec2.connect_to_region("us-east-1")
>>> statuses = conn.get_all_instance_status()
```

---

3 Or maybe it's *~/.bashrc*? I've never figured out the difference between the various Bash dotfiles.

4 You might need to use sudo or activate a virtualenv to install this package, depending on how you installed Ansible.

```
>>> statuses
[]
```

Dynamic Inventory

If your servers live on EC2, you don't want to keep a separate copy of these servers in an Ansible inventory file, because that file is going to go stale as you spin up new servers and tear down old ones.

It's much simpler to track your EC2 servers by taking advantage of Ansible's support for dynamic inventory to pull information about hosts directly from EC2. Ansible ships with a dynamic inventory script for EC2, although I recommend you just grab the latest one from the Ansible GitHub repository.[5]

You need two files:

ec2.py
> The actual inventory script (*http://bit.ly/1Fw6bQu*)

ec2.ini
> The configuration file for the inventory script (*http://bit.ly/1Fw6f2y*)

Previously, we had a *playbooks/hosts* file, which served as our inventory. Now, we're going to use a *playbooks/inventory* directory. We'll place *ec2.py* and *ec2.ini* into that directory, and set *ec2.py* as executable. Example 12-3 shows one way to do that.

Example 12-3. Installing the EC2 dynamic inventory script

```
$ cd playbooks/inventory
$ wget https://raw.githubusercontent.com/ansible/ansible/devel/plugins/inventory/ec2.py
$ wget https://raw.githubusercontent.com/ansible/ansible/devel/plugins/inventory/ec2.ini
$ chmod +x ec2.py
```

 If you are running Ansible on a Linux distribution that uses Python 3.x as the default Python (e.g., Arch Linux), then the *ec2.py* will not work unmodified because it is a Python 2.x script.

Make sure your system has Python 2.x installed and then modify the first line of *ec2.py* from this:

```
#!/usr/bin/env python
```

to this:

```
#!/usr/bin/env python2
```

---

5 And, to be honest, I have no idea where the package managers install this file.

If you've set up your environment variables as described in the previous section, you should be able to confirm that the script is working by running:

```
$ ./ec2.py --list
```

The script should output information about your various EC2 instances. The structure should look something like this:

```json
{
  "_meta": {
    "hostvars": {
      "ec2-203-0-113-75.compute-1.amazonaws.com": {
        "ec2_id": "i-i2345678",
        "ec2_instance_type": "c3.large",
        ...
      }
    }
  },
  "ec2": [
    "ec2-203-0-113-75.compute-1.amazonaws.com",
    ...
  ],
  "us-east-1": [
    "ec2-203-0-113-75.compute-1.amazonaws.com",
    ...
  ],
  "us-east-1a": [
    "ec2-203-0-113-75.compute-1.amazonaws.com",
    ...
  ],
  "i-12345678": [
    "ec2-203-0-113-75.compute-1.amazonaws.com",
  ],
  "key_mysshkeyname": [
    "ec2-203-0-113-75.compute-1.amazonaws.com",
    ...
  ],
  "security_group_ssh": [
    "ec2-203-0-113-75.compute-1.amazonaws.com",
    ...
  ],
  "tag_Name_my_cool_server": [
    "ec2-203-0-113-75.compute-1.amazonaws.com",
    ...
  ],
  "type_c3_large": [
    "ec2-203-0-113-75.compute-1.amazonaws.com",
    ...
  ]
}
```

Inventory Caching

When Ansible executes the EC2 dynamic inventory script, the script has to make requests against one or more EC2 endpoints to retrieve this information. Because this can take time, the script will cache the information the first time it is invoked by writing to the following files:

- *$HOME/.ansible/tmp/ansible-ec2.cache*
- *$HOME/.ansible/tmp/ansible-ec2.index*

On subsequent calls, the dynamic inventory script will use the cached information until the cache expires.

You can modify the behavior by editing the *cache_max_age* configuration option in the *ec2.ini* configuration file. It defaults to 300 seconds (5 minutes). If you don't want caching at all, you can set it to 0:

```
[ec2]
...
cache_max_age = 0
```

You can also force the inventory script to refresh the cache by invoking it with the `--refresh-cache` flag:

```
$ ./ec2.py --refresh-cache
```

 If you create or destroy instances, the EC2 dynamic inventory script will not reflect these changes unless the cache expires, or you manually refresh the cache.

Other Configuration Options

The *ec2.ini* file includes a number of configuration options that control the behavior of the dynamic inventory script. Because the file itself is well-documented with comments, I won't cover those options in detail here.

Auto-Generated Groups

The EC2 dynamic inventory script will create the following groups:

Table 12-1. Generated EC2 groups

Type	Example	Ansible group name
Instance	i-123456	i-123456
Instance type	c1.medium	type_c1_medium
Security group	ssh	security_group_ssh
Keypair	foo	key_foo
Region	us-east-1	us-east-1
Tag	env=staging	tag_env_staging
Availability zone	us-east-1b	us-east-1b
VPC	vpc-14dd1b70	vpc_id_vpc-14dd1b70
All ec2 instances	N/A	ec2

The only legal characters in a group name are alphanumeric, hyphen, and under-score. The dynamic inventory script will convert any other character into underscore.

For example, if you had an instance with a tag:

```
Name=My cool server!
```

Ansible would generate the group name `tag_Name_my_cool_server_`.

Defining Dynamic Groups with Tags

Recall that the dynamic inventory script automatically creates groups based on things such as instance type, security group, keypair, and tags. EC2 tags are the most convenient way of creating Ansible groups because you can define them however you like.

For example, you could tag all of your webservers with:

```
type=web
```

Ansible will automatically create a group called *tag_type_web* that contains all of the servers tagged with a name of `type` and a value of `web`.

EC2 allows you to apply multiple tags to an instance. For example, if you have separate staging and production environments, you can tag your production web servers like this:

```
env=production
type=web
```

Now you can refer to production machines as `tag_env_production` and your web-servers as `tag_type_web`. If you want to refer to your production webservers, use the Ansible intersection syntax, like this:

```
hosts: tag_env_production:&tag_type_web
```

Applying Tags to Existing Resources

Ideally, you'd tag your EC2 instances as soon as you create them. However, if you're using Ansible to manage existing EC2 instances, you will likely already have a number of instances running that you need to tag. Ansible has an `ec2_tag` module that will allow you to add tags to your instances.

For example, if you wanted to tag an instance with `env=prodution` and `type=web`, you could do it in a simple playbook as shown in Example 12-4.

Example 12-4. Adding EC2 tags to instances

```
- name: Add tags to existing instances
  hosts: localhost
  vars:
    web_production:
      - i-123456
      - i-234567
    web_staging:
      - i-ABCDEF
      - i-333333
  tasks:
    - name: Tag production webservers
      ec2_tag: resource={{ item }} region=us-west-1
      args:
        tags: { type: web, env: production }
      with_items: web_production

    - name: Tag staging webservers
      ec2_tag: resource={{ item }} region=us-west-1
      args:
        tags: { type: web, env: staging }
      with_items: web_staging
```

This example uses the inline syntax for YAML dictionaries when specifying the tags (`{ type: web, env: production}`) in order to make the playbook more compact, but the regular YAML dictionary syntax would have worked as well:

```
tags:
  type: web
  env: production
```

Nicer Group Names

Personally, I don't like the name `tag_type_web` for a group. I'd prefer to just call it web.

To do this, we need to add a new file to the *playbooks/inventory* directory that will have information about groups. This is just a traditional Ansible inventory file, which we'll call *playbooks/inventory/hosts* (see Example 12-5).

Example 12-5. playbooks/inventory/hosts

```
[web:children]
tag_type_web

[tag_type_web]
```

Once you do this, you can refer to web as a group in your Ansible plays.

 You must define the empty `tag_type_web` group in your static inventory file, even though the dynamic inventory script also defines this group. If you forget it, Ansible will fail with the error:

```
ERROR: child group is not defined: (tag_type_web)
```

EC2 Virtual Private Cloud (VPC) and EC2 Classic

When Amazon first launched EC2 back in 2006, all of the EC2 instances were effectively connected to the same flat network.[6] Every EC2 instance had a private IP address and a public IP address.

In 2009, Amazon introduced a new feature called *Virtual Private Cloud* (VPC). VPC allows users to control how their instances are networked together, and whether they will be publicly accessible from the Internet or isolated. Amazon uses the term "VPC" to describe the virtual networks that users can create inside of EC2. Amazon uses the term "EC2-VPC" to refer to instances that are launched inside of VPCs, and "EC2-Classic" to refer to instances that are not launched inside of VPCs.

Amazon actively encourages users to use EC2-VPC. For example, some instance types, such as t2.micro, are only available on EC2-VPC. Depending on when your AWS account was created and which EC2 regions you've previously launched instan-

---

6 Amazon's internal network is divided up into subnets, but users do not have any control over how instances are allocated to subnets.

ces in, you might not have access to EC2-Classic at all. Table 12-2 describes which accounts have access to EC2-Classic.[7]

Table 12-2. Do I have access to EC2-Classic?

My account was created	Access to EC2-Classic
Before March 18, 2013	Yes, but only in regions you've used before
Between March 18, 2013, and December 4, 2013	Maybe, but only in regions you've used before
After December 4, 2013	No

The main difference between having support for EC2-Classic versus only having access to EC2-VPC is what happens when you create a new EC2 instance and do not explicitly associate a VPC ID with that instance. If your account has EC2-Classic enabled, then the new instance is not associated with a VPC. If your account does not have EC2-Classic enabled, then the new instance is associated with the default VPC.

Here's one reason why you should care about the distinction: in EC2-Classic, all instances are permitted to make outbound network connections to any host on the Internet. In EC2-VPC, instances are not permitted to make outbound network connections by default. If a VPC instance needs to make outbound connections, it must be associated with a security group that permits outbound connections.

For the purposes of this chapter, I'm going to assume EC2-VPC only, so I will associate instances with a security group that enables outbound connections.

Configuring ansible.cfg for Use with ec2

When I'm using Ansible to configure EC2 instances, I add the following lines in my *ansible.cfg*:

```
[defaults]
remote_user = ubuntu
host_key_checking = False
```

I always use Ubuntu images, and on those images you are supposed to SSH as the *ubuntu* user. I also turn off host key checking, since I don't know in advance what the host keys are for new instances.[8]

---

7 Go to Amazon (*http://amzn.to/1Fw6v1D*) for more details on VPC and whether you have access to EC2-Classic (*http://amzn.to/1Fw6w5M*) in a region.

8 It's possible to retrieve the host key by querying EC2 for the instance console output, but I must admit that I never bothing doing this because I've never gotten around to writing a proper script that parses out the host key from the console output.

Launching New Instances

The `ec2` module allows you to launch new instances on EC2. It's one of the most complex Ansible modules because it supports so many arguments.

Example 12-6 shows a simple playbook for launching an Ubuntu 14.04 EC2 instance.

Example 12-6. Simple playbook for creating an EC2 instance

```
- name: Create an ubuntu instance on Amazon EC2
  hosts: localhost
  tasks:
  - name: start the instance
    ec2:
      image: ami-8caa1ce4
      region: us-east-1
      instance_type: m3.medium
      key_name: mykey
      group: [web, ssh, outbound]
      instance_tags: { Name: ansiblebook, type: web, env: production }
```

Let's go over what these parameters mean.

The `image` parameter refers to the Amazon Machine Image (AMI) ID, which you must always specify. As described earlier in the chapter, an image is basically a filesystem that contains an installed operating system. The example just used, *ami-8caa1ce4*, refers to an image that has the 64-bit version of Ubuntu 14.04 installed on it.

The `region` parameter specifies the geographical region where the instance will be launched.[9]

The `instance_type` parameter describes the amount of CPU cores, memory, and storage your instance will have. EC2 doesn't let you choose arbitrary combinations of cores, memory, and storage. Instead, Amazon defines a collection of instance types.[10] The preceding example uses the *t2.medium* instance type. This is a 64-bit instance type with 1 core, 3.75 GB of RAM, and 4 GB of SSD-based storage.

> Not all images are compatible with all instance types. I haven't actually tested whether ami-8caa1ce4 works with m3.medium. Caveat lector!

---

9 Visit Amazon (*http://amzn.to/1Fw6OcE*) for a list of the regions that it supports.

10 There's also a handy (unofficial) website (*http://www.ec2instances.info*) that provides a single table with all of the available EC2 instance types.

The `key_name` parameter refers to an SSH key pair. Amazon uses SSH key pairs to provide users with access to their servers. Before you start your first server, you must either create a new SSH key pair, or upload the public key of a key pair that you have previously created. Regardless of whether you create a new key pair or you upload an existing one, you must give a name to your SSH key pair.

The `group` parameter refers to a list of security groups associated with an instance. These groups determine what kinds of inbound and outbound network connections are permitted.

The `instance_tags` parameter associates metadata with the instance in the form of EC2 tags, which are key-value pairs. In the preceding example, we set the following tags:

```
Name=ansiblebook
type=web
env=production
```

EC2 Key Pairs

In Example 12-6, we assumed that Amazon already knew about an SSH key pair named *mykey*. Let's see how we can use Ansible to create new key pairs.

Creating a New Key

When you create a new key pair, Amazon generates a private key and the corresponding public key; then it sends you the private key. Amazon does not keep a copy of the private key, so you've got to make sure that you save it after you generate it. Here's how you would create a new key with Ansible:

Example 12-7. Create a new SSH key pair

```
- name: create a new keypair
  hosts: localhost
  tasks:
  - name: create mykey
    ec2_key: name=mykey region=us-west-1
    register: keypair

  - name: write the key to a file
    copy:
      dest: files/mykey.pem
      content: "{{ keypair.key.private_key }}"
      mode: 0600
    when: keypair.changed
```

In Example 12-7, we invoke the ec2_key to create a new key pair. We then use the copy module with the content parameter in order to save the SSH private key to a file.

If the module creates a new key pair, then the variable keypair that is registered will contain a value that looks like this:

```
"keypair": {
  "changed": true,
  "invocation": {
    "module_args": "name=mykey",
    "module_name": "ec2_key"
  },
  "key": {
    "fingerprint": "c5:33:74:84:63:2b:01:29:6f:14:a6:1c:7b:27:65:69:61:f0:e8:b9",
    "name": "mykey",
    "private_key": "-----BEGIN RSA PRIVATE KEY-----\nMIIEowIBAAKCAQEAjAJpvhY3QGKh
...
0PkCRPl8ZHKtShKESIsG3WC\n-----END RSA PRIVATE KEY-----"
  }
}
```

If the key pair already existed, then the variable keypair that is registered will contain a value that looks like this:

```
"keypair": {
  "changed": false,
  "invocation": {
    "module_args": "name=mykey",
    "module_name": "ec2_key"
  },
  "key": {
    "fingerprint": "c5:33:74:84:63:2b:01:29:6f:14:a6:1c:7b:27:65:69:61:f0:e8:b9",
    "name": "mykey"
  }
}
```

Because the private_key value will not be present if the key already exists, we need to add a when clause to the copy invocation to make sure that we only write a private key file to disk if there is actually a private key file to write.

We add the line:

```
when: keypair.changed
```

to only write the file to disk if there was a change of state when ec2_key was invoked (i.e., that a new key was created). Another way we could have done it would be to check for the existence of the private_key value, like this:

```
- name: write the key to a file
  copy:
    dest: files/mykey.pem
```

```
content: "{{ keypair.key.private_key }}"
mode: 0600
when: keypair.key.private_key is defined
```

We use the Jinja2 `defined` test[11] to check if `private_key` is present.

Upload an Existing Key

If you already have an SSH public key, you can upload that to Amazon and associate it with a keypair:

```
- name: create a keypair based on my ssh key
  hosts: localhost
  tasks:
  - name: upload public key
    ec2_key: name=mykey key_material="{{ item }}"
    with_file: ~/.ssh/id_rsa.pub
```

Security Groups

Example 12-6 assumed that the *web*, *SSH*, and *outbound* security groups already existed. We can use the `ec2_group` module to ensure that these security groups have been created before we use them.

Security groups are similar to firewall rules: you specify rules about who is allowed to connect to the machine and how.

In Example 12-8, we specify the *web* group as allowing anybody on the Internet to connect to ports 80 and 443. For the *SSH* group, we allow anybody on the Internet to connect on port 22. For the *outbound* group, we allow outbound connections to anywhere on the Internet. We need outbound connections enabled in order to download packages from the Internet.

Example 12-8. Security groups

```
- name: web security group
  ec2_group:
    name: web
    description: allow http and https access
    rules:
      - proto: tcp
        from_port: 80
        to_port: 80
        cidr_ip: 0.0.0.0/0
      - proto: tcp
```

---

11 For more information on Jinja2 tests, see the Jinja2 documentation page on built-in tests (*http://bit.ly/1Fw77nO*).

```
        from_port: 443
        to_port: 443
        cidr_ip: 0.0.0.0/0

- name: ssh security group
  ec2_group:
    name: ssh
    description: allow ssh access
    rules:
      - proto: tcp
        from_port: 22
        to_port: 22
        cidr_ip: 0.0.0.0/0

- name: outbound group
  ec2_group:
    name: outbound
    description: allow outbound connections to the internet
    region: "{{ region }}"
    rules_egress:
      - proto: all
        cidr_ip: 0.0.0.0/0
```

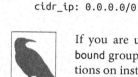 If you are using EC2-Classic, you don't need to specify the out‐
bound group, since EC2-Classic does not restrict outbound connec‐
tions on instances.

If you haven't used security groups before, the parameters to the rules dictionary bear
some explanation. Table 12-3 provides a quick summary of the parameters for secu‐
rity group connection rules.

Table 12-3. Security group rule parameters

Parameter	Description
proto	IP protocol (tcp, udp, icmp) or "all" to allow all protocols and ports
cidr_ip	Subnet of IP addresses that are allowed to connect, using CIDR notation
from_port	The first port in the range of permitted ports
to_port	The last port in the range of permitted ports

Permitted IP Addresses

Security groups allow you to restrict which IP addresses are permitted to connect to
an instance. You specify a subnet using classless interdomain routing (CIDR) nota‐

tion. An example of a subnet specified with CIDR notation is *203.0.113.0/24*,[12] which means that the first 24 bits of the IP address must match the first 24 bits of *203.0.113.0*. People sometimes just say "/24" to refer to the size of a CIDR that ends in /24.

A /24 is a nice value because it corresponds to the first three octets of the address, namely *203.0.113*.[13] What this means is that any IP address that starts with *203.0.113* is in the subnet, meaning any IP address in the range *203.0.113.0* to *203.0.113.255*.

If you specify *0.0.0.0/0*, that means that any IP address is permitted to connect.

Security Group Ports

One of the things that I find confusing about EC2 security groups is the `from port` and `to port` notation. EC2 allows you to specify a range of ports that you are allowed to access. For example, you could indicate that you are allowing TCP connections on any port from 5900 to 5999 by specifying:

```
- proto: tcp
  from_port: 5900
  to_port: 5999
  cidr_ip: 0.0.0.0/0
```

However, I often find the from/to notation confusing, because I almost never specify a range of ports.[14] Instead, I usually want to enable non-consecutive ports, such as 80 and 443. Therefore, in almost every case, the `from_port` and `to_port` parameters are going to be the same.

The `c2_group` module has a number of other parameters, including specifying inbound rules using security group IDs, as well as specifying outbound connection rules. Check out the module's documentation for more details.

Getting the Latest AMI

In Example 12-6, we explicitly specified the AMI like this:

```
image: ami-8caa1ce4
```

---

12 This example happens to correspond to a special IP address range named TEST-NET-3, which is reserved for examples. It's the example.com of IP subnets.

13 Subnets that are /8, /16, and /24 make great examples because the math is much easier than, say, /17 or /23.

14 Astute observers might have noticed that ports 5900-5999 are commonly used by the VNC remote desktop protocol, one of the few applications where specifying a range of ports makes sense.

However, if you want to launch the latest Ubuntu 14.04 image, you don't want to hardcode the AMI like this. That's because Canonical[15] frequently makes minor updates to Ubuntu, and every time it makes a minor update, it generates a new AMI. Just because `ami-8caa1ce4` corresponds to the latest release of Ubuntu 14.04 yesterday doesn't mean it will correspond to the latest release of Ubuntu 14.04 tomorrow.

Ansible ships with a nifty little module called *ubuntu_ami_search* (written by yours truly) that will retrieve the AMI that corresponds to a given operating system release. Example 12-9 shows this module in action:

Example 12-9. Retrieving the latest Ubuntu AMI

```
- name: Create an ubuntu instance on Amazon EC2
  hosts: localhost
  tasks:
  - name: Get the ubuntu trusty AMI
    ec2_ami_search: distro=ubuntu release=trusty region=us-west-1
    register: ubuntu_image

  - name: start the instance
    ec2:
      image: "{{ ubuntu_image.ami }}"
      instance_type: m3.medium
      key_name: mykey
      group: [web, ssh, outbound]
      instance_tags: { type: web, env: production }
```

Currently, the module only supports looking up Ubuntu AMIs.

Adding a New Instance to a Group

Sometimes I like to write a single playbook that launches an instance and then runs a playbook against that instance.

Unfortunately, before you've run the playbook, the host doesn't exist yet. Disabling caching on the dynamic inventory script won't help here, because Ansible only invokes the dynamic inventory script at the beginning of playbook execution, which is before the host exists.

You can add a task that uses the `add_host` module to add the instance to a group, as shown in Example 12-10.

---

15 Canonical is the company that runs the Ubuntu project.

Example 12-10. Adding an instance to groups

```
- name: Create an ubuntu instance on Amazon EC2
  hosts: localhost
  tasks:
  - name: start the instance
    ec2:
      image: ami-8caa1ce4
      instance_type: m3.medium
      key_name: mykey
      group: [web, ssh, outbound]
      instance_tags: { type: web, env: production }
    register: ec2

  - name: add the instance to web and production groups
    add_host: hostname={{ item.public_dns_name }} groups=web,production
    with_items: ec2.instances

- name: do something to production webservers
  hosts: web:&production
  tasks:
  - ...
```

Return Type of the ec2 Module

The ec2 module returns a dictionary with three fields, shown in Table 12-4.

Table 12-4. Return value of ec2 module

Parameter	Description
instance_ids	List of instance ids
instances	List of instance dicts
tagged_instances	List of instance dicts

If the user passes the exact_count parameter to the ec2 module, then the module might not create new instances, as described in "Creating Instances the Idempotent Way" on page 225. In this case, the instance_ids and instances fields will be populated only if the module creates new instances. However, the tagged_instances field will contain instance dicts for all of the instances that match the tags, whether they were just created or already existed.

An instance dict contains the fields shown in Table 12-5.

Table 12-5. Contents of instance dicts

Parameter	Description
id	Instance id
ami_launch_index	Instance index within a reservation (between 0 and N-1) if N launched
private_ip	Internal IP address (not routable outside of EC2)
private_dns_name	Internal DNS name (not routable outside of EC2)
public_ip	Public IP address
public_dns_name	Public DNS name
state_code	Reason code for the state change
architecture	CPU architecture
image_id	AMI
key_name	Key pair name
placement	Location where the instance was launched
kernel	AKI (Amazon kernel image)
ramdisk	ARI (Amazon ramdisk image)
launch_time	Time instance was launched
instance_type	Instance type
root_device_type	Type of root device (ephemeral, EBS)
root_device_name	Name of root device
state	State of instance
hypervisor	Hypervisor type

For more details on what these fields mean, check out the Boto[16] documentation for the `boto.ec2.instance.Instance` (*http://bit.ly/1Fw7HSO*) class or the documentation for the output of the `run-instances` command of Amazon's command-line tool (*http://amzn.to/1Fw7Jd9*).[17]

Waiting for the Server to Come Up

While IaaS clouds like EC2 are remarkable feats of technology, they still require a finite amount of time to create new instances. What this means is that you can't run a playbook against an EC2 instance immediately after you've submitted a request to create it. Instead, you need to wait for the EC2 instance to come up.

The `ec2` module supports a `wait` parameter. If it's set to "yes," then the `ec2` task will not return until the instance has transitioned to the running state:

```
- name: start the instance
  ec2:
    image: ami-8caa1ce4
    instance_type: m3.medium
    key_name: mykey
    group: [web, ssh, outbound]
    instance_tags: { type: web, env: production }
    wait: yes
  register: ec2
```

Unfortunately, waiting for the instance to be in the running state isn't enough to ensure that you can actually execute a playbook against a host. You still need to wait until the instance has advanced far enough in the boot process that the SSH server has started and is accepting incoming connections.

The `wait_for` module is designed for this kind of scenario. Here's how you would use the `ec2` and `wait_for` modules in concert to start an instance and then wait until the instance is ready to receive SSH connections:

```
- name: start the instance
  ec2:
    image: ami-8caa1ce4
    instance_type: m3.medium
    key_name: mykey
    group: [web, ssh, outbound]
    instance_tags: { type: web, env: production }
    wait: yes
  register: ec2
```

---

16 Boto is the Python library that Ansible uses to communicate with EC2.

17 The command-line tool is documented at *http://aws.amazon.com/cli/*.

```
- name: wait for ssh server to be running
  wait_for: host={{ item.public_dns_name }} port=22 search_regex=OpenSSH
  with_items: ec2.instances
```

This invocation of `wait_for` uses the `search_regex` argument to look for the string `OpenSSH` after connecting to the host. This `regex` takes advantage of the fact that a fully functioning SSH server will return a string that looks something like Example 12-11 when an SSH client first connects.

Example 12-11. Initial response of an SSH server running on Ubuntu

```
SSH-2.0-OpenSSH_5.9p1 Debian-5ubuntu1.4
```

We could invoke the `wait_for` module to just check if port 22 is listening for incoming connections. However, sometimes an SSH server has gotten far enough along in the startup process that it is listening on port 22, but is not fully functional yet. Waiting for the initial response ensures that the `wait_for` module will only return when the SSH server has fully started up.

Creating Instances the Idempotent Way

Playbooks that invoke the `ec2` module are not generally idempotent. If you were to execute Example 12-6 multiple times, then EC2 will create multiple instances.

You can write idempotent playbooks with the `ec2` module by using the `count_tag` and `exact_count` parameters.

Let's say we want to write a playbook that starts three instances. We want this playbook to be idempotent, so if three instances are already running, we want the playbook to do nothing. Example 12-12 shows what it would look like:

Example 12-12. Idempotent instance creation

```
- name: start the instance
  ec2:
    image: ami-8caa1ce4
    instance_type: m3.medium
    key_name: mykey
    group: [web, ssh, outbound]
    instance_tags: { type: web, env: production }
    exact_count: 3
    count_tag: { type: web }
```

The `exact_count: 3` parameter tells Ansible to ensure that exactly three instances are running that match the tags specified in `count_tag`. In our example, I only specified one tag for `count_tag`, but it does support multiple tags.

When running this playbook for the first time, Ansible will check how many instances are currently running that are tagged with type=web. Assuming there are no such instances, Ansible will create three new instances and tag them with type=web and env=production.

When running this playbook the next time, Ansible will check how many instances are currently running that are tagged with type=web. It will see that there are three instances running and will not start any new instances.

Putting It All Together

Example 12-13 shows the playbook that create three EC2 instances and configures them as web servers. The playbook is idempotent, so you can safely run it multiple times, and it will create new instances only if they haven't been created yet.

Note how we use the tagged_instances return value of the ec2 module, instead of the instances return value, for reasons described in "Return Type of the ec2 Module" on page 222.

Example 12-13. ec2-example.yml: Complete EC2 playbook

```
---
- name: launch webservers
  hosts: localhost
  vars:
    region: us-west-1
    instance_type: t2.micro
    count: 3
  tasks:
  - name: ec2 keypair
    ec2_key: name=mykey key_material="{{ item }}" region={{ region }}
    with_file: ~/.ssh/id_rsa.pub

  - name: web security group
    ec2_group:
      name: web
      description: allow http and https access
      region: "{{ region }}"
      rules:
        - proto: tcp
          from_port: 80
          to_port: 80
          cidr_ip: 0.0.0.0/0
        - proto: tcp
          from_port: 443
          to_port: 443
          cidr_ip: 0.0.0.0/0

  - name: ssh security group
```

```
    ec2_group:
      name: ssh
      description: allow ssh access
      region: "{{ region }}"
      rules:
        - proto: tcp
          from_port: 22
          to_port: 22
          cidr_ip: 0.0.0.0/0

  - name: outbound security group
    ec2_group:
      name: outbound
      description: allow outbound connections to the internet
      region: "{{ region }}"
      rules_egress:
        - proto: all
          cidr_ip: 0.0.0.0/0

  - name: Get the ubuntu trusty AMI
    ec2_ami_search: distro=ubuntu release=trusty virt=hvm region={{ region }}
    register: ubuntu_image

  - name: start the instances
    ec2:
      region: "{{ region }}"
      image: "{{ ubuntu_image.ami }}"
      instance_type: "{{ instance_type }}"
      key_name: mykey
      group: [web, ssh outbound]
      instance_tags: { Name: ansiblebook, type: web, env: production }
      exact_count: "{{ count }}"
      count_tag: { type: web }
      wait: yes
    register: ec2

  - name: add the instance to web and production groups
    add_host: hostname={{ item.public_dns_name }} groups=web,production
    with_items: ec2.tagged_instances
    when: item.public_dns_name is defined

  - name: wait for ssh server to be running
    wait_for: host={{ item.public_dns_name }} port=22 search_regex=OpenSSH
    with_items: ec2.tagged_instances
    when: item.public_dns_name is defined

- name: configure webservers
  hosts: web:&production
  sudo: True
  roles:
    - web
```

Specifying a Virtual Private Cloud

So far, we've been launching our instances into the default virtual private cloud (VPC). Ansible also allows us to create new VPCs and launch instances into them.

What Is a VPC?

Think of a VPC as an isolated network. When you create a VPC, you specify an IP address range. It must be a subset of one of the private address ranges (*10.0.0.0/8, 172.16.0.0/12*, or *192.168.0.0/16*).

You carve up your VPC into subnets, which have IP ranges that are subsets of the IP range of your entire VPC. In Example 12-14, the VPC has the IP range *10.0.0.0/16*, and we associate two subnets: *10.0.0.0/24* and *10.0.10/24*.

When you launch an instance, you assign it to a subnet in a VPC. You can configure your subnets so that your instances get either public or private IP addresses. EC2 also allows you to define routing tables for routing traffic between your subnets and to create Internet gateways for routing traffic from your subnets to the Internet.

Configuring networking is a complex topic that's (way) outside the scope of this book. For more info, check out Amazon's EC2 documentation on VPC (*http://amzn.to/1Fw89Af*).

Example 12-14 shows how to create a VPC with two subnets.

Example 12-14. create-vpc.yml: Creating a vpc

```
- name: create a vpc
  ec2_vpc:
    region: us-west-1
    internet_gateway: True
    resource_tags: { Name: "Book example", env: production }
    cidr_block: 10.0.0.0/16
    subnets:
      - cidr: 10.0.0.0/24
        resource_tags:
          env: production
          tier: web
      - cidr: 10.0.1.0/24
        resource_tags:
          env: production
          tier: db
    route_tables:
      - subnets:
        - 10.0.0.0/24
        - 10.0.1.0/24
        routes:
```

```
    - dest: 0.0.0.0/0
      gw: igw
```

Creating a VPC is idempotent; Ansible uniquely identifies the VPC based on a combination of the `resource_tags` and the `cidr_block` parameters. Ansible will create a new VPC if no existing VPC matches the resource tags and CIDR block.[18]

Admittedly, Example 12-14 is a simple example from a networking perspective, as we've just defined two subnets that are both connected to the Internet. A more realistic example would have one subnet that's routable to the Internet, and another subnet that's not routable to the Internet, and we'd have some rules for routing traffic between the two subnets.

Example 12-15 shows a complete example of creating a VPC and launching instances into it.

Example 12-15. ec2-vpc-example.yml: Complete EC2 playbook that specifies a VPC

```
---
- name: launch webservers into a specific vpc
  hosts: localhost
  vars:
    instance_type: t2.micro
    count: 1
    region: us-west-1
  tasks:
  - name: create a vpc
    ec2_vpc:
      region: "{{ region }}"
      internet_gateway: True
      resource_tags: { Name: book, env: production }
      cidr_block: 10.0.0.0/16
      subnets:
        - cidr: 10.0.0.0/24
          resource_tags:
            env: production
            tier: web
        - cidr: 10.0.1.0/24
          resource_tags:
            env: production
            tier: db
      route_tables:
        - subnets:
          - 10.0.0.0/24
          - 10.0.1.0/24
          routes:
```

---

18 As of this writing, a bug (*http://bit.ly/1Fw8eUI*) in Ansible causes it to incorrectly report a state of changed each time this module is invoked, even if it does not a create a VPC only.

```
          - dest: 0.0.0.0/0
            gw: igw
      register: vpc

- set_fact: vpc_id={{ vpc.vpc_id }}

- name: set ec2 keypair
  ec2_key: name=mykey key_material="{{ item }}"
  with_file: ~/.ssh/id_rsa.pub

- name: web security group
  ec2_group:
    name: vpc-web
    region: "{{ region }}"
    description: allow http and https access
    vpc_id: "{{ vpc_id }}"
    rules:
      - proto: tcp
        from_port: 80
        to_port: 80
        cidr_ip: 0.0.0.0/0
      - proto: tcp
        from_port: 443
        to_port: 443
        cidr_ip: 0.0.0.0/0

- name: ssh security group
  ec2_group:
    name: vpc-ssh
    region: "{{ region }}"
    description: allow ssh access
    vpc_id: "{{ vpc_id }}"
    rules:
      - proto: tcp
        from_port: 22
        to_port: 22
        cidr_ip: 0.0.0.0/0

- name: outbound security group
  ec2_group:
    name: vpc-outbound
    description: allow outbound connections to the internet
    region: "{{ region }}"
    vpc_id: "{{ vpc_id }}"
    rules_egress:
      - proto: all
        cidr_ip: 0.0.0.0/0

- name: Get the ubuntu trusty AMI
  ec2_ami_search: distro=ubuntu release=trusty virt=hvm region={{ region }}
  register: ubuntu_image
```

```
- name: start the instances
  ec2:
    image: "{{ ubuntu_image.ami }}"
    region: "{{ region }}"
    instance_type: "{{ instance_type }}"
    assign_public_ip: True
    key_name: mykey
    group: [vpc-web, vpc-ssh, vpc-outbound]
    instance_tags: { Name: book, type: web, env: production }
    exact_count: "{{ count }}"
    count_tag: { type: web }
    vpc_subnet_id: "{{ vpc.subnets[0].id}}"
    wait: yes
  register: ec2

- name: add the instance to web and production groups
  add_host: hostname={{ item.public_dns_name }} groups=web,production
  with_items: ec2.tagged_instances
  when: item.public_dns_name is defined

- name: wait for ssh server to be running
  wait_for: host={{ item.public_dns_name }} port=22 search_regex=OpenSSH
  with_items: ec2.tagged_instances
  when: item.public_dns_name is defined

- name: configure webservers
  hosts: web:&production
  sudo: True
  roles:
    - web
```

 Unfortunately, as of this writing, the Ansible ec2 module can't handle the case where you have security groups with the same name in different VPCs. This means we can't have an SSH security group defined in multiple VPCs, because the module will try to associate all of the SSH security groups when we launch an instance. In our example, I've used different names for these security groups. I'm hoping this will be fixed in a future version of the module.

Dynamic Inventory and VPC

Oftentimes, when using a VPC, you will place some instances inside of a private subnet that is not routable from the Internet. When you do this, there is no public IP address associated with the instance.

In this case, you might want to run Ansible from an instance inside of your VPC. The Ansible dynamic inventory script is smart enough that it will return internal IP addresses for VPC instances that don't have public IP addresses.

See Appendix C for details on how you can use IAM roles to run Ansible inside of a VPC without needing to copy EC2 credentials to the instance.

Building AMIs

There are two approaches you can take to creating custom Amazon machine images (AMIs) with Ansible. You can use the `ec2_ami` module, or you can use a third-party tool called Packer that has support for Ansible.

With the ec2_ami Module

The `ec2_ami` module will take a running instance and snapshot it into an AMI. Example 12-16 shows this module in action.

Example 12-16. Creating an AMI with the ec2_ami module

```
- name: create an AMI
  hosts: localhost
  vars:
    instance_id: i-dac5473b
  tasks:
    - name: create the AMI
      ec2_ami:
        name: web-nginx
        description: Ubuntu 14.04 with nginx installed
        instance_id: "{{ instance_id }}"
        wait: yes
      register: ami

    - name: output AMI details
      debug: var=ami
```

With Packer

The `ec2_ami` module works just fine, but you have to write some additional code to create and terminate the instance.

There's an open source tool called Packer (*https://www.packer.io*) that will automate the creation and termination of an instance for you. Packer also happens to be written by Mitchell Hashimoto, the creator of Vagrant.

Packer can create different types of images and works with different configuration management tools. This chapter focuses on using Packer to create AMIs using Ansible, but you can also use Packer to create images for other IaaS clouds, such as Google Compute Engine, DigitalOcean, or OpenStack. It can even be used to create Vagrant boxes and Docker containers. It also supports other configuration management tools, such as Chef, Puppet, and Salt.

To use Packer, you create a configuration file in JSON format and then use the `packer` command-line tool to create the image using the configuration file.

Example 12-17 shows a sample Packer configuration file that uses Ansible to create an AMI with our web role.

Example 12-17. web.json

```json
{
  "builders": [
    {
      "type": "amazon-ebs",
      "region": "us-west-1",
      "source_ami": "ami-50120b15",
      "instance_type": "t2.micro",
      "ssh_username": "ubuntu",
      "ami_name": "web-nginx-{{timestamp}}",
      "tags": {
        "Name": "web-nginx"
      }
    }
  ],
  "provisioners": [
    {
      "type": "shell",
      "inline": [
        "sleep 30",
        "sudo apt-get update",
        "sudo apt-get install -y ansible"
      ]
    },
    {
      "type": "ansible-local",
      "playbook_file": "web-ami.yml",
      "role_paths": [
        "/Users/lorinhochstein/dev/ansiblebook/ch12/playbooks/roles/web"
      ]
    }
  ]
}
```

Use the `packer build` command to create the AMI:

```
$ packer build web.json
```

The output looks like this:

```
==> amazon-ebs: Inspecting the source AMI...
==> amazon-ebs: Creating temporary keypair: packer 546919ba-cb97-4a9e-1c21-389633
dc0779
==> amazon-ebs: Creating temporary security group for this instance...
...
```

```
==> amazon-ebs: Stopping the source instance...
==> amazon-ebs: Waiting for the instance to stop...
==> amazon-ebs: Creating the AMI: web-nginx-1416174010
    amazon-ebs: AMI: ami-963fa8fe
==> amazon-ebs: Waiting for AMI to become ready...
==> amazon-ebs: Adding tags to AMI (ami-963fa8fe)...
    amazon-ebs: Adding tag: "Name": "web-nginx"
==> amazon-ebs: Terminating the source AWS instance...
==> amazon-ebs: Deleting temporary security group...
==> amazon-ebs: Deleting temporary keypair...
Build 'amazon-ebs' finished.

==> Builds finished. The artifacts of successful builds are:
--> amazon-ebs: AMIs were created:

us-west-1: ami-963fa8fe
```

Example 12-17 has two sections: builders and provisioners. The builders section refers to the type of image being created. In our case, we are creating an Elastic Block Store–backed (EBS) Amazon Machine Image, so we use the amazon-ebs builder.

Packer needs to start a new instance to create an AMI, so you need to configure Packer with all of the information you typically need when creating an instance: EC2 region, AMI, and instance type. Packer doesn't need to be configured with a security group because it will create a temporary security group automatically, and then delete that security group when it is finished. Like Ansible, Packer needs to be able to SSH to the created instance. Therefore, you need to specify the SSH username in the Packer configuration file.

You also need to tell Packer what to name your instance, as well as any tags you want to apply to your instance. Because AMI names must be unique, we use the {{time stamp}} function to insert a Unix timestamp. A Unix timestamp encodes the date and time as the number of seconds since Jan. 1, 1970, UTC. See the Packer documentation (*http://bit.ly/1Fw9hEc*) for more information about the functions that Packer supports.

Because Packer needs to interact with EC2 to create the AMI, it needs access to your EC2 credentials. Like Ansible, Packer can read your EC2 credentials from environment variables, so you don't need to specify them explicitly in the configuration file, although you can if you prefer.

The provisioners section refers to the tools used to configure the instance before it is captured as an image. Packer supports an Ansible local provisioner: it runs Ansible on the instance itself. That means that Packer needs to copy over all of the necessary Ansible playbooks and related files before it runs, and it also means that Ansible must be installed on the instance before it executes Ansible.

Packer supports a shell provisioner that lets you run arbitrary commands on the instance. Example 12-17 uses this provisioner to install Ansible as an Ubuntu `apt` package. To avoid a race situation with trying to install packages before the operating system is fully booted up, the shell provisioner in our example is configured to wait for 30 seconds before installing Ansible.

Example 12-18 shows the web-ami.yml playbook we use for configuring an instance. It's a simple playbook that applies the `web` role to the local machine. Because it uses the `web` role, the configuration file must explicitly specify the location of the directory that contains the `web` role so that Packer can copy the `web` role's files to the instance.

Example 12-18. web-ami.yml

```
- name: configure a webserver as an ami
  hosts: localhost
  sudo: True
  roles:
    - web
```

Instead of selectively copying over roles, we can also tell Packer to just copy our entire playbooks directory instead. In that case, the configuration file would look like Example 12-19.

Example 12-19. web-pb.json copying over the entire playbooks directory

```
{
  "builders": [
    {
      "type": "amazon-ebs",
      "region": "us-west-1",
      "source_ami": "ami-50120b15",
      "instance_type": "t2.micro",
      "ssh_username": "ubuntu",
      "ami_name": "web-nginx-{{timestamp}}",
      "tags": {
        "Name": "web-nginx"
      }
    }
  ],
  "provisioners": [
    {
      "type": "shell",
      "inline": [
        "sleep 30",
        "sudo apt-get update",
        "sudo apt-get install -y ansible"
      ]
    },
    {
```

```
    "type": "ansible-local",
    "playbook_file": "web-ami.yml",
    "playbook_dir": "/Users/lorinhochstein/dev/ansiblebook/ch12/playbooks"
  }
 ]
}
```

 As of this writing, Packer doesn't support SSH agent forwarding. Check GitHub (*http://bit.ly/1Fw9neU*) for the current status of this issue.

Packer has a lot more functionality than we can cover here. Check out its documentation (*https://www.packer.io/docs/*) for more details.

Other Modules

Ansible supports even more of EC2, as well as other AWS services. For example, you can use Ansible to launch CloudFormation stacks with the `cloudformation` module, put files into S3 with the `s3` module, modify DNS records with the `route53` module, create autoscaling groups with the `ec2_asg` module, create autoscaling configuration with the `ec2_lc` module, and more.

Using Ansible with EC2 is a large enough topic that you could write a whole book about it. In fact, Yan Kurniawan is writing a book on Ansible and AWS. After digesting this chapter, you should have enough knowledge under your belt to pick up these additional modules without difficulty.

## CHAPTER 13

Docker

The Docker project has taken the IT world by storm. I can't think of another technology that was so quickly embraced by the community. This chapter covers how to use Ansible to create Docker images and deploy Docker containers.

What Is a Container?

A container is a form of virtualization. When you use virtualization to run processes in a guest operating system, these guest processes have no visibility into the host operating system that runs on the physical hardware. In particular, processes running in the guest are not able to directly access physical resources, even if these guest processes are provided with the illusion that they have root access.

Containers are sometimes referred to as *operating system virtualization* to distinguish them from *hardware virtualization* technologies.

In hardware virtualization, a program called the *hypervisor* virtualizes an entire physical machine, including a virtualized CPU, memory, and devices such as disks and network interfaces. Because the entire machine is virtualized, hardware virtualization is very flexible. In particular, you can run an entirely different operating system in the guest than in the host (e.g., running a Windows Server 2012 guest inside of a RedHat Enterprise Linux host), and you can suspend and resume a virtual machine just like you can a physical machine. This flexibility brings with it additional overhead needed to virtualize the hardware.

With operating system virtualization (containers), the guest processes are isolated from the host by the operating system. The guest processes run on the same kernel as the host. The host operating system is responsible for ensuring that the guest processes are fully isolated from the host. When running a Linux-based container program like Docker, the guest processes also must be Linux programs. However, the overhead is much lower than that of hardware virtualization, because you are running only a single operating system. In particular, processes start up much more quickly inside containers than inside virtual machines.

Docker is more than just containers. Think of Docker as being a platform where containers are a building block. To use an analogy, containers are to Docker what virtual machines are to IaaS clouds. The other two major pieces that make up Docker are its image format and the Docker API.

You can think of Docker images as similar to virtual machine images. A Docker image contains a filesystem with an installed operating system, along with some metadata. One important difference is that Docker images are layered. You create a new Docker image by taking an existing Docker image and modifying it by adding, modifying, and deleting files. The representation for the new Docker image contains a reference to the original Docker image, as well as the file system differences between the original Docker image and the new Docker image. As an example, the official nginx docker image (*http://bit.ly/1Fw9JCf*) is built as layers on top of the official Debian Wheezy image. The layered approach means that Docker images are smaller than traditional virtual machine images, so it's faster to transfer Docker images over the Internet than it would be to transfer a traditional virtual machine image. The Docker project maintains a registry of publicly available images (*https://regis try.hub.docker.com*).

Docker also supports a remote API, which enables third-party tools to interact with it. In particular, Ansible's `docker` module uses the Docker remote API.

The Case for Pairing Docker with Ansible

Docker containers make it easier to package your application into a single image that's easy to deploy in different places, which is why the Docker project has embraced the metaphor of the shipping container. Docker's remote API simplifies the automation of software systems that run on top of Docker.

There are two areas where Ansible simplifies working with Docker. One is in the orchestration of Docker containers. When you deploy a "Dockerized" software app, you're typically creating multiple Docker containers that contain different services. These services need to communicate with each other, so you need to connect the appropriate containers correctly and ensure they start up in the right order. Initially, the Docker project did not provide orchestration tools, so third-party tools emerged to fill in the gap. Ansible was built for doing orchestration, so it's a natural fit for deploying your Docker-based application.

The other area is the creation of Docker images. The official way to create your own Docker images is by writing special text files called *Dockerfiles*, which resemble shell scripts. For simpler images, Dockerfiles work just fine. However, when you start to create more-complex images, you'll quickly miss the power that Ansible provides. Fortunately, you can use Ansible to create playbooks.

Docker Application Life Cycle

Here's what the typical life cycle of a Docker-based application looks like:

1. Create Docker images on your local machine.
2. Push Docker images up from your local machine to the registry.
3. Pull Docker images down to your remote hosts from the registry.
4. Start up Docker containers on the remote hosts, passing in any configuration information to the containers on startup.

You typically create your Docker image on your local machine, or on a continuous integration system that supports creating Docker images, such as Jenkins or CircleCI. Once you've created your image, you need to store it somewhere it will be convenient for downloading onto your remote hosts.

Docker images typically reside in a repository called a *registry*. The Docker project runs a registry called *Docker Hub*, which can host both public and private Docker images, and where the Docker command-line tools have built-in support for pushing images up to a registry and for pulling images down from a registry.

Once your Docker image is in the registry, you connect to a remote host, pull down the container image, and then run the container. Note that if you try to run a container whose image isn't on the host, Docker will automatically pull down the image from the registry, so you do not need to explicitly issue a command to download an image from the registry.

When you use Ansible to create the Docker images and start the containers on the remote hosts, the application lifecycle looks like this:

1. Write Ansible playbooks for creating Docker images.
2. Run the playbooks to create Docker images on your local machine.
3. Push Docker images up from your local machine to the registry.
4. Write Ansible playbooks to pull Docker images down to remote hosts and start up Docker containers on remote hosts, passing in configuration information.
5. Run Ansible playbooks to start up the containers.

Dockerizing Our Mezzanine Application

We'll use our Mezzanine example and deploy it inside of Docker containers. Recall that our application involves the following services:

- Postgres database
- Mezzanine (web application)
- Memcached (in-memory cache to improve performance)
- nginx (web server)

We could deploy all of these services into the same container. However, for pedagogical purposes, I'm going to run each service in a separate container, as shown in Figure 13-1. Deploying each service in a separate container makes for a more complex deployment, but it allows me to demonstrate how you can do more complex things with Docker and Ansible.

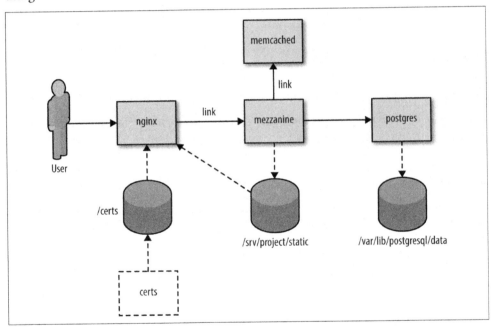

Figure 13-1. Deploying Mezzanine as Docker containers

Each box represents a Docker container that runs a service. Containers that communicate with each other using TCP/IP are connected by solid lines. The nginx container is the only one that must respond to requests from the outside world. It proxies web requests to the Mezzanine application, so it connects to the Mezzanine container. The Mezzanine container must access the database, so it connects to the Postgres container. It must also connect to the Memcached container in order to access the in-memory cache provided by Memcached to improve performance.

The cylinders represent Docker volumes that containers export and import. For example, the Mezzanine container exports the volume */srv/project/static*, and the nginx container imports this volume.

The nginx service must serve static content such as JavaScript, CSS, and images, including files uploaded by Mezzanine users. (Recall that Mezzanine is a CMS that allows users to upload files such as images.) These files are in the Mezzanine container, not the nginx container. To share files across these containers, we configure the Mezzanine container to store the static file content in a volume, and we mount the volume into the nginx container.

Containers that share volumes (in our deployment, *nginx* and *mezzanine*) must be running on the same host, but otherwise we could deploy each container on a separate host. In a real deployment, we'd likely deploy Memcached on the same host as Mezzanine, and we'd put Postgres on a separate host. In our example, I'm going to use *container linking* (see "Linking Docker Containers" on page 241) to link the nginx, Mezzanine, and Memcached containers together (hence the *link* annotation on the diagram). Mezzanine will communicate with Postgres over the port exposed by the Postgres container, in order to demonstrate both ways of connecting together containers that run on the same host.

Linking Docker Containers

If two Docker containers are running on the same host, you can use a feature called *linking containers* so that the two containers can be networked together. Linking is unidirectional, so if container *A* is linked to container *B*, then processes in *A* can connect to network services running in *B*.

Docker will inject special environment variables into one of the containers. These variables contain IP addresses and ports so that one container can access services in the other container, as well as update the */etc/hosts* file so that one container can access the other by hostname. For more details, see the official Docker documentation about container (*https://docs.docker.com/userguide/dockerlinks/*).

Finally, there's a dashed box in the diagram labeled "certs." This is a Docker data volume that contains the TLS certificates. Unlike the other containers, this one is stopped; it exists only to store the certificate files.

Creating Docker Images with Ansible

In this chapter, I'm going to use the method recommended by the Ansible project for creating images with Ansible. In a nutshell, the method is:

1. Use an official Ansible base image that has Ansible installed in it.
2. In the Dockerfile, copy the playbooks into the image.
3. Invoke Ansible from the Dockerfile.

Note that we won't be creating all of our images with Ansible. In one case, we'll be able to use an existing image right off-the-shelf…er…Docker registry. In other cases, we'll build the Docker image with a traditional Dockerfile.

We need to create Docker images for each of the boxes depicted in Figure 13-1.

Mezzanine

Our Mezzanine container image is the most complex one, and we'll be using Ansible to configure it.

The official Ansible base images are hosted on the Docker registry (*https://regis try.hub.docker.com/repos/ansible/*). As of this writing, there are two base images available:

- ansible/centos7-ansible (CentOS 7)
- ansible/ubuntu14.04-ansible (Ubuntu 14.04).

We'll be using the Ubuntu 14.04 image. To create this image, I have a *mezzanine* directory that contains the following files:

- *Dockerfile*
- *ansible/mezzanine-container.yml*
- *ansible/files/gunicorn.conf.py*
- *ansible/files/local_settings.py*
- *ansible/files/scripts/setadmin.py*
- *ansible/files/scripts/setsite.py*

There's the Dockerfile for building the Docker image, the playbook itself (*mezzanine-container.yml*), and several other files that we're going to copy into the image.

Example 13-1 shows what the Dockerfile looks like for building the Mezzanine image.

Example 13-1. Mezzanine Dockerfile

```
FROM ansible/ubuntu14.04-ansible:stable
MAINTAINER Lorin Hochstein <lorin@ansiblebook.com>

ADD ansible /srv/ansible
WORKDIR /srv/ansible

RUN ansible-playbook mezzanine-container.yml -c local

VOLUME /srv/project/static

WORKDIR /srv/project

EXPOSE 8000
CMD ["gunicorn_django", "-c", "gunicorn.conf.py"]
```

We copy the playbook and associated files into the container and then execute the playbook. We also create a mount point for */srv/project/static*, the directory that contains the static content that the nginx container will serve.

Finally, we expose port 8000 and specify `gunicorn_django` as the default command for the container, which will run Mezzanine using the Gunicorn application server. Example 13-2 shows the playbook we use to configure the container.

Example 13-2. mezzanine-container.yml

```
- name: Create Mezzanine container
  hosts: local
  vars:
    mezzanine_repo_url: https://github.com/lorin/mezzanine-example.git
    mezzanine_proj_path: /srv/project
    mezzanine_reqs_path: requirements.txt
    script_path: /srv/scripts
  tasks:
  - name: install apt packages
    apt: pkg={{ item }} update_cache=yes cache_valid_time=3600
    with_items:
      - git
      - gunicorn
      - libjpeg-dev
      - libpq-dev
      - python-dev
      - python-pip
      - python-psycopg2
      - python-setuptools

  - name: check out the repository on the host
    git:
      repo: "{{ mezzanine_repo_url }}"
      dest: "{{ mezzanine_proj_path }}"
```

```
        accept_hostkey: yes

  - name: install required python packages
    pip: name={{ item }}
    with_items:
        - south
        - psycopg2
        - django-compressor
        - python-memcached

  - name: install requirements.txt
    pip: requirements={{ mezzanine_proj_path }}/{{ mezzanine_reqs_path }}

  - name: generate the settings file
    copy: src=files/local_settings.py dest={{ mezzanine_proj_path }}/
    local_settings.py

  - name: set the gunicorn config file
    copy: src=files/gunicorn.conf.py dest={{ mezzanine_proj_path }}/gunicorn.conf.py

  - name: collect static assets into the appropriate directory
    django_manage: command=collectstatic app_path={{ mezzanine_proj_path }}
    environment:
        # We can't run collectstatic if the secret key is blank,
        # so we just pass in an arbitrary one
        SECRET_KEY: nonblanksecretkey

  - name: script directory
    file: path={{ script_path }} state=directory

  - name: copy scripts for setting site id and admin at launch time
    copy: src=files/scripts/{{ item }} dest={{ script_path }}/{{ item }} mode=0755
    with_items:
        - setadmin.py
        - setsite.py
```

The Example 13-2 playbook is similar to the playbook from Chapter 6, with the following differences:

- We don't install Postgres, nginx, Memcached, or Supervisor, which is discussed in Chapter 5, into the image.

- We don't use templates to generate *local_settings.py* and *gunicorn.conf.py*.

- We don't run the Django syncdb or migrate commands.

- We copy *setadmin.py* and *setsite.py* scripts into the container instead of executing them.

We don't install the other services into the image because those services are implemented by separate images, except for Supervisor.

Why We Don't Need Supervisor

Recall that our deployment of Mezzanine originally used Supervisor to manage our application server (Gunicorn). This meant that Supervisor was responsible for starting and stopping the Gunicorn process.

In our Mezzanine Docker container, we don't need a separate program for starting and stopping the Gunicorn process. That's because Docker is itself a system designed for starting and stopping processes.

Without Docker, we would use Supervisor to start Gunicorn:

```
$ supervisorctl start gunicorn_mezzanine
```

With Docker, we start up a container containing Gunicorn, and we use Ansible to do something like this:

```
$ docker run lorin/mezzanine:latest
```

We don't use templates to generate *local_settings.py* because when we build the image, we don't know what the settings will be. For example, we don't know what the database host, port, username, and password values should be. Even if we did, we don't want to hardcode them in the image, because we want to be able to use the same image in our development, staging, and production environments.

What we need is a service discovery mechanism so that we can determine what all of these settings should be when the container starts up. There are many different ways of implementing service discovery, including using a service discovery tool such as etcd, Consul, Apache ZooKeeper, or Eureka. We're going to use environment variables, since Docker lets us specify environment variables when we start containers. Example 13-3 shows the *local_settings.py* file we are using for the image.

Example 13-3. local_settings.py

```
from __future__ import unicode_literals
import os

SECRET_KEY = os.environ.get("SECRET_KEY", "")
NEVERCACHE_KEY = os.environ.get("NEVERCACHE_KEY", "")
ALLOWED_HOSTS = os.environ.get("ALLOWED_HOSTS", "")

DATABASES = {
    "default": {
        # Ends with "postgresql_psycopg2", "mysql", "sqlite3" or "oracle".
        "ENGINE": "django.db.backends.postgresql_psycopg2",
```

```
        # DB name or path to database file if using sqlite3.
        "NAME": os.environ.get("DATABASE_NAME", ""),
        # Not used with sqlite3.
        "USER": os.environ.get("DATABASE_USER", ""),
        # Not used with sqlite3.
        "PASSWORD": os.environ.get("DATABASE_PASSWORD", ""),
        # Set to empty string for localhost. Not used with sqlite3.
        "HOST": os.environ.get("DATABASE_HOST", ""),
        # Set to empty string for default. Not used with sqlite3.
        "PORT": os.environ.get("DATABASE_PORT", "")
    }
}

SECURE_PROXY_SSL_HEADER = ("HTTP_X_FORWARDED_PROTOCOL", "https")

CACHE_MIDDLEWARE_SECONDS = 60

CACHE_MIDDLEWARE_KEY_PREFIX = "mezzanine"

CACHES = {
    "default": {
        "BACKEND": "django.core.cache.backends.memcached.MemcachedCache",
        "LOCATION": os.environ.get("MEMCACHED_LOCATION", "memcached:11211"),
    }
}

SESSION_ENGINE = "django.contrib.sessions.backends.cache"

TWITTER_ACCESS_TOKEN_KEY = os.environ.get("TWITTER_ACCESS_TOKEN_KEY ", "")
TWITTER_ACCESS_TOKEN_SECRET = os.environ.get("TWITTER_ACCESS_TOKEN_SECRET ", "")
TWITTER_CONSUMER_KEY = os.environ.get("TWITTER_CONSUMER_KEY ", "")
TWITTER_CONSUMER_SECRET = os.environ.get("TWITTER_CONSUMER_SECRET ", "")
TWITTER_DEFAULT_QUERY = "from:ansiblebook"
```

Note how most of the settings in Example 13-3 make reference to an environment variable by calling os.environ.get.

For most of the settings, we don't use a meaningful default value if the environment variable doesn't exist. There is one exception, the location of the memcached server:

```
    "LOCATION": os.environ.get("MEMCACHED_LOCATION", "memcached:11211"),
```

I do this so that the default will handle the case where we use container linking. If I link the Memcached container with the name *memcached* at runtime, then Docker will automatically resolve the memcached hostname to the IP address of the Memcached container.

Example 13-4 shows the Gunicorn configuration file. We could probably get away with hardcoding 8000 as the port, but instead I've allowed the user to override this by defining the GUNICORN_PORT environment variable.

Example 13-4. gunicorn.conf.py

```
from __future__ import unicode_literals
import multiprocessing
import os

bind = "0.0.0.0:{}".format(os.environ.get("GUNICORN_PORT", 8000))
workers = multiprocessing.cpu_count() * 2 + 1
loglevel = "error"
proc_name = "mezzanine"
```

The *setadmin.py* and *setsite.py* files are unchanged from the originals in Examples 6-17 and 6-18. We copy these into the container so that we can invoke them at deployment time. In our original playbook, we copied these files to the host at deploy time and executed them, but Docker doesn't yet support a simple way to copy files into a container at runtime, so instead we just copied them into the image at build-time.

The Other Container Images

Our Mezzanine example uses some additional Docker images that we do not use Ansible to configure.

Postgres

We need an image that runs the Postgres service. Fortunately, the Postgres project has an official image in the Docker registry (*https://registry.hub.docker.com/_/postgres/*). I'm going to use an official image, so there's no need for us to create our own. Specifically, I'm going to use the image that contains Postgres version 9.4, which is named postgres:9.4.

Memcached

There's no official Memcached image, but the Dockerfile to build one is very simple, as shown in Example 13-5.

Example 13-5. Dockerfile for Memcached

```
FROM ubuntu:trusty
MAINTAINER lorin@ansiblebook.com

# Based on the Digital Ocean tutorial: http://bit.ly/1qJ8CXP

# Update the default application repository sources list
RUN apt-get update

# Install Memcached
```

```
RUN apt-get install -y memcached

# Port to expose (default: 11211)
EXPOSE 11211

# Default Memcached run command arguments
CMD ["-m", "128"]

# Set the user to run Memcached daemon
USER daemon

# Set the entrypoint to memcached binary
ENTRYPOINT memcached
```

Nginx

There is an official Dockerfile Nginx image (*http://bit.ly/1Dfau2Z*) that we can use.
We need to use our own configuration file for nginx so that it reverse proxies to the
Mezzanine application. The official nginx image is configured so that we could put
our custom *nginx.conf* file on the local filesystem of the host and mount it into the
container. However, I prefer to create a self-contained Docker image that doesn't
depend on configuration files that are outside of the container.

We can build a new image using the official image as a base and add our custom
nginx configuration file into it. Example 13-6 shows the Dockerfile and Example 13-7
shows the custom nginx configuration file we use.

Example 13-6. Dockerfile for custom nginx Docker image

```
FROM nginx:1.7

RUN rm /etc/nginx/conf.d/default.conf \
       /etc/nginx/conf.d/example_ssl.conf
COPY nginx.conf /etc/nginx/conf.d/mezzanine.conf
```

Example 13-7. nginx.conf for nginx Docker image

```
upstream mezzanine {
    server mezzanine:8000;
}

server {

    listen 80;

    listen 443 ssl;

    client_max_body_size 10M;
    keepalive_timeout     15;
```

```
    ssl_certificate      /certs/nginx.crt;
    ssl_certificate_key  /certs/nginx.key;
    ssl_session_cache    shared:SSL:10m;
    ssl_session_timeout  10m;
    ssl_ciphers (too long to show here);
    ssl_prefer_server_ciphers on;

    location / {
        proxy_redirect     off;
        proxy_set_header   Host                    $host;
        proxy_set_header   X-Real-IP               $remote_addr;
        proxy_set_header   X-Forwarded-For         $proxy_add_x_forwarded_for;
        proxy_set_header   X-Forwarded-Protocol    $scheme;
        proxy_pass         http://mezzanine;
    }

    location /static/ {
        root           /srv/project;
        access_log     off;
        log_not_found  off;
    }

    location /robots.txt {
        root           /srv/project/static;
        access_log     off;
        log_not_found  off;
    }

    location /favicon.ico {
        root           /srv/project/static/img;
        access_log     off;
        log_not_found  off;
    }
}
```

Nginx doesn't natively support reading in configuration from environment variables, so we need to use a well-known path for the location of the static content (*/srv/project/static*). We specify the location of the Mezzanine service as *mezzanine:8000*; when we link the nginx container to the Mezzanine container; then Docker will ensure that the *mezzanine* hostname resolves to the Mezzanine container's IP address.

Certs

The *certs* Docker image is a file that contains the TLS certificate used by nginx. In a real scenario, we'd use a certificate issued from a certificate authority. But for the purposes of demonstration, the Dockerfile for this image generates a self-signed certificate for *http://192.168.59.103.xip.io*, as shown in Example 13-8.

Example 13-8. Dockerfile for certs image

```
FROM ubuntu:trusty
MAINTAINER lorin@ansiblebook.com

# Create self-signed cert for 192.168.59.103
RUN apt-get update
RUN apt-get install -y openssl

RUN mkdir /certs

WORKDIR /certs

RUN openssl req -new -x509 -nodes -out nginx.crt \
    -keyout nginx.key -subj '/CN=192.168.59.103.xip.io' -days 3650

VOLUME /certs
```

Building the Images

I did not use Ansible itself to build the Docker images. Instead, I just built them on the command line. For example, to build the Mezzanine image, I wrote:

```
$ cd mezzanine
$ docker build -t lorin/mezzanine .
```

Ansible does contain a module for building Docker images, called `docker_image`. However, that module has been deprecated because building images isn't a good fit for a tool like Ansible. Image building is part of the build process of an application's lifecycle; building Docker images and pushing them up an image registry is the sort of thing that your continuous integration system should be doing, not your configuration management system.

Deploying the Dockerized Application

We use the docker module for deploying the application. As of this writing, there are several known issues with the docker module that ships with Ansible.

- The volumes_from parameter does not work with recent versions of Docker.

- It does not support Boot2Docker, a commonly used tool for running Docker on OS X.

- It does not support the wait parameter that I use in some examples in this section.

There are proposed fixes for all of these issues awaiting review in the Ansible project. Hopefully by the time you read this, these issues all will have been fixed. There is also a pending pull request to support detach=no, which has the same behavior as wait=yes in the examples here. In the meantime, I have included a custom version of the docker module in the code sample repository that has fixes for these issues. The file is *ch13/playbooks/library/docker.py*.

Example 13-10 shows the entire playbook that orchestrates the Docker containers in our Mezzanine deployment. The sensitive data is in a separate file, shown in Example 13-11. You can think of this as a development setup, because all of the services are running on the control machine.

Note that I'm running this on Mac OS X using Boot2Docker, so the Docker containers actually run inside of a virtual machine, rather than on localhost. This also means that I can invoke Docker without needing it to be root. If you're running this on Linux, you'll need to use sudo or run this as root for it to work.

Since this is a large playbook, let's break it down.

Starting the Database Container

Here's how we start the container that runs the Postgres database.

```
- name: start the postgres container
  docker:
    image: postgres:9.4
    name: postgres
    publish_all_ports: True
    env:
      POSTGRES_USER: "{{ database_user }}"
      POSTGRES_PASSWORD: "{{ database_password }}"
```

Whenever you start a Docker container, you must specify the image. If you don't have the `postgres:9.4` image installed locally, then Docker will download it for you the first time it runs. We specify `publish_all_ports` so that Docker will open up the ports that this container is configured to expose; in this case, that's port 5432.

The container is configured by environment variables, so we pass the username and password that should have access to this service. The Postgres image will automatically create a database with the same name as the user.

Retrieving the Database Container IP Address and Mapped Port

When we started up our Postgres container, we could have explicitly mapped the container's database port (5432) to a known port on the host. (We'll do this for the nginx container.) Since we didn't, Docker will select an arbitrary port on the host that maps to 5432 inside of the container.

Later on in the playbook, we're going to need to know what this port is, because we need to wait for the Postgres service to start before we bring up Mezzanine, and we're going to do that by checking to see if there's anything listening on that port.

We could configure the Mezzanine container to connect on the mapped port, but instead I decided to have the Mezzanine container connect to port 5432 on the Postgres container's IP address, which gives me an excuse to demonstrate how to retrieve a Docker container's IP address.

When the Docker module starts one or more containers, it sets information about the started container(s) as facts. This means that we don't need to use the `register` clause to capture the result of invoking this module; we just need to know the name of the fact that contains the information we're looking for.

The name of the fact with the information is `docker_containers`, which is a list of dictionaries that contains information about the container. It's the same output you'd see if you used the `docker inspect` command. Example 13-9 shows an example of the value of the `docker_containers` fact after we start a postgres container.

Example 13-9. docker_containers fact after starting postgres container

```
[
    {
        "AppArmorProfile": "",
        "Args": [
            "postgres"
        ],
        "Config": {
            "AttachStderr": false,
```

```
            "AttachStdin": false,
            "AttachStdout": false,
            "Cmd": [
                "postgres"
            ],
            "CpuShares": 0,
            "Cpuset": "",
            "Domainname": "",
            "Entrypoint": [
                "/docker-entrypoint.sh"
            ],
            "Env": [
                "POSTGRES_PASSWORD=password",
                "POSTGRES_USER=mezzanine",
                "PATH=/usr/lib/postgresql/9.4/bin:/usr/local/sbin:/usr/local/bin:
/usr/sbin:/usr/bin:/sbin:/bin",
                "LANG=en_US.utf8",
                "PG_MAJOR=9.4",
                "PG_VERSION=9.4.0-1.pgdg70+1",
                "PGDATA=/var/lib/postgresql/data"
            ],
            "ExposedPorts": {
                "5432/tcp": {}
            },
            "Hostname": "71f40ec4b58c",
            "Image": "postgres",
            "MacAddress": "",
            "Memory": 0,
            "MemorySwap": 0,
            "NetworkDisabled": false,
            "OnBuild": null,
            "OpenStdin": false,
            "PortSpecs": null,
            "StdinOnce": false,
            "Tty": false,
            "User": "",
            "Volumes": {
                "/var/lib/postgresql/data": {}
            },
            "WorkingDir": ""
        },
        "Created": "2014-12-25T22:59:15.841107151Z",
        "Driver": "aufs",
        "ExecDriver": "native-0.2",
        "HostConfig": {
            "Binds": null,
            "CapAdd": null,
            "CapDrop": null,
            "ContainerIDFile": "",
            "Devices": null,
            "Dns": null,
            "DnsSearch": null,
```

```
            "ExtraHosts": null,
            "IpcMode": "",
            "Links": null,
            "LxcConf": null,
            "NetworkMode": "",
            "PortBindings": {
                "5432/tcp": [
                    {
                        "HostIp": "0.0.0.0",
                        "HostPort": ""
                    }
                ]
            },
            "Privileged": false,
            "PublishAllPorts": false,
            "RestartPolicy": {
                "MaximumRetryCount": 0,
                "Name": ""
            },
            "SecurityOpt": null,
            "VolumesFrom": [
                "data-volume"
            ]
        },
        "HostnamePath": "/mnt/sda1/var/lib/docker/containers/71f40ec4b58c3176030274a
fb025fbd3eb130fe79d4a6a69de473096f335e7eb/hostname",
        "HostsPath": "/mnt/sda1/var/lib/docker/containers/71f40ec4b58c3176030274afb0
25fbd3eb130fe79d4a6a69de473096f335e7eb/hosts",
        "Id": "71f40ec4b58c3176030274afb025fbd3eb130fe79d4a6a69de473096f335e7eb",
        "Image": "b58a816df10fb20c956d39724001d4f2fabddec50e0d9099510f0eb579ec8a45",
        "MountLabel": "",
        "Name": "/high_lovelace",
        "NetworkSettings": {
            "Bridge": "docker0",
            "Gateway": "172.17.42.1",
            "IPAddress": "172.17.0.12",
            "IPPrefixLen": 16,
            "MacAddress": "02:42:ac:11:00:0c",
            "PortMapping": null,
            "Ports": {
                "5432/tcp": [
                    {
                        "HostIp": "0.0.0.0",
                        "HostPort": "49153"
                    }
                ]
            }
        },
        "Path": "/docker-entrypoint.sh",
        "ProcessLabel": "",
        "ResolvConfPath": "/mnt/sda1/var/lib/docker/containers/71f40ec4b58c3176030274
afb025fbd3eb130fe79d4a6a69de473096f335e7eb/resolv.conf",
```

```
    "State": {
        "Error": "",
        "ExitCode": 0,
        "FinishedAt": "0001-01-01T00:00:00Z",
        "OOMKilled": false,
        "Paused": false,
        "Pid": 9625,
        "Restarting": false,
        "Running": true,
        "StartedAt": "2014-12-25T22:59:16.219732465Z"
    },
    "Volumes": {
        "/var/lib/postgresql/data": "/mnt/sda1/var/lib/docker/vfs/dir/4ccd3150c8d
74b9b0feb56df928ac915599e12c3ab573cd4738a18fe3dc6f474"
    },
    "VolumesRW": {
        "/var/lib/postgresql/data": true
    }
    }
]
```

If you wade through this output, you can see that the IP address and mapped port are in the `NetworkSettings` part of the structure:

```
"NetworkSettings": {
    "Bridge": "docker0",
    "Gateway": "172.17.42.1",
    "IPAddress": "172.17.0.12",
    "IPPrefixLen": 16,
    "MacAddress": "02:42:ac:11:00:0c",
    "PortMapping": null,
    "Ports": {
        "5432/tcp": [
            {
                "HostIp": "0.0.0.0",
                "HostPort": "49153"
            }
        ]
    }
},
```

Here's how we extract out the IP address (*172.17.0.12*) and the mapped port number (*49153*) and assign them to variables using the `set_fact` module: [source,yaml+jinja]

```
- name: capture database ip address and mapped port
  set_fact:
    database_host: "{{ docker_containers[0].NetworkSettings.IPAddress }}"
    mapped_database_port: "{{ docker_containers[0].NetworkSettings.Ports[
'5432/tcp'][0].HostPort}}"
```

Waiting for the Database to Start Up

The documentation for the official Postgres Docker image (*https://regis try.hub.docker.com/_/postgres/*) contains the following caveat:

> If there is no database when postgres starts in a container, then postgres will create the default database for you. While this is the expected behavior of postgres, this means that it will not accept incoming connections during that time. This may cause issues when using automation tools, such as fig, that start several containers simultaneously.

This is a great use case for the `wait_for` module, which will block playbook execution until the service accepts TCP connection requests:

```
- name: wait for database to come up
  wait_for: host={{ docker_host }} port={{ mapped_database_port }}
```

Note the use of the `docker_host` variable for specifying the host running Docker. Here's how this variable is defined up in the `vars` section. I've added a line break for clarity, but it should all be on one line.

```
docker_host: "{{ lookup('env', 'DOCKER_HOST') |
  regex_replace('^tcp://(.*):\\d+$', '\\\\1') | default('localhost', true) }}"
```

The issue is that the Docker host will depend on whether you're running on Linux, and therefore running Docker directly on your control machine, or whether you're running on Mac OS X, and are using Boot2Docker to run Docker inside of a virtual machine.

If you're running Docker locally, then `docker_host` should be set to `localhost`. If you're running Boot2Docker, then it should be set to the IP address of the virtual machine.

If you're running Boot2Docker, then you need to have an environment variable named `DOCKER_HOST` defined. Here's what mine looks like:

```
DOCKER_HOST=tcp://192.168.59.103:2375
```

I need to extract the *192.168.59.103* part of that, if `DOCKER_HOST` is defined. If it's not defined, then I want to default to localhost.

I used the `env` lookup plug-in to retrieve the value of the `DOCKER_HOST` environment variable:

```
lookup('env', 'DOCKER_HOST')
```

To extract the IP address, I used the `regex_replace` filter, which is a custom Jinja2 filter defined by Ansible that allows you to do regular expression (note the number of backslashes required):

```
regex_replace('^tcp://(.*):\\d+$', '\\\\1')
```

Finally, I used the standard `default` Jinja2 filter to set a default value of `localhost` for the variable `docker_host` if the `DOCKER_HOST` environment variable wasn't defined. Because the env lookup returns an empty string, I needed to pass `true` as the second argument to the `default` filter to get it to work properly. See the Jinja2 documentation (*http://bit.ly/1DfbzI7*) for more details:

```
default('localhost', true)
```

Initializing the Database

To initialize the database, we need to run the Django `syncdb` and `migrate` commands. (In Django 1.7, you only need to run `migrate`, but Mezzanine defaults to Django 1.6).

We need to run the Mezzanine container for this, but instead of running Gunicorn, we want to pass it the appropriate `syncdb` and `migrate` commands, as well as run the *setsite.py* and *setadmin.py* scripts to set the site ID and the admin password.

```
- name: initialize database
  docker:
    image: lorin/mezzanine:latest
    command: python manage.py {{ item }} --noinput
    wait: yes
    env: "{{ mezzanine_env }}"
  with_items:
    - syncdb
    - migrate

- name: set the site id
  docker:
    image: lorin/mezzanine:latest
    command: /srv/scripts/setsite.py
    env: "{{ setsite_env.update(mezzanine_env) }}{{ setsite_env }}"
    wait: yes

- name: set the admin password
  docker:
    image: lorin/mezzanine:latest
    command: /srv/scripts/setadmin.py
    env: "{{ setadmin_env.update(mezzanine_env) }}{{ setadmin_env }}"
    wait: yes
```

We use the `command` parameter to specify the `syncdb` and `migrate` commands.

We use the `wait` parameter so that the module will block until the process completes. Otherwise, we could have a race condition where the database setup has not completed yet when we start up Mezzanine.

Note the use of the `env` parameter to pass environment variables with the configuration information, including how to connect to the database service. I put all of the environment variables into a `mezzanine_env` variable that's defined like this:

```
mezzanine_env:
  SECRET_KEY: "{{ secret_key }}"
  NEVERCACHE_KEY: "{{ nevercache_key }}"
  ALLOWED_HOSTS: "*"
  DATABASE_NAME: "{{ database_name }}"
  DATABASE_USER: "{{ database_user }}"
  DATABASE_PASSWORD: "{{ database_password }}"
  DATABASE_HOST: "{{ database_host }}"
  DATABASE_PORT: "{{ database_port }}"
  GUNICORN_PORT: "{{ gunicorn_port }}"
```

When we set the site ID, we need to add the additional two environment variables, which I defined in a `setsite_env` variable:

```
setsite_env:
  PROJECT_DIR: "{{ project_dir }}"
  WEBSITE_DOMAIN: "{{ website_domain }}"
```

We need to combine the `mezzanine_env` and `setsite_env` dicts into a single dict and pass that to the `env` parameter.

Unfortunately, there's no simple way to combine two dicts in Ansible, but there's a workaround. Jinja2 has an `update` method that lets you merge one dictionary into another. The problem is that calling this doesn't return the merged dictionary; it just updates the state of the dictionary. Therefore, you need to call the `update` method, and then you need to evaluate the variable. The resulting `env` parameter looks like this:

```
env: "{{ setsite_env.update(mezzanine_env) }}{{ setsite_env }}"
```

Starting the Memcached Container

Starting the Memcached container is straightforward. We don't even need to pass it environment variables since Memcached doesn't need any configuration information. We also don't need to publish any ports since only the Mezzanine container will connect to it via linking.

```
- name: start the memcached container
  docker:
    image: lorin/memcached:latest
    name: memcached
```

Starting the Mezzanine Container

We link the Mezzanine container with the Memcached container and pass it configuration information via the environment.

We also run another container with the same image to run `cron`, since Mezzanine uses `cron` to update information from Twitter:

```
- name: start the mezzanine container
  docker:
    image: lorin/mezzanine:latest
    name: mezzanine
    env: "{{ mezzanine_env }}"
    links: memcached

- name: start the mezzanine cron job
  docker:
    image: lorin/mezzanine:latest
    name: mezzanine
    env: "{{ mezzanine_env }}"
    command: cron -f
```

Starting the Certificate Container

We start the container that holds the TLS certificates. Recall that this container
doesn't run a service, but we need to start it so that we can mount the volume into the
nginx container.

```
- name: start the cert container
  docker:
    image: lorin/certs:latest
    name: certs
```

Starting the Nginx Container

Finally, we start the Nginx container. This container needs to expose ports 80 and 443
to the world. It also needs to mount volumes for the static content and the TLS certificates. Finally, we link it to the Mezzanine container so that the Mezzanine hostname
will resolve to the container that runs Mezzanine:

```
- name: run nginx
  docker:
    image: lorin/nginx-mezzanine:latest
    ports:
      - 80:80
      - 443:443
    name: nginx
    volumes_from:
      - mezzanine
      - certs
    links: mezzanine
```

And that's it! If you're running Docker locally on your Linux machine, you should
now be able to access Mezzanine at *http://localhost* and *https://localhost*. If you're running Boot2Docker on OS X, you should be able to access it at the IP address of your
Boot2Docker VM, which you can get by doing:

```
boot2docker ip
```

On my machine, it's at *http://192.168.59.103* and *https://192.168.59.103*, or you can use xip.io and access it at *https://192.168.59.103.xip.io.f1326.20*.

The Entire Playbook

Example 13-10 shows the entire playbook, and Example 13-11 shows the contents of the *secrets.yml* file.

Example 13-10. run-mezzanine.yml

```
#!/usr/bin/env ansible-playbook
---
- name: run mezzanine from containers
  hosts: localhost
  vars_files:
    - secrets.yml
  vars:
    # The postgres container uses the same name for the database
    # and the user
    database_name: mezzanine
    database_user: mezzanine
    database_port: 5432
    gunicorn_port: 8000
    docker_host: "{{ lookup('env', 'DOCKER_HOST') |
regex_replace('^tcp://(.*):\\d+$', '\\\\1') | default('localhost', true) }}"
    project_dir: /srv/project
    website_domain: "{{ docker_host }}.xip.io"
    mezzanine_env:
      SECRET_KEY: "{{ secret_key }}"
      NEVERCACHE_KEY: "{{ nevercache_key }}"
      ALLOWED_HOSTS: "*"
      DATABASE_NAME: "{{ database_name }}"
      DATABASE_USER: "{{ database_user }}"
      DATABASE_PASSWORD: "{{ database_password }}"
      DATABASE_HOST: "{{ database_host }}"
      DATABASE_PORT: "{{ database_port }}"
      GUNICORN_PORT: "{{ gunicorn_port }}"
    setadmin_env:
      PROJECT_DIR: "{{ project_dir }}"
      ADMIN_PASSWORD: "{{ admin_password }}"
    setsite_env:
      PROJECT_DIR: "{{ project_dir }}"
      WEBSITE_DOMAIN: "{{ website_domain }}"

  tasks:
    - name: start the postgres container
      docker:
        image: postgres:9.4
        name: postgres
        publish_all_ports: True
```

```yaml
        env:
          POSTGRES_USER: "{{ database_user }}"
          POSTGRES_PASSWORD: "{{ database_password }}"

      - name: capture database ip address and mapped port
        set_fact:
          database_host: "{{ docker_containers[0].NetworkSettings.IPAddress }}"
          mapped_database_port: "{{ docker_containers[0].NetworkSettings.Ports[
'5432/tcp'][0].HostPort}}"

      - name: wait for database to come up
        wait_for: host={{ docker_host }} port={{ mapped_database_port }}

      - name: initialize database
        docker:
          image: lorin/mezzanine:latest
          command: python manage.py {{ item }} --noinput
          wait: True
          env: "{{ mezzanine_env }}"
        with_items:
          - syncdb
          - migrate
        register: django

      - name: set the site id
        docker:
          image: lorin/mezzanine:latest
          command: /srv/scripts/setsite.py
          env: "{{ setsite_env.update(mezzanine_env) }}{{ setsite_env }}"
          wait: yes

      - name: set the admin password
        docker:
          image: lorin/mezzanine:latest
          command: /srv/scripts/setadmin.py
          env: "{{ setadmin_env.update(mezzanine_env) }}{{ setadmin_env }}"
          wait: yes

      - name: start the memcached container
        docker:
          image: lorin/memcached:latest
          name: memcached

      - name: start the mezzanine container
        docker:
          image: lorin/mezzanine:latest
          name: mezzanine
          env: "{{ mezzanine_env }}"
          links: memcached

      - name: start the mezzanine cron job
        docker:
```

```
    image: lorin/mezzanine:latest
    name: mezzanine
    env: "{{ mezzanine_env }}"
    command: cron -f

- name: start the cert container
  docker:
    image: lorin/certs:latest
    name: certs

- name: run nginx
  docker:
    image: lorin/nginx-mezzanine:latest
    ports:
      - 80:80
      - 443:443
    name: nginx
    volumes_from:
      - mezzanine
      - certs
    links: mezzanine
```

Example 13-11. secrets.yml

```
database_password: password
secret_key: randomsecretkey
nevercache_key: randomnevercachekey
admin_password: password
```

Because the Docker project is relatively young, much of the tooling is still in flux, and Docker deployment patterns are still evolving. Many of these emerging tools likely will have functionality that overlaps with Ansible when it comes to orchestrating containers.

Even if another tool emerges to dominate the world of Docker orchestration, I still believe Ansible will continue to be a useful tool for operators and developers.

## CHAPTER 14

Debugging Ansible Playbooks

Let's face it: mistakes happen. Whether it's a bug in a playbook, or a config file on your control machine with the wrong configuration value, eventually something's going to go wrong. In this last chapter, I'll review some techniques you can use to help track down those errors.

Debugging SSH Issues

Sometimes, Ansible fails to make a successful SSH connection with the host. When this happens, it's helpful to see exactly what arguments Ansible is passing to the underlying SSH client so that you can reproduce the problem manually on the command line.

If you invoke `ansible-playbook` with the `-vvv` argument, you can see the exact SSH commands that Ansible invokes. This can be handy for debugging.

Example 14-1 shows some sample Ansible output for executing a module that copies a file.

Example 14-1. Example output when verbose flags are enabled

```
TASK: [copy TLS key] *********************************************************
<127.0.0.1> ESTABLISH CONNECTION FOR USER: vagrant
<127.0.0.1> ESTABLISH CONNECTION FOR USER: vagrant
<127.0.0.1> EXEC ['ssh', '-C', '-tt', '-q', '-o', 'ControlMaster=auto', '-o',
'ControlPersist=60s', '-o', 'ControlPath=/Users/lorinhochstein/.ansible/cp/
ansible-ssh-%h-%p-%r', '-o', 'Port=2222', '-o', u'IdentityFile="/Users/
lorinhochstein/.vagrant.d/insecure_private_key"', '-o', 'KbdInteractive
Authentication=no', '-o', 'PreferredAuthentications=gssapi-with-mic,gssapi-keyex,
hostbased,publickey', '-o', 'PasswordAuthentication=no', '-o', 'User=vagrant',
'-o', 'ConnectTimeout=10', u'127.0.0.1', u'/bin/sh -c \'sudo -k && sudo -H -S -p
"[sudo via ansible, key=ypkyixkznvqmrbmlhezlnlujtdhrcoam] password: " -u root
```

```
/bin/sh -c \'"\'"\'echo SUDO-SUCCESS-ypkyixkznvqmrbmlhezlnlujtdhrcoam; rc=0;
[ -r "/etc/nginx/ssl/nginx.key" ] || rc=2; [ -f "/etc/nginx/ssl/nginx.key" ] ||
rc=1; [ -d "/etc/nginx/ssl/nginx.key" ] && echo 3 && exit 0; (/usr/bin/md5sum
/etc/nginx/ssl/nginx.key 2>/dev/null) || (/sbin/md5sum -q /etc/nginx/ssl/nginx.key
2>/dev/null) || (/usr/bin/digest -a md5 /etc/nginx/ssl/nginx.key 2>/dev/null) ||
(/sbin/md5 -q /etc/nginx/ssl/nginx.key 2>/dev/null) || (/usr/bin/md5 -n /etc/
nginx/ssl/nginx.key 2>/dev/null) || (/bin/md5 -q /etc/nginx/ssl/nginx.key
2>/dev/null) || (/usr/bin/csum -h MD5 /etc/nginx/ssl/nginx.key 2>/dev/null) ||
(/bin/csum -h MD5 /etc/nginx/ssl/nginx.key 2>/dev/null) || (echo "${rc}
/etc/nginx/ssl/nginx.key")\'"\'"\'\'']
```

Sometimes you might need to use -vvvv when debugging a connection issue, in order
to see an error message that the SSH client is throwing.

For example, if the host doesn't have SSH running, you'll see an error that looks like
this:

```
testserver | FAILED => SSH encountered an unknown error. The output was:
OpenSSH_6.2p2, OSSLShim 0.9.8r 8 Dec 2011
debug1: Reading configuration data /etc/ssh_config
debug1: /etc/ssh_config line 20: Applying options for *
debug1: /etc/ssh_config line 102: Applying options for *
debug1: auto-mux: Trying existing master
debug1: Control socket "/Users/lorinhochstein/.ansible/cp/ansible-ssh-127.0.0.1-
2222-vagrant" does not exist
debug2: ssh_connect: needpriv 0
debug1: Connecting to 127.0.0.1 [127.0.0.1] port 2222.
debug2: fd 3 setting O_NONBLOCK
debug1: connect to address 127.0.0.1 port 2222: Connection refused
ssh: connect to host 127.0.0.1 port 2222: Connection refused
```

If you have host key verification enabled, and the host key in ~/.ssh/known_hosts
doesn't match the host key of the server, then using -vvvv will output an error that
looks like this:

```
@@@@@@@@@@@@@@@@@@@@@@@@@@@@@@@@@@@@@@@@@@@@@@@@@@@@@@@@@@@@@
@    WARNING: REMOTE HOST IDENTIFICATION HAS CHANGED!    @
@@@@@@@@@@@@@@@@@@@@@@@@@@@@@@@@@@@@@@@@@@@@@@@@@@@@@@@@@@@@@
IT IS POSSIBLE THAT SOMEONE IS DOING SOMETHING NASTY!
Someone could be eavesdropping on you right now (man-in-the-middle attack)!
It is also possible that a host key has just been changed.
The fingerprint for the RSA key sent by the remote host is
c3:99:c2:8f:18:ef:68:fe:ca:86:a9:f5:95:9e:a7:23.
Please contact your system administrator.
Add correct host key in /Users/lorinhochstein/.ssh/known_hosts to get rid of this
message.
Offending RSA key in /Users/lorinhochstein/.ssh/known_hosts:1
RSA host key for [127.0.0.1]:2222 has changed and you have requested strict
checking.
Host key verification failed.
```

If that's the case, you should delete the offending entry from your *~/.ssh/known_hosts* file.

The Debug Module

We've used the `debug` module several times in this book. It's Ansible's version of a `print` statement. As shown in Example 14-2, you can use it to print out either the value of a variable or an arbitrary string.

Example 14-2. The debug module in action

```
- debug: var=myvariable
- debug: msg="The value of myvariable is {{ var }}"
```

As we discussed in Chapter 4, you can print out the values of all the variables associated with the current host by invoking:

```
- debug: var=hostvars[inventory_hostname]
```

The Assert Module

The `assert` module will fail with an error if a specified condition is not met. For example, to fail the playbook if there's no `eth1` interface:

```
- name: assert that eth1 interface exists
  assert:
    that: ansible_eth1 is defined
```

When debugging a playbook, it can be helpful to insert assertions so that a failure happens as soon as some assumption you've made has been violated.

If you want to check on the status of some file on the host's file system, then it's useful to call the `stat` module first and make some assertion based on the return value of that module:

```
- name: stat /opt/foo
  stat: path=/opt/foo
  register: st

- name: assert that /opt/foo is a directory
  assert:
    that: st.stat.isdir
```

The `stat` module collects information about the state of a file path. It returns a dictionary that contains a *stat* field with the values shown in Table 14-1.

Table 14-1. stat module return values

Field	Description
atime	Last access time of path, in Unix timestamp format
ctime	Creation time of path, in Unix timestamp format
dev	Numerical ID of the device that the inode resides on
exists	True if path exists
gid	Numerical group ID of path owner
inode	Inode number
isblk	True if path is block special device file
ischr	True if path is character special device file
isdir	True if path is a directory
isfifo	True if path is a FIFO (named pipe)
isgid	True if set-group-ID bit is set on file
islnk	True if path is a symbolic link
isreg	True if path is a regular file
issock	True if path is a Unix domain socket
isuid	True if set-user-ID bit is set on file
mode	File mode as a string, in octal (e.g. "1777")
mtime	Last modification time of path, in Unix timestamp format
nlink	Number of hard links to the file
pw_name	Login name of file owner
rgrp	True if group read permission enabled
roth	True if other read permission enabled
rusr	True if user read permission enabled

Field	Description
size	File size in bytes, if regular file
uid	Numerical user ID of path owner
wgrp	True if group write permission enabled
woth	True if other write permission enabled
wusr	True if user write permission enabled
xgrp	True if group execute permission enabled
xoth	True if other execute permission enabled
xusr	True if user execute permission enabled

Checking Your Playbook Before Execution

The `ansible-playbook` command supports several flags that allow you to sanity check your playbook before you execute it.

Syntax Check

The `--syntax-check` flag, as shown in Example 14-3, will check that your playbook's syntax is valid, but it will not execute it.

Example 14-3. syntax check

```
$ ansible-playbook --syntax-check playbook.yml
```

List Hosts

The `--list-hosts` flag, as shown in Example 14-4, will output the hosts that the playbook will run against, but it will not execute the playbook.

Example 14-4. list hosts

```
$ ansible-playbook --list-hosts playbook.yml
```

Sometimes you get the dreaded error:

`ERROR: provided hosts list is empty`

There must be one host explicitly specified in your inventory, or you'll get this error, even if your playbook only runs against the localhost. If your inventory is initially empty (perhaps because you're using a dynamic inventory script and haven't launched any hosts yet), you can work around this by explicitly adding the following line to your inventory:

`localhost ansible_connection=local`

List Tasks

The `--list-tasks` flag, shown in Example 14-5, will output the tasks that the playbook will run against. It will not execute the playbook.

Example 14-5. list tasks

```
$ ansible-playbook --list-tasks playbook.yml
```

Recall that we used this flag in Example 6-1 to list the tasks in our first Mezzanine playbook.

Check Mode

The `-C` and `--check` flags will run Ansible in check mode (sometimes known as *dry-run*), which tells you whether each task in the playbook would modify the host, but does not make any actual changes to the server.

```
$ ansible-playbook -C playbook.yml
$ ansible-playbook --check playbook.yml
```

One of the challenges with using check mode is that later parts of a playbook might only succeed if earlier parts of the playbook were actually executed. Running check mode on Example 6-27 yields the error shown in Example 14-6 because the task depended on an earlier task installing the Git program on the host.

Example 14-6. Check mode failing on a correct playbook

```
PLAY [Deploy mezzanine] ************************************************

GATHERING FACTS *******************************************************
ok: [web]

TASK: [install apt packages] ******************************************
changed: [web] => (item=git,libjpeg-dev,libpq-dev,memcached,nginx,postgresql,py
thon-dev,python-pip,python-psycopg2,python-setuptools,python-virtualenv,supervi
sor)
```

```
TASK: [check out the repository on the host] ********************************
failed: [web] => {"failed": true}
msg: Failed to find required executable git

FATAL: all hosts have already failed -- aborting
```

See Chapter 10 for more details on how modules implement check mode.

Diff (Show File Changes)

The -D and -diff flags will output differences for any files that will be changed on the remote machine. It's a helpful option to use in conjunction with --check to show how Ansible would change the file if it were run normally.

```
$ ansible-playbook -D --check playbook.yml
$ ansible-playbook --diff --check playbook.yml
```

If Ansible would modify any files (e.g., using modules such as copy, template, and lineinfile), then it will show the changes in .diff format, like this:

```
TASK: [set the gunicorn config file] ****************************************
--- before: /home/vagrant/mezzanine-example/project/gunicorn.conf.py
+++ after: /Users/lorinhochstein/dev/ansiblebook/ch06/playbooks/templates/gunicor
n.conf.py.j2
@@ -1,7 +1,7 @@
 from __future__ import unicode_literals
 import multiprocessing

 bind = "127.0.0.1:8000"
 workers = multiprocessing.cpu_count() * 2 + 1
-loglevel = "error"
+loglevel = "warning"
 proc_name = "mezzanine-example"
```

Limiting Which Tasks Run

Sometimes you don't want Ansible to run every single task in your playbook, particularly when you're first writing and debugging the playbook. Ansible provides several command-line options that let you control which tasks run.

Step

The --step flag, shown in Example 14-7, will have Ansible prompt you before running each task, like this:

```
Perform task: install packages (y/n/c):
```

You can choose to execute the task (y), skip it (n), or tell Ansible to continue running the rest of the playbook without prompting you (c).

Example 14-7. step

```
$ ansible-playbook --step playbook.yml
```

Start-at-Task

The `--start-at-task taskname` flag, shown in Example 14-8, tells Ansible to start running the playbook at the specified task, instead of at the beginning. This can be very handy if one of your tasks failed because there was a bug in one of your tasks, and you want to re-run your playbook starting at the task you just fixed.

Example 14-8. start-at-task

```
$ ansible-playbook --start-at-task="install packages" playbook.yml
```

Tags

Ansible allows you to add one or more tags to a task or a play. For example, here's a play that's tagged with foo and a task that's tagged with bar and quux:

```
- hosts: myservers
  tags:
    - foo
  tasks:
    - name: install editors
      apt: name={{ item }}
      with_items:
        - vim
        - emacs
        - nano

    - name: run arbitrary command
      command: /opt/myprog
      tags:
        - bar
        - quux
```

Use the `-t tagnames` or `--tags tagnames` flag to tell Ansible to only run plays and tasks that have certain tags. Use the `--skip-tags tagnames` flag to tell Ansible to skip plays and tasks that have certain tags. See Example 14-9.

Example 14-9. Running or skipping tags

```
$ ansible-playbook -t foo,bar playbook.yml
$ ansible-playbook --tags=foo,bar playbook.yml
$ ansible-playbook --skip-tags=baz,quux playbook.yml
```

Onward

As this chapter ends, so does our journey together. And yet, your journey with Ansible is just beginning. I hope that you'll come to enjoy working with it as much as I do, and that the next time you encounter colleagues who is in clear need of an automation tool, you'll show them how Ansible can make their lives easier.

SSH

Because Ansible uses SSH as its transport mechanism, you'll need to understand some of SSH's features to take advantage of them with Ansible.

Native SSH

By default, Ansible uses the native SSH client installed on your operating system. This means that Ansible can take advantage of all of the typical SSH features, including Kerberos and jump hosts. If you have a *~/.ssh/config* file with custom configurations for your SSH setup, Ansible will respect these settings.

SSH Agent

There's a handy program called *ssh-agent* that simplifies working with SSH private keys.

When ssh-agent is running on your machine, you can add private keys to it using the ssh-add command.

```
$ ssh-add /path/to/keyfile.pem
```

> The SSH_AUTH_SOCK environment variable must be set, or the ssh-add command will not be able to communicate with ssh-agent. See "Starting Up ssh-agent" on page 274.

You can use the -L flag with the ssh_add program to see which keys have been added to your agent, as shown in Example A-1. This example shows that there are two keys in the agent.

Example A-1. Listing the keys in the agent

```
$ ssh-add -L
ssh-rsa AAAAB3NzaC1yc2EAAAADAQABAAAABAQDWAfog5tz4W9bPVbPDlNC8HWMfhjTgKOhpSZYI+clc
 e3/pz5viqsHDQIjzSImoVzIOTV0tOIfE8qMkqEYk7igESccCy0zN9VnD6EfYVkEx1C+xqkCtZTEVuQn
 d+4qyo222EAVkHm6bAhgyoA9nt9Um9WFO0045yHZL2Do9Z7KXTS4xOqeGF5vv7SiuKcsLjORPcWcYqC
 fYdrdUdRD9dFq7zFKmpCPJqNwDQDrXbgaTOe+H6cu2f4RrJLp88WY8voB3zJ7avv68eOgah82dovSgw
 hcsZp4SycZSTy+WqZQhzLogaifvtdgdzaooxNtsm+qRvQJyHkwdoXR6nJgt /Users/lorinhochste
 in/.ssh/id_rsa
ssh-rsa AAAAB3NzaC1yc2EAAAABIwAAAQEA6NF8iallvQVp22WDkTkyrtvp9eWW6A8YVr+kz4TjGYe7
 gHzIw+niNltGEFHzD8+v1I2YJ6oXevct1YeS0o9HZyN1Q9qgCgzUFtdOKLv6IedplqoPkcmF0aYet2P
 kEDo3MlTBckFXPITAMzF8dJSIFo9D8HfdOV0IAdx4O7PtixWKn5y2hMNG0zQPyUecp4pzC6kivAIhyf
 HilFR61RGL+GPXQ2MWZWFYbAGjyiYJnAmCP3NOTd0jMZEnDkbUvxhMmBYSdETk1rRgm+R4LOzFUGaHq
 HDFIPKcF96hrucXzcWyLbIbEgE98OHlnVYCzRdK8jlqm8tehUc9c9WhQ== insecure_private_key
```

When you try to make a connection to a remote host, and you have ssh-agent running, the SSH client will try to use the keys stored in ssh-agent to authenticate with the host.

Using an SSH agent has several advantages:

- The SSH agent makes it easier to work with encrypted SSH private keys. If you use an encrypted SSH private key, then the private key file is protected with a password. When you use this key to make an SSH connection to a host, then you will be prompted to type in the password. With an encrypted private key, even if somebody got access to your private SSH key, they wouldn't be able to use it without the password. If you use an encrypted SSH private key, and you aren't using an SSH agent, then you have to type in the encryption password each time you use the private key. If you are using an SSH agent, then you only have to type the private key password when you add the key to the agent.

- If you are using Ansible to manage hosts that use different SSH keys, using an SSH agent simplifies your Ansible configuration files; you don't have to explicitly specify the *ansible_ssh_private_key_file* on your hosts as we did back in Example 1-1.

- If you need to make an SSH connection from your remote host to a different host (e.g., cloning a private Git repository over SSH), you can take advantage of *agent forwarding* so that you don't have to copy private SSH keys over to the remote host. We explain agent forwarding next.

Starting Up ssh-agent

How you start up the SSH agent varies depending on which operating system you're running.

Mac OS X

Mac OS X comes preconfigured to run ssh-agent, so there's nothing you need to do.

Linux

If you're running on Linux, you'll need to start up ssh-agent yourself and ensure its environment variables are set correctly. If you invoke ssh-agent directly, it will output the environment variables you'll need to set. For example:

```
$ ssh-agent
SSH_AUTH_SOCK=/tmp/ssh-YI7PBGlkOteo/agent.2547; export SSH_AUTH_SOCK;
SSH_AGENT_PID=2548; export SSH_AGENT_PID;
echo Agent pid 2548;
```

You can automatically export these environment variables by invoking ssh-agent like this:

```
$ eval $(ssh-agent)
```

You'll also want to ensure that you only have one instance of ssh-agent running at a time. There are various helper tools on Linux, such as *Keychain* and *Gnome Keyring*, for managing ssh-agent startup for you, or you can modify your *.profile* file to ensure that ssh-agent starts up exactly once in each login shell. Configuring your account for ssh-agent is beyond the scope of this book, so I recommend you consult your Linux distribution's documentation for more details on how to set this up.

Agent Forwarding

If you are cloning a Git repository over SSH, you'll need to use an SSH private key recognized by your Git server. I like to avoid copying private SSH keys to my hosts, in order to limit the damage in case a host ever gets compromised.

One way to avoid copying SSH private keys around is to use the ssh-agent program on your local machine, with agent forwarding. If you SSH from your laptop to host *A*, and you have agent forwarding enabled, then agent forwarding allows you to SSH from host *A* to host *B* using the private key that resides on your laptop.

Figure A-1 shows an example of agent forwarding in action. Let's say you want to check out a private repository from GitHub, using SSH. You have ssh-agent running on your laptop, and you've added your private key using the ssh-add command.

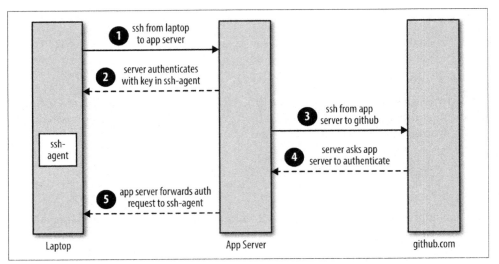

Figure A-1. Agent forwarding in action

If you were manually SSHing to the app server, you would call the `ssh` command with the `-A` flag, which enables agent forwarding:

```
$ ssh -A myuser@myappserver.example.com
```

On the app server, you check out a Git repository using an SSH URL:

```
$ git clone git@github.com:lorin/mezzanine-example.git
```

Git will connect via SSH to GitHub. The GitHub SSH server will try to authenticate against the SSH client on the app server. The app server doesn't know your private key. However, because you enabled agent forwarding, the SSH client on the app server will connect back to ssh-agent running on your laptop, which will handle the authentication.

There are a couple of issues you need to keep in mind in using agent forwarding with Ansible.

First, you need to tell Ansible to enable agent forwarding when it connects to remote machines, because SSH does not enable agent forwarding by default.

You can enable agent forwarding for all nodes you SSH to by adding the following lines to your *~/.ssh/config* file on your control machine:

```
Host *
    ForwardAgent yes
```

Or, if you only want to enable agent forwarding for a specific server, add this:

```
Host appserver.example.com
    ForwardAgent yes
```

If, instead, you only want to enable agent forwarding for Ansible, then you can edit your *ansible.cfg* file by adding it to the `ssh_args` parameter in the `ssh_connection` section:

```
[ssh_connection]
ssh_args = -o ControlMaster=auto -o ControlPersist=60s -o ForwardAgent=yes
```

Here, I used the more verbose `-o ForwardAgent=yes` flag instead of the shorter `-A` flag, but it does the same thing.

The `ControlMaster` and `ControlPersist` settings are needed for a performance optimization called *SSH multiplexing*. They are on by default, but if you override the `ssh_args` variable, then you need to explicitly specify them or you will disable this performance boost. We discuss SSH multiplexing in Chapter 9.

Sudo and Agent Forwarding

When you enable agent forwarding, the remote machine sets the `SSH_AUTH_SOCK` environment variable, which contains a path to a UNIX-domain socket (e.g., */tmp/ ssh-FShDVu5924/agent.5924*). However, if you do sudo, then the `SSH_AUTH_SOCK` environment variable won't carry over unless you explicitly configure sudo to allow this behavior.

To allow the `SSH_AUTH_SOCK` variable to carry over via sudo to the root user, we can add the following line either to the */etc/sudoers* file or (on Debian-based distributions like Ubuntu) to its own file in the */etc/sudoers.d* directory.

```
Defaults>root env_keep+=SSH_AUTH_SOCK
```

Let's call this file *99-keep-ssh-auth-sock-env* and put it in the files directory on our local machine.

Validating Files

The `copy` and `template` modules support a `validate` clause. This clause lets you specify a program to run against the file that Ansible will generate. Use `%s` as a placeholder for the filename. For example:

```
validate: visudo -cf %s
```

When the `validate` clause is present, Ansible will copy the file to a temporary directory first and then run the specified validation program. If the validation program returns success (0), then Ansible will copy the file from the temporary location to the proper destination. If the validation program returns a non-zero return code, Ansible will return an error that looks like this:

```
failed: [myhost] => {"checksum": "ac32f572f0a670c3579ac2864cc3069ee8a19588",
"failed": true}
```

```
   msg: failed to validate: rc:1 error:

   FATAL: all hosts have already failed -- aborting
```

Since a bad sudoers file can keep us from accessing it as root, it's always a good idea to validate a sudoers file using the *visudo* program. For a cautionary tale about invalid sudoers files, see Ansible contributor Jan-Piet Mens's blog post, "Don't try this at the office: /etc/sudoers." (*http://bit.ly/1DfeQY7*).

```
- name: copy the sudoers file so we can do agent forwarding
  copy:
    src: files/99-keep-ssh-auth-sock-env
    dest: /etc/sudoers.d/99-keep-ssh-auth-sock-env
    owner: root group=root mode=0440
    validate: visudo -cf %s
```

Unfortunately, it's not currently possible to sudo as a non-root user and use agent forwarding. For example, let's say you wanted to sudo from the ubuntu user to a deploy user. The problem is that the UNIX-domain socket pointed to be the SSH_AUTH_SOCK is owned by the ubuntu user and won't be readable or writeable by the deploy user.

As a workaround, you can always invoke the Git module as root and then change the permissions with the file module, as shown in Example A-2.

Example A-2. Cloning as root and changing permissions

```
- name: verify the config is valid sudoers file
  local_action: command visudo -cf files/99-keep-ssh-auth-sock-env
  sudo: True

- name: copy the sudoers file so we can do agent forwarding
  copy: >
    src=files/99-keep-ssh-auth-sock-env
    dest=/etc/sudoers.d/99-keep-ssh-auth-sock-env
    owner=root group=root mode=0440
    validate='visudo -cf %s'
  sudo: True

- name: check out my private git repository
  git: repo=git@github.com:lorin/mezzanine-example.git dest={{ proj_path }}
  sudo: True

- name: set file ownership
  file: >
    path={{ proj_path }} state=directory recurse=yes
    owner={{ user }} group={{ user }}
  sudo: True
```

Host Keys

Every host that runs an SSH server has an associated host key. The host key acts like a signature that uniquely identifies the host. Host keys exist to prevent man-in-the-middle attacks. If you're cloning a Git repository over SSH from GitHub, you don't really know whether the server that claims to be github.com is really GitHub's server, or is an impostor that used DNS spoofing to pretend to be github.com. Host keys allow you to check that the server that claims to be github.com really is github.com. This means that you need to have the host key (a copy of what the signature should look like) before you try to connect to the host.

Ansible will check the host key by default, although you can disable this behavior in *ansible.cfg*, like this:

```
[defaults]
host_key_checking = False
```

Host key checking also comes into play with the `git` module. Recall in Chapter 6 how the `git` module took an `accept_hostkey` parameter:

```
- name: check out the repository on the host
  git: repo={{ repo_url }} dest={{ proj_path }} accept_hostkey=yes
```

The `git` module can hang when cloning a Git repository using the SSH protocol if host key checking is enabled on the host and the Git server's SSH host key is not known to the host.

The simplest approach is to use the `accept_hostkey` parameter to tell Git to automatically accept the host key if it isn't known, which is the approach we use in Example 6-5.

Many people simply accept the host key and don't worry about these types of man-in-the-middle attacks. That's what we did in our playbook, by specifying `accept_host key=yes` as an argument when invoking the `git` module. However, if you are more security conscious and don't want to automatically accept the host key, then you can manually retrieve and verify GitHub's host key, and then add it to the system-wide */etc/ssh/known_hosts* file or, for a specific user, to the user's *~/.ssh/known_hosts* file.

To manually verify GitHub's SSH host key, you'll need to get the SSH host key fingerprint from the Git server using some kind of out-of-band channel. If you're using GitHub as your Git server, you can look up its SSH key fingerprint (*http://bit.ly/1DffcxK*) on the GitHub website.

As of this writing, GitHub's RSA fingerprint is `16:27:ac:a5:76:28:2d:36:63:1b:56:4d:eb:df:a6:48`, but don't take my word for it—go check the website.

Next, you need to retrieve the full SSH host key. You can use the ssh-keyscan program to retrieve the host key associated with the host with hostname `github.com`. I like to put files that Ansible will deal with in the *files* directory, so let's do that:

```
$ mkdir files
$ ssh-keyscan github.com > files/known_hosts
```

The output looks like this:

```
github.com ssh-rsa
AAAAB3NzaC1yc2EAAAABIwAAAQEAq2A7hRGmdnm9tUDbO9IDSwBK6TbQa+PXYPCPy6rbTrTtw7PHkccK
rpp0yVhp5HdEIcKr6pLlVDBfOLX9QUsyCOV0wzfjIJNlGEYsdlLJizHhbn2mUjvSAHQqZETYP81eFzLQ
NnPHt4EVVUh7VfDESU84KezmD5QlWpXLmvU31/yMf+Se8xhHTvKSCZIFImWwoG6mbUoWf9nzpIoaSjB+
weqqUUmpaaasXVal72J+UX2B+2RPW3RcT0eOzQgqlJL3RKrTJvdsjE3JEAvGq3lGHSZXy28G3skua2Sm
Vi/w4yCE6gbODqnTWlg7+wC604ydGXA8VJiS5ap43JXiUFFAaQ==
```

For the more paranoid, the `ssh-keyscan` command supports an `-H` flag so that the hostname won't show up in the *known_hosts* file. Even if somebody gets access to your known hosts file, they can't tell what the hostnames are. When using this flag, the output looks like this:

```
|1|BI+Z8H3hzbcmTWna9R4orrwrNrg=|wCxJf50pTQ83JFzyXG4aNLxEmzc= ssh-rsa AAAAB3NzaC1y
c2EAAAABIwAAAQEAq2A7hRGmdnm9tUDbO9IDSwBK6TbQa+PXYPCPy6rbTrTtw7PHkccKrpp0yVhp5HdEI
cKr6pLlVDBfOLX9QUsyCOV0wzfjIJNlGEYsdlLJizHhbn2mUjvSAHQqZETYP81eFzLQNnPHt4EVVUh7Vf
DESU84KezmD5QlWpXLmvU31/yMf+Se8xhHTvKSCZIFImWwoG6mbUoWf9nzpIoaSjB+weqqUUmpaaasXVa
l72J+UX2B+2RPW3RcT0eOzQgqlJL3RKrTJvdsjE3JEAvGq3lGHSZXy28G3skua2SmVi/w4yCE6gbODqnT
Wlg7+wC604ydGXA8VJiS5ap43JXiUFFAaQ==
```

You then need to verify that the host key in the *files/known_hosts* file matches the fingerprint you found on GitHub. You can check with the *ssh-keygen* program:

```
$ ssh-keygen -lf files/known_hosts
```

The output should match the RSA fingerprint advertised on the website, like this:

```
2048 16:27:ac:a5:76:28:2d:36:63:1b:56:4d:eb:df:a6:48 github.com (RSA)
```

Now that you are confident that you have the correct host key for your Git server, you can use the copy module to copy it to */etc/ssh/known_hosts*.

```
- name: copy system-wide known hosts
  copy: src=files/known_hosts dest=/etc/ssh/known_hosts owner=root group=root
  mode=0644
```

Alternatively, you can copy it to a specific user's *~/.ssh/known_hosts*. Example A-3 shows how to copy the known hosts file from the control machine to the remote hosts.

Example A-3. Adding known host

```
- name: ensure the ~/.ssh directory exists
  file: path=~/.ssh state=directory
```

```
- name: copy known hosts file
  copy: src=files/known_hosts dest=~/.ssh/known_hosts mode=0600
```

A Bad Host Key Can Cause Problems, Even with Key Checking Disabled

If you have disabled host key checking in Ansible by setting host_key_checking to false in your *ansible.cfg* file, and the host key for the host that Ansible is trying to connect to does not match the key entry in your *~/.ssh/known_hosts* file, then agent forwarding won't work. Trying to clone a Git repository will then result in an error that looks like this:

```
TASK: [check out the repository on the host] ********************************
failed: [web] => {"cmd": "/usr/bin/git ls-remote git@github.com:lorin/
mezzanine- example.git -h refs/heads/HEAD", "failed": true, "rc": 128}
stderr: Permission denied (publickey).
fatal: Could not read from remote repository.

Please make sure you have the correct access rights
and the repository exists.

msg: Permission denied (publickey).
fatal: Could not read from remote repository.

Please make sure you have the correct access rights
and the repository exists.

FATAL: all hosts have already failed -- aborting
```

This can happen if you're using Vagrant, and you destroy a Vagrant machine and then create a new one, because the host key changes every time you create a new Vagrant machine. You can check if agent forwarding is working by doing this:

```
$ ansible web -a "ssh-add -l"
```

If it's working, you'll see output like:

```
web | success | rc=0 >>
2048 e5:ec:48:d3:ec:5e:67:b0:22:32:6e:ab:dd:91:f9:cf /Users/lorinhochstein/
.ssh/id_rsa (RSA)
```

If it's not working, you'll see output like:

```
web | FAILED | rc=2 >>
Could not open a connection to your authentication agent.
```

If this happens to you, then delete the appropriate entry from your *~/.ssh/known_hosts* file.

Note that because of SSH multiplexing, Ansible maintains an open SSH connection to the host for 60 seconds, and you need to wait for this connection to expire, or you won't see the effect of modifying the *known_hosts* file.

Clearly, there's a lot more work involved in verifying an SSH host key than blindly accepting it. As is often the case, there's a trade-off between security and convenience.

Default Settings

Ansible defines a number of settings. You can override the default values of these settings in the Ansible configuration file or as an environment variable.

The configuration file is broken up into the following sections:

- defaults
- ssh_connection
- paramiko
- accelerate

Table B-1. Defaults section

Config name	Environment variable	Default value
hostfile	ANSIBLE_HOSTS	/etc/ansible/hosts
library	ANSIBLE_LIBRARY	(none)
roles_path	ANSIBLE_ROLES_PATH	/etc/ansible/roles
remote_tmp	ANSIBLE_REMOTE_TEMP	$HOME/.ansible/tmp
module_name	(none)	command
pattern	(none)	*
forks	ANSIBLE_FORKS	5
module_args	ANSIBLE_MODULE_ARGS	(empty string)

Config name	Environment variable	Default value
module_lang	ANSIBLE_MODULE_LANG	en_US.UTF-8
timeout	ANSIBLE_TIMEOUT	10
poll_interval	ANSIBLE_POLL_INTERVAL	15
remote_user	ANSIBLE_REMOTE_USER	current user
ask_pass	ANSIBLE_ASK_PASS	false
private_key_file	ANSIBLE_PRIVATE_KEY_FILE	(none)
sudo_user	ANSIBLE_SUDO_USER	root
ask_sudo_pass	ANSIBLE_ASK_SUDO_PASS	false
remote_port	ANSIBLE_REMOTE_PORT	(none)
ask_vault_pass	ANSIBLE_ASK_VAULT_PASS	false
vault_password_file	ANSIBLE_VAULT_PASSWORD_FILE	(none)
ansible_managed	(none)	Ansible managed: {file} modified on %Y-%m-%d %H:%M:%S by {uid} on {host}
syslog_facility	ANSIBLE_SYSLOG_FACILITY	LOG_USER
keep_remote_files	ANSIBLE_KEEP_REMOTE_FILES	true
sudo	ANSIBLE_SUDO	false
sudo_exe	ANSIBLE_SUDO_EXE	sudo
sudo_flags	ANSIBLE_SUDO_FLAGS	-H
hash_behaviour	ANSIBLE_HASH_BEHAVIOUR	replace
jinja2_extensions	ANSIBLE_JINJA2_EXTENSIONS	(none)
su_exe	ANSIBLE_SU_EXE	su
su	ANSIBLE_SU	false
su_flag	ANSIBLE_SU_FLAGS	(empty string)

Config name	Environment variable	Default value
su_user	ANSIBLE_SU_USER	root
ask_su_pass	ANSIBLE_ASK_SU_PASS	false
gathering	ANSIBLE_GATHERING	implicit
action_plugins	ANSIBLE_ACTION_PLUGINS	/usr/share/ansible_plugins/action_plugins
cache_plugins	ANSIBLE_CACHE_PLUGINS	/usr/share/ansible_plugins/cache_plugins
callback_plugins	ANSIBLE_CALLBACK_PLUGINS	/usr/share/ansible_plugins/callback_plugins
connection_plugins	ANSIBLE_CONNECTION_PLUGINS	/usr/share/ansible_plugins/connection_plugins
lookup_plugins	ANSIBLE_LOOKUP_PLUGINS	/usr/share/ansible_plugins/lookup_plugins
vars_plugins	ANSIBLE_VARS_PLUGINS	/usr/share/ansible_plugins/vars_plugins
filter_plugins	ANSIBLE_FILTER_PLUGINS	/usr/share/ansible_plugins/filter_plugins
log_path	ANSIBLE_LOG_PATH	(empty string)
fact_caching	ANSIBLE_CACHE_PLUGIN	memory
fact_caching_connection	ANSIBLE_CACHE_PLUGIN_CONNECTION	(none)
fact_caching_prefix	ANSIBLE_CACHE_PLUGIN_PREFIX	ansible_facts
fact_caching_timeout	ANSIBLE_CACHE_PLUGIN_TIMEOUT	86400 (seconds)
force_color	ANSIBLE_FORCE_COLOR	(none)
nocolor	ANSIBLE_NOCOLOR	(none)
nocows	ANSIBLE_NOCOWS	(none)
display_skipped_hosts	DISPLAY_SKIPPED_HOSTS	true
error_on_undefined_vars	ANSIBLE_ERROR_ON_UNDEFINED_VARS	true
host_key_checking	ANSIBLE_HOST_KEY_CHECKING	true
system_warnings	ANSIBLE_SYSTEM_WARNINGS	true
deprecation_warnings	ANSIBLE_DEPRECATION_WARNINGS	true

Config name	Environment variable	Default value
callable_whitelist	ANSIBLE_CALLABLE_WHITELIST	(empty list)
command_warnings	ANSIBLE_COMMAND_WARNINGS	false
bin_ansible_callbacks	ANSIBLE_LOAD_CALLBACK_PLUGINS	false

 If you installed Ansible using a package manager, then default paths for the plug-ins might be different than those listed here, since the downstream package manager might have modified the default locations of Ansible-related files from what is specified in the upstream Ansible project.

Table B-2. ssh_connection section

Config name	Environment variable	Default value
ssh_args	ANSIBLE_SSH_ARGS	-o ControlMaster=auto -o ControlPersist=60s -o ControlPath="$ANSIBLE_SSH_CONTROL_PATH"
control_path	ANSIBLE_SSH_CONTROL_PATH	%(directory)s/ansible-ssh-%%h-%%p-%%r
pipelining	ANSIBLE_SSH_PIPELINING	false
scp_if_ssh	ANSIBLE_SCP_IF_SSH	false

Ansible substitutes the %(directory)s variable in the _control_path config file to *$HOME/.ansible/cp.*

Table B-3. paramiko section

Config name	Environment variable	Default value
record_host_keys	ANSIBLE_PARAMIKO_RECORD_HOST_KEYS	true
pty	ANSIBLE_PARAMIKO_PTY	true

Table B-4. accelerate section

Config name	Environment variable	Default value
accelerate_keys_dir	ACCELERATE_KEYS_DIR	\~/.fireball.keys
accelerate_keys_dir_perms	ACCELERATE_KEYS_DIR_PERMS	700
accelerate_keys_file_perms	ACCELERATE_KEYS_FILE_PERMS	600
accelerate_multi_key	ACCELERATE_MULTI_KEY	false

Using IAM Roles for EC2 Credentials

If you're going to run Ansible inside of a VPC, you can take advantage of Amazon's Identity and Access Management (IAM) roles so that you do not even need to set environment variables to pass your EC2 credentials to the instance.

Amazon's IAM roles let you define users and groups and control what those users and groups are permitted to do with EC2 (e.g., get information about your running instances, create instances, create images). You can also assign IAM roles to running instances, so you can effectively say: "This instance is allowed to start other instances."

When you make requests against EC2 using a client program that supports IAM roles, and an instance is granted permissions by an IAM role, the client will fetch the credentials from the EC2 instance metadata service (*http://amzn.to/1Cu0fTl*) and use those to make requests against the EC2 service end point.

You can create an IAM role through the Amazon Web Services (AWS) management console, or at the command line using the AWS Command Line Interface tool, or AWS CLI (*http://aws.amazon.com/cli/*).

AWS Management Console

Here's how you would use the AWS management console to create an IAM role that has "Power User Access," meaning that it is permitted to do pretty much anything with AWS except to modify IAM users and groups.

1. Log in to the AWS management console (*https://console.aws.amazon.com*).
2. Click on "Identity & Access Management."
3. Click on "Roles" at the left.

4. Click the "Create New Role" button.

5. Give your role a name. I like to use "ansible" as the name for the role for my instance that will run Ansible.

6. Under "AWS Service Roles," select "Amazon EC2."

7. Select "Power User Access." The web interface should then show you a policy name and a policy document, and give you an opportunity to edit them if you like. The default policy name will look something like *PowerUserAccess-ansible-201411182152*, and the policy document is a JSON string that should look like Example C-1.

8. Click "Next Step."

9. Click "Create Role."

Example C-1. IAM power user policy document

```
{
  "Version": "2012-10-17",
  "Statement": [
    {
      "Effect": "Allow",
      "NotAction": "iam:*",
      "Resource": "*"
    }
  ]
}
```

When you create a role through the web interface, AWS also automatically creates an *instance profile* with the same name as the role (e.g., "ansible"), and associates the role with the instance profile name. When you create an instance with the ec2 module, if you pass the instance profile name as the instance_profile_name parameter, then the created instance will have the permissions of that role.

Command-Line

You can also create the role and the instance profile using the AWS CLI tool, but it's a bit more work. You need to:

1. Create a role, specifying the trust policy. The trust policy describes the entities that can assume the role and the access conditions for the role.

2. Create a policy that describes what the role is permitted to do. In our case, we want to create the equivalent of the power user, where the role can perform any AWS-related action except manipulate IAM roles and groups.

3. Create an instance profile.

4. Associate the role with the instance profile.

You'll need to create two IAM policy files first, which are in JSON format. The trust policy is shown in Example C-2. This is the same trust policy that AWS automatically generates when you create the role via the web interface.

The role policy that describes what the role is allowed to do is shown in Example C-3.

Example C-2. trust-policy.json

```
{
  "Version": "2012-10-17",
  "Statement": [
    {
      "Sid": "",
      "Effect": "Allow",
      "Principal": {
        "Service": "ec2.amazonaws.com"
      },
      "Action": "sts:AssumeRole"
    }
  ]
}
```

Example C-3. power-user.json

```
{
  "Version": "2012-10-17",
  "Statement": [
    {
      "Effect": "Allow",
      "NotAction": "iam:*",
      "Resource": "*"
    }
  ]
}
```

Example C-4 shows how you'd create an instance profile on the command line, once you've created the files shown in Examples C-2 and C-3.

Example C-4. Creating an instance profile at the command line

```
# Make sure that trust-policy.json and power-user.json are in the
# current directory, or change the file:// arguments to include the
# complete path

$ aws iam create-role --role-name ansible --assume-role-policy-document \
  file://trust-policy.json
$ aws iam put-role-policy --role-name ansible --policy-name \
  PowerUserAccess-ansible-20141118 --policy-document file://power-user.json
```

```
$ aws iam create-instance-profile --instance-profile-name ansible
$ aws iam add-role-to-instance-profile --instance-profile-name ansible \
  --role-name ansible
```

As you can see, it's much simpler to do this via the web interface, but if you want to automate this, then you can use the command line instead. Check out the AWS Identity and Access Management User Guide (*http://docs.aws.amazon.com/IAM/latest/UserGuide*) for more details on IAM.

Once you've created the instance profile, you can then launch an EC2 instance with that instance profile. You can do this with the ec2 module using the instance_pro file_name parameter:

```
- name: launch an instance with iam role
  ec2:
    instance_profile_name: ansible
    # Other parameters not shown
```

If you SSH into this instance, you can query the EC2 metadata service to confirm that this instance is associated with the Ansible profile. The output should look something like this:

```
$ curl http://169.254.169.254/latest/meta-data/iam/info
{
  "Code" : "Success",
  "LastUpdated" : "2014-11-17T02:44:03Z",
  "InstanceProfileArn" : "arn:aws:iam::549704298184:instance-profile/ansible",
  "InstanceProfileId" : "AIPAINM7F44YGDNIBHPYC"
}
```

You can also directly inspect the credentials, although it's not something you need to do. The Boto library will automatically retrieve these credentials when the Ansible ec2 modules or dynamic inventory script executes:

```
$ curl http://169.254.169.254/latest/meta-data/iam/security-credentials/ansible
{
  "Code" : "Success",
  "LastUpdated" : "2015-02-09T21:45:20Z",
  "Type" : "AWS-HMAC",
  "AccessKeyId" : "ASIAIYXCUETJPY42AC2Q",
  "SecretAccessKey" : "ORp9gldiymIKH9+rFtWEx8BjGRteNTQSRnLnlmWq",
  "Token" : "AQoDYXdzEGca4AMPC5W69pvtENpXjw79oH9...",
  "Expiration" : "2015-02-10T04:10:36Z"
}
```

These credentials are temporary, and Amazon will rotate them automatically for you.

You can now use this instance as your control machine, without needing to specify your credentials via environment variables. The Ansible ec2 modules will automatically retrieve the credentials from the metadata service.

Glossary

Alias

When the name of a host in the inventory is different from the actual hostname of the host.

AMI

Amazon Machine Image, a virtual machine image in the Amazon Elastic Compute Cloud, also known as *EC2*.

Ansible, Inc.

The company that manages the Ansible project.

Ansible Galaxy

A repository (*https://galaxy.ansible.com*) of Ansible roles contributed by the community.

Ansible Tower

A proprietary web-based dashboard and REST interface for controlling Ansible, sold by Ansible, Inc.

Check mode

An optional mode when running a playbook. When check mode is enabled, and when Ansible executes a playbook, it will not make any changes to remote hosts. Instead, it will simply report whether each task would have changed the state of the host. Sometimes referred to as "dry run" mode.

CIDR

Classless Inter-Domain Routing, a notation for specifying a range of IP addresses, used when defining Amazon EC2 security groups.

Configuration management

A process for ensuring that servers are in the proper state for doing their job.

By state, we mean things like the configuration files for server applications have the correct values, the proper files are present, the correct services are running, the expected user accounts are present, permissions are set correctly, and so on.

Convergence

A property of configuration management systems where the system will execute multiple times against a server in order to get the server to reach the desired state, with each execution bringing the server closer to the desired state. Convergence is most closely associated with the CFEngine configuration management system. Convergence doesn't really apply to Ansible, which puts servers into desired states after a single execution.

Complex arguments

Arguments passed to modules that are of type list or dictionary.

Container

A form of server virtualization where the virtualization is implemented at the operating system level, so that the virtual machine instance shares the same kernel as the host. Docker is the most well-known container technology.

Control machine

The computer that you run Ansible on that is used to control the remote hosts.

Control socket

A Unix domain socket that SSH clients will use to connect to a remote host when SSH multiplexing is enabled.

ControlPersist

A synonym for SSH multiplexing.

Declarative

A type of programming language where the programmer describes the desired output, not the procedure for how to compute the output. Ansible's playbooks are declarative. SQL is another example of a declarative language. Contrast with *procedural* languages, such as Java and Python.

Deployment

The process of bringing software up onto a live system.

DevOps

IT buzzword that gained popularity in the mid-2010s.

Dry run

See *Check mode*.

DSL

Domain-specific language. In systems that use DSLs, the user interacts with the systems by writing text files in the domain-specific language and then runs those files through the system. DSLs are not as powerful as general-purpose programming language, but (if designed well) they are easier to read and write than general-purpose programming language. Ansible exposes a DSL that uses YAML syntax.

Dynamic inventory

Source that provides Ansible with information about hosts and groups at playbook execution time.

EBS

Elastic block store. On Amazon EC2, an EBS refers to a persistent disk that can be attached to instances.

Fact

A variable that contains information about a specific host.

Facter

A tool used by Puppet to retrieve information about a host. Ansible will invoke Facter when gathering facts about a host, if Facter is installed.

Glob

A glob is a pattern used by Unix shells to match against filenames. For example, *.txt is a glob that would match all files that end in .txt.

Group

A named collection of hosts.

Handler

Similar to a task, except that handlers only execute in response to a task that is configured to notify the handler on change of state.

Host

A remote server managed by Ansible.

IAM

Identity and Access Management, a feature of Amazon's Elastic Compute Cloud that allows you to manage user and group permissions.

Idempotent

An action is idempotent if executing the action multiple times has the same effect as executing it once.

Instance

A virtual machine. The term is commonly used to refer to a virtual machine running inside an infrastructure-as-a-service cloud, such as Amazon's Elastic Cloud Compute (EC2).

Inventory

The list of hosts and groups

Lookups

Code that executes on the control machine to obtain some configuration data needed by Ansible while a playbook is running.

Module

Modules are Ansible scripts that perform one specific task. Examples include creating a user account, installing a package, or starting a service. Most Ansible modules are idempotent.

Ohai

A tool used by Chef to retrieve information about a host. Ansible will invoke Ohai when gathering facts about a host, if Ohai is installed.

Orchestration

Performing a series of tasks in a well-specified order on a collection of servers. Orchestration is often needed for performing deployments.

Pattern

Ansible syntax for describing which hosts to run a play against.

Play

Associates a set of hosts with a list of tasks to perform on that host.

Playbook

An Ansible script. It specifies a list of plays and a collection of hosts to execute the plays against.

Registered variable

A variable created by using the register clause in a task.

Role

An Ansible mechanism for bundling together a collection of tasks, handlers, files, templates, and variables.

For example, an nginx role might contain tasks for installing the nginx package, generating the nginx configuration file, copying TLS certificate files, and starting the nginx service.

SSH multiplexing

A feature of the OpenSSH SSH client that can reduce the time it takes to make an SSH connection when making multiple SSH connections to the same machine. Ansible uses SSH multiplexing by default to improve performance.

Task

The unit of work in an Ansible play. A task specifies a module and its arguments, as well as an optional name and some additional optional parameters.

TLS

Transport Layer Security, a protocol used to secure communications between web servers and browsers. TLS superseded an earlier protocol called *Secure Sockets Layer* (SSL). Many people refer to TLS incorrectly as SSL.

Transport

The protocol and implementation Ansible uses to connect to the remote host. The default transport is SSH.

Vault

A mechanism used by Ansible for encrypting sensitive data on disk. Typically used to safely store secret data in a version control system.

Vagrant

A tool for managing virtual machines, intended for use by developers to create reproducible development environments.

Virtualenv

A mechanism for installing Python packages into an environment that can be activated and deactivated. Enables a user to install Python packages without root access and without polluting the global Python package library on the machine.

VPC

Virtual private cloud. A term used by Amazon EC2 to describe an isolated network you can create for your EC2 instances.

Bibliography

- [ansible-aws] Kurniawan, Yan. *Ansible for AWS*. Leanpub, 2015 (forthcoming).

- [cloudsysadmin] Limoncelli, Thomas A.; Hogan, Christina J.; Chalup, Strata R. *The Practice of Cloud System Administration: Designing and Operating Large Distributed Systems*. Addison-Wesley Professional, 2014.

- [dataintensive] Kleppmann, Martin. *Designing Data-Intensive Applications*. O'Reilly Media, 2015.

- [nist] Mell, Peter; Grance, Timothy. *The NIST Definition of Cloud Computing*. NIST Special Publication 800-145, 2011.

- [openssh] *OpenSSH/Cookbook/Multiplexing*, Wikibooks, *http://bit.ly/1bpeV0y*, October 28, 2014.

- [pragprog] Hunt, Andrew; Thomas, David. *The Pragmatic Programmer: From Journeyman to Master*. Addison-Wesley, 1999.

- [tastetest] Jaynes, Matt. *Taste Test: Puppet, Chef, Salt, Ansible*. Publisher, 2014.

- [vagrant] Hashimoto, Mitchell. *Vagrant: Up and Running*. O'Reilly Media, 2013.

- [webops] Shafer, Andrew Clay. *Agile Infrastructure* in *Web Operations: Keeping the Data on Time*. O'Reilly Media, 2010.

Index

X

xgrp return value, 265
xip.io, 105
xusr return value, 265

Y

YAML, 28-30
yes, true vs., 23

About the Author

Lorin Hochstein was born and raised in Montreal, Quebec, though you'd never guess he was a Canadian by his accent, other than his occasional tendency to say "close the light." He is a recovering academic, having spent two years on the tenure track as an assistant professor of computer science and engineering at the University of Nebraska-Lincoln, and another four years as a computer scientist at the University of Southern California's Information Sciences Institute. He earned his BEng. in Computer Engineering at McGill University, his MS in Electrical Engineering at Boston University, and his PhD in Computer Science at the University of Maryland, College Park. He is currently a Senior Software Engineer at SendGrid, where he works on new product development for SendGrid Labs.

Colophon

The animal on the cover of *Ansible: Up and Running* is a Holstein Friesian *(Bos primigenius)*, often shortened to Holstein in North America and Friesian in Europe. This breed of cattle originated in Europe in what is now the Netherlands, bred with the goal of obtaining animals that could exclusively eat grass—the area's most abundant resource—resulting in a high-producing, black-and-white dairy cow. Holstein-Friesians were introduced to the US from 1621 to 1664, but American breeders didn't become interested in the breed until the 1830s.

Holsteins are known for their large size, distinct black-and-white markings, and their high production of milk. The black and white coloring is a result of artificial selection by the breeders. Healthy calves weigh 90–100 pounds at birth; mature Holsteins can weigh up to 1280 pounds and stand at 58 inches tall. Heifers of this breed are typically bred by 13 to 15 months; their gestation period is nine and a half months.

This breed of cattle averages about 2022 gallons of milk per year; pedigree animals average 2146 gallons per year, and can produce up to 6898 gallons in a lifetime.

In September 2000, the Holstein became the center of controversy when one of its own, Hanoverhill Starbuck, was cloned from frozen fibroblast cells recovered one month before his death, birthing Starbuck II. The cloned calf was born 21 years and 5 months after the original Starbuck.

Many of the animals on O'Reilly covers are endangered; all of them are important to the world. To learn more about how you can help, go to *animals.oreilly.com*.

The cover image is from Lydekker's *Royal Natural History, Vol. 2*. The cover fonts are URW Typewriter and Guardian Sans. The text font is Adobe Minion Pro; the heading font is Adobe Myriad Condensed; and the code font is Dalton Maag's Ubuntu Mono.

Have it your way.

Get even more for your money.

Join the O'Reilly Community, and register the O'Reilly books you own. It's free, and you'll get:

- $4.99 ebook upgrade offer
- 40% upgrade offer on O'Reilly print books
- Membership discounts on books and events
- Free lifetime updates to ebooks and videos
- Multiple ebook formats, DRM FREE
- Participation in the O'Reilly community
- Newsletters
- Account management
- 100% Satisfaction Guarantee

Signing up is easy:

1. Go to: oreilly.com/go/register
2. Create an O'Reilly login.
3. Provide your address.
4. Register your books.

Note: English-language books only

To order books online:
oreilly.com/store

For questions about products or an order:
orders@oreilly.com

To sign up to get topic-specific email announcements and/or news about upcoming books, conferences, special offers, and new technologies:
elists@oreilly.com

For technical questions about book content:
booktech@oreilly.com

To submit new book proposals to our editors:
proposals@oreilly.com

O'Reilly books are available in multiple DRM-free ebook formats. For more information:
oreilly.com/ebooks

O'REILLY®

- debug: var=login
- debug:

register? 70

parser

handlers
- name: restart apache
  service: name=nginx state=restarted

TODO facts: ansible server1 -m setup

cmd: ARGUMENTS

SHOW LOOPS

TODO
set up other two hosts
break up command.
CONDITIONAL LINE IN FILE
? DO I NEED HOST ON EVERY STANZA/PLAY?
raw, cmd, shell

ansible-galaxy install   158 + 160

script command 174
P177 NOTIFIER CHANGED & TRUE   ALERTS

CPSIA information can be obtained at www.ICGtesting.com
Printed in the USA
BVOW09s0208110216

436305BV00004B/7/P